# Effective Project
## and Change Sponsorship

GETTING THE MOST FROM YOUR STRATEGIC INVESTMENTS

## Ori Schibi, PMP, CMP, PMI-ACP

J.ROSS
PUBLISHING

ISBN-13: 978-1-60427-174-4

Printed and bound in the U.S.A. Printed on acid-free paper.

10 9 8 7 6 5 4 3 2 1

**Library of Congress Cataloging-in-Publication Data**
Names: Schibi, Ori, 1971– author.
Title: Effective project and change sponsorship : getting the most from your
   strategic investments / Ori Schibi.
Description: 1 Edition. | PLANTATION : J. Ross Publishing, 2020. | Includes
   bibliographical references and index.
Identifiers: LCCN 2020027366 (print) | LCCN 2020027367 (ebook) | ISBN
   9781604271744 (paperback) | ISBN 9781604278255 (epub)
Subjects: LCSH: Project management. | Strategic planning. | Business planning.
Classification: LCC HD69.P75 S3485 2020  (print) | LCC HD69.P75  (ebook) |
   DDC 658.4/04—dc23
LC record available at https://lccn.loc.gov/2020027366
LC ebook record available at https://lccn.loc.gov/2020027367

Direct all inquiries to J. Ross Publishing, Inc., 300 S. Pine Island Rd., Suite 305,
Plantation, FL 33324.

Phone: (954) 727-9333
Fax: (561) 892-0700
Web: www.jrosspub.com

# CONTENTS

*This book is dedicated to:*

*My wonderful wife, Eva*

*Incredible mom*

*Remarkable daughters—Kayla and Maya*

*I am inspired and empowered by your endless love and support*

*Love you all*

# INTRODUCTION

In their search for improved efficiency and performance, an increasing number of organizations have started to realize that the challenges surrounding project and change *sponsorship* are a major cause preventing them from improving their bottom lines. This book looks at the gaps, issues, and problems with both project and change sponsorship, and offers practical approaches and solutions to these challenges. This includes how to better define the exact role of the sponsor and his/her responsibilities and boundaries, as well as focusing on increasing the awareness around what effective project and change sponsorship looks like.

When it comes to project and change management, there are misconceptions surrounding the area of sponsorship. Project and change sponsorship are rarely packaged together under the same umbrella, and while they are two different things, the sponsors of projects and those of change initiatives have similar roles, responsibilities, and characteristics. This book deals with both *types* of sponsorship—change and project. It also explores the role of the sponsor in agile projects, including the sponsor's relationship with the product owner and other stakeholders.

## BOOK OBJECTIVES

This book examines project and change sponsorship: the need for an effective sponsor, the challenges with sponsorship as we know it, and the benefits that effective sponsorship introduces to organizations. It explains how improving the practices around sponsorship can create a ripple effect across the entire organization. In a similar fashion to a positive interpretation of the butterfly effect, all it takes are some small adjustments to sponsorship in order to yield significant organizational benefits.

This guide offers a unique approach on how to organize thoughts and ideas around the roles of the project and the change sponsor, and introduces structure around what the sponsor should look for, measure, ask about, and do at different stages of the project or the change initiative. Readers will explore the types of challenges that sponsors face and the way these challenges manifest—for easier and earlier detection. We will identify the root causes of sponsorship-related issues as a key step to systematic problem solving. Many will be surprised to learn that most sponsorship-related problems stem from a limited number of root causes. Furthermore, most of the root causes are related to common types of organizational problems that bring us back to the basics, such as time management, prioritization, and accountability.

From here, this book applies techniques to guide readers through the process of finding short-term fixes to problems, along with an approach for long-term resolutions that will become preventive measures. Many of the concepts in this book are simple and straightforward, yet most organizations have not made a consolidated attempt, in context, to fix them once and for all.

## WHAT MAKES THIS BOOK DIFFERENT?

This book is a valuable repository of knowledge, concepts, and techniques for project and change sponsors—guiding them to success. It is essentially the first attempt to incorporate the good from project management, business analysis, change management, and agile while creating awareness and knowledge of the sponsorship role. In addition to the context those four areas offer, this book also provides a look into how to become a more effective manager (a sponsor's "day job"), which will help free up time, focus, and capacity for senior managers to become better sponsors.

This unique guide details the role of the sponsor in the context of organizational change—posing critical questions that the sponsor needs to introduce in order to ensure that there is clarity about the reason for the change, the change objectives, and the change outcome. There is also a discussion on how to build a clear and meaningful vision, as well as how to ensure that once the change is *done*, the organization is ready for the next one.

## THE STRUCTURE OF THIS BOOK

*Chapter 1* provides an overview of what sponsorship is, along with a discussion on the two *aspects* of sponsorship that this book covers: project (including sponsorship in agile environments) and change. The chapter continues with a review of the common challenges that sponsors face, as well as the challenges that organizations face as a result of deficiencies in project and change sponsorships. It will provide a high-level overview of the main causes that lead to sponsorship-related problems, and this will lead to a discussion on the context around sponsorship—including governance, portfolio management, and the project management office (PMO). The chapter also features a comparison between project and change sponsorship, along with the nuances, subtleties, and differences between these areas. It then explores how to deliver organizational success by connecting project and change management, including how sponsors should deal with their respective change managers, project managers, and teams. Finally, the chapter provides some practical advice on how to establish a meaningful feedback loop so the sponsor can remain informed and maintain context.

*Chapter 2* focuses on where to begin the process of *fixing* the problems and challenges around sponsorship. It starts with a list of challenges in the form of short scenarios, or vignettes, that represent common situations around sponsorship in many organizations. It then progresses to exploring common symptoms or signs that allow practitioners to easily identify when these conditions present themselves—or are about to. Early detection of these items helps us become more proactive in search of a solution. The chapter then takes a deeper look into a set of likely root causes that lead to, or at least contribute to, the challenges that were introduced.

*Chapter 3* serves as the core of the tangible actions and considerations for the project and change sponsor. It looks at behaviors and activities that make sponsorship more effective and covers the role of the sponsor in helping the organization manage resources. The chapter also offers possible actions to take in light of the situations presented through the vignettes in Chapter 2. The possible actions are broken into two categories: (1) short-term remedies to the challenges that plague or are imposed by weak project sponsorship and (2) long-term fixes that, if applied properly and in context, can serve as a set of preventive measures for the future.

*Chapter 4* is about dealing with stakeholders. It starts by emphasizing the importance of setting and managing stakeholder expectations and it moves into an application of techniques related to forming and maintaining relationships, setting expectations and boundaries, and establishing lines of communication. These areas serve as critical success factors that are a *must* for becoming an effective sponsor. The chapter offers unique and practical insights on how to deal with various stakeholder groups, how to identify and accommodate communication styles and preferences, and how to build a cross-project/cross-initiative collaboration mechanism. On a more tactical note, it explores how to form reporting guidelines, escalations, and thresholds, and helps determine the right level of involvement for the sponsor. Lastly, the chapter offers a discussion on what happens (or should happen) to an initiative if the sponsor changes.

*Chapter 5* covers the unique aspects that change sponsorship introduces. The chapter starts with a mechanism that helps by asking questions concerning the reasons for the change (why), the change vision, and the desired outcome of the change initiative. It then reviews the notion of whether the change brings the organization to a level of sufficient readiness for the next change and proceeds to explore the role of the sponsor in ensuring that changes do not override each other and that people throughout the organization do not suffer from change fatigue. The chapter also provides a discussion having to do with the relationship between the change sponsor and the change manager, the change agent, and the change subjects (or victims).

*Chapter 6* takes a deeper look into project sponsorship, the project charter, and ways to improve the relationship and collaboration between the project sponsor and the project manager (PM). The chapter covers the notion that sponsors should establish a stronger orientation toward *product* thinking, rather than *project* thinking, allowing success to be meaningful and long-lasting. Product thinking also allows for a more effective lessons learned process that includes a post-implementation review. It then goes through a brief agile discussion that includes the role of the sponsor in agile environments and the sponsor's interactions with key agile team members, including the product owner, the PM (or coach/Scrum Master), the BA (business analyst), and team members. The chapter covers the relationship between the sponsor and the product owner, considerations around the need for a *proxy sponsor*, and the sponsor's interaction with other agile stakeholders.

*Chapter 7* provides key tips and concepts for the effective sponsor, including innovative thoughts around time management, capacity management, prioritization, urgency measurement, and leadership. It then goes through a brief review of a day in a life of the sponsor and continues the critical discussion of effectively working with the PM.

*Chapter 8* revisits some of the key concepts introduced throughout and closes by looking ahead at the future of sponsorship and project/change initiatives. This includes the idea of integrating certain aspects of project and change management and PMO/CMOs (change management offices).

Note that throughout this book, the sponsor is referred to as the "project sponsor," "change sponsor," or "initiative sponsor." In some sections, there will be specific distinctions between the project sponsor and the change sponsor. However, when it comes to change initiatives and to projects, both require similar needs from the sponsor since most change initiatives are broken down into projects.

## IMPORTANT TAKEAWAYS

Addressing the area of change and project sponsorship will help organizations start to fix actual problems, as opposed to addressing just the symptoms and afflictions. The key benefits of this book include:

- Helping sponsors become more effective at both their *day-job* role as well as in their role as sponsors and leaders
- Introducing ideas to help sponsors better understand their (and their teams') capacity and, in turn, prioritize more effectively
- Defining roles and responsibilities and setting realistic expectations
- Enhancing cross-project and cross-initiative collaboration to reduce, or even remove, silos

- Learning how to recognize common challenges that impact sponsorship and performance
- Identifying root causes and underlying trends that lead to challenging situations
- Improving the ability to effectively gather and apply lessons as part of continuous improvement
- Incorporating post-implementation reviews to evaluate an initiatives' success level in comparison with the initial intent, business case, and selection criteria
- Ensuring the sponsor picks the best PM and that they act as a cohesive unit (*one entity*)
- Learning how to establish and communicate a clear, inspiring, and measurable vision for initiatives and, in turn, the ability to *extend* the vision to a clear definition of success
- Managing communication and stakeholder expectations to improve stakeholder and team member alignment with the initiative's objectives
- Establishing mechanisms to provide real-time support to team members, while reducing redundancies in guidance, communication, and clarifications

This long list of improvements is achievable and has been proven to enhance performance in multiple organizations. The keys to success are to approach it consistently, avoid taking shortcuts, and ensure that it is initiated from—and supported by—senior management.

# FOREWORD

Over the past decade, I have become very interested in how projects can help organizations deliver their strategy. What I have seen is that most organizations do a good job of *creating* their strategy, but *implementing* it is another question. Many organizations struggle to implement their strategy; some with disastrous results. Why is this?

In today's world, every organization is challenged by technology disrupters, new business models, and diversity. Firms are facing competition from not only organizations around the corner, but from all over the world. The creation of the world wide web in the early 1990s opened up a whole new way for organizations to communicate with customers. Suddenly, an organization could sell to customers across the globe. The internet is just one example of new technologies that are being introduced constantly and, in many cases, feature new business models as well. These new technologies are disrupting the way organizations do business and shorten the life of their products. The result is organizations need to change and implement new strategies to take advantage of these changes, to respond to competitors, and to respond to customer needs. However, organizations do not just implement the strategy, organizations must implement their strategy quickly, with laser focus, while reacting to a constantly changing environment.

While doing research for a book I co-authored, *Gen P: New Generation of Product Owners Who Care about Customers*, I found there are several reasons why organizations struggle to implement their strategy. In this book, Ori Schibi addresses two of the reasons: change and sponsorship.

To implement a strategy successfully requires an organization to change. Projects, by their very nature, deliver new products or services. For that product or service to realize benefits, the organization and potentially their customers must change. Two of the keys to successful organizational change is strong leadership and effective communication. For an organization to change, leaders need to be advocates for the change and be able to effectively communicate to staff and customers why the change is necessary and critical for success. How the product is created by the project will help the organization achieve its strategy. Strong leadership shown by the sponsor of the change is required to overcome the resistance to change of organizational culture and fear of the unknown. If an organization does not change, then the organization will fail.

Projects deliver products that are required by organizations to achieve their strategy. Studies done by the Project Management Institute have shown that two of the most important keys for project success are communication and links to strategy. A key element that links effective communication to strategy is having an effective project sponsor. A project sponsor has two key roles to ensure project success, which Ori addresses in detail in this book. The first role of a project sponsor is to ensure the project is linked to the organization's strategy, and the second is to advocate for the project within the organization and to customers. An effective sponsor must have excellent communication skills to clear project roadblocks, resolve issues, motivate the project team, and support the project manager in ensuring success and strategic implementation.

*Effective Project and Change Sponsorship* explores the role and the skills that a valuable project sponsor must have to ensure successful projects. In today's ever-changing world, a world with increased competition and technology disruptors, every project needs an effective project sponsor. I recommend that every project and change sponsor read this book to gain the skills they need to support their teams and, more important, support the implementation of the organization's strategy.

Peter Monkhouse
Co-founder, NewGenP
Past Chair, PMI Board of Directors
Toronto, Canada

# ABOUT THE AUTHOR

Ori Schibi, MBA, PMP, PMI-ACP, SMC, CMP, Agile-PM, is president of PM Konnectors, an international consulting practice based in Toronto. With a focus on disciplined agile practices, project management, change management, and organizational agility, PM Konnectors provides a variety of services which delivers tangible value and quick turnaround to their clients. Many large to mid-sized organizations in diverse industries and levels of governments have benefited from their wide range of innovative business solutions.

Mr. Schibi is a thought-leader and subject matter expert in organizational change, agile, and project management. He is the author of *Managing Stakeholder Expectations for Project Success* and co-author of *Effective PM and BA Role Collaboration* and *Agile Business Analysis*. Ori is also a speaker and consultant with over 25 years of proven experience in driving value creation, improving organizational agility, and effectively dealing with complex programs to stabilize business, create growth and value, and lead sustainable change.

Web
Added
Value™

This book has free material available for download from the
Web Added Value™ resource center at *www.jrosspub.com*

At J. Ross Publishing we are committed to providing today's professional with practical, hands-on tools that enhance the learning experience and give readers an opportunity to apply what they have learned. That is why we offer free ancillary materials available for download on this book and all participating Web Added Value™ publications. These online resources may include interactive versions of the material that appears in the book or supplemental templates, worksheets, models, plans, case studies, proposals, spreadsheets and assessment tools, among other things. Whenever you see the WAV™ symbol in any of our publications, it means bonus materials accompany the book and are available from the Web Added Value Download Resource Center at www.jrosspub.com.

Downloads for *Effective Project and Change Sponsorship: Getting the Most from Your Strategic Investments* include an initial impact audit and tools for stakeholder analysis, among other valuable documents.

# 1

---

# INTRODUCTION TO SPONSORSHIP

---

## WHAT IS SPONSORSHIP?

Before diving into the challenges surrounding the role of project and change sponsorship, let's take a quick look at the basics of what sponsorship is all about.

All projects and change initiatives should have a sponsor, who *owns* the initiative and oversees it—often this person is the initiator and the one who introduces it. The sponsor is also viewed as a representative of the customer for whom the project or initiative is being undertaken. When referring to projects, the sponsor is typically expected to secure funding and resources, define the success criteria, approve changes, and make decisions. It is expected that the sponsor will promote the initiative and ensure that it gets the right amount of focus, attention, and priority from the organization because the initiative needs to compete for limited resources with other initiatives and priorities. The sponsor should be accountable for actions, performance, and results since the buck stops with the sponsor—he/she will have to shoulder the blame for unsatisfactory results.

In most cases, sponsors are members of the management layer of the organization, though their seniority varies based on the organizational structure, the circumstances, along with the size, profile, and importance of the initiatives they oversee. The sponsor may be a member of senior management—or even an executive. Project sponsor and change sponsor are rarely titles that are found in organizations since these are roles that are performed by the managers who end up sponsoring the initiatives. In most cases, the person who acts as a sponsor has a day job, and the role of a sponsor has to be performed in addition to the regular or ongoing job of that individual.

In the context of sports, the word sponsorship refers to providing a brand sponsorship to a team or an individual, while in other settings, sponsoring is about providing funding. It is believed that it was brought into organizations suggesting ownership; corporate accountability; and support of an activity, a project, an initiative, or a result—usually by the sponsor tapping into his/her budget to provide the funding. Either way, it is also common to view the sponsor as a person who puts his/her name to something, as in putting their reputation on the line.

A project sponsor is an individual in the organization who represents the customer; has seniority, authority, and clout; and who justifies and enables a project/initiative to take place. It is important to note that the sponsor can also be an internal organization, a committee, or a team of individuals. The sponsor oversees the initiative and maintains a two-way accountability—coming from the organization toward the project/initiative and by the project toward the organization. The accountability ensures a successful delivery of the initiative toward the corporate goals and enables the initiative to move forward through the allocation of funding, resources, and priorities.

With the exception of small organizations where the sponsor may also be the project manager (PM) or the change manager, the sponsor typically should not be the same person who acts as a PM or a change manager because the roles are different. Although these two roles work together on the same initiatives, they are performed at different capacities and they serve different purposes. Table 1.1 provides a high-level comparison between the role of the sponsor and that of the project or the change manager.

Since the sponsor is a member of senior levels of the organization, the project/change initiatives he/she oversees are typically tactical elements that support a strategic direction or initiative. In many cases, projects are components of an organizational change; whether referred to as a project or a change, the sponsored initiatives are part of a bigger picture within the organization. For example, there may be a technology implementation to automate a process or eliminate the use of paper as part of a modernization initiative, or there could be a reorganization as part of a merger.

Here are some additional roles and expectations that a sponsor must fulfill:

- Represent the initiative at the senior management level to ensure funding, support, and bandwidth
- Support the communication process of the project/initiative (for escalation or for certain communications—for example, with more senior stakeholders)

**Table 1.1**  Sponsor versus project and change managers

|  | Sponsor | Project or Change Manager |
|---|---|---|
| **Day-to-day management of the work** | No | Yes |
| **Funding** | Approving | Requesting and managing |
| **Deliverables** | Accepting | Producing |
| **Mandates and thresholds** | Defining | Working within |

- Provide advice and make decisions (specifically when it is beyond the project/change manager's authority)
- Contribute to, or write, the project charter
- Articulate the project/change manager's level of authority, as well as set boundaries between the sponsor and the respective roles
- Be there to support the project/change manager
- Review and approve artifacts, as required
- Serve as an escalation point for decisions, exceptions, changes, and problems
- Maintain an overview of the initiative, without being involved in the details
- Ensure the initiative gets the funding, resources, and attention it needs
- Make sure the project/change manager is aware of any organizational or external factors as well as changes to the product/mandate/needs that may impact the initiative
- Accept or reject deliverables and provide feedback and guidance

As a leader and a mentor, the sponsor should act as a filter to protect the initiative; a motivator for the project/change manager; and a seller of the initiative outward, throughout the organization, and with the customer. It is important that the sponsor provides the project/change manager with context that helps reveal the rationale behind actions and decisions. The sponsor is not there to sugarcoat the information in an effort to make their project/change manager feel better, but rather he/she should act as a partner, despite the hierarchy and the reporting lines.

Understanding what the role of the sponsor entails is not difficult, but the majority of sponsors struggle to fulfill this role as intended. While there is a variety of reasons as to why the role of the sponsor is not performed as expected, the challenges are commonly driven by a lack of awareness of the importance of the role, poor definition of the role, and a lack of time since the day job of the individual who acts as a sponsor consumes more time than expected. The result is that the capacity allocated to sponsoring an initiative is limited and often not sufficient to the project/change needs.

## CHALLENGES WITH THE ROLE OF THE SPONSOR AND THE SYMPTOMS OF THESE CHALLENGES

Every role in any organization faces challenges in the way it is defined and performed; some challenges are technical, and are related to the work itself, while others are related to communication and interactions with others. It is common that the challenges pertaining to a specific role or profession are addressed within their respective areas—by associations and through job descriptions and role definitions, or other guidelines and best practices (e.g., project management, business analysis, change management, accounting, or human resources). With sponsorship, however, it is different since sponsorship is not recognized as a distinct role or as a profession. Sponsorship is often a *side role* for managers—one that comes in addition to one's official title—and there is little guidance or direction to help perform this role effectively or even define it in a consistent manner.

For the most part, sponsorship is referred to in the context of projects. Most information about this role refers to it in the context of project management—and mostly from the PM's point of view. Further, there are multiple associations that oversee their respective professions—for example, the Project Management Institute (PMI), the International Institute for Business Analysis, Prosci for Change Management, and the Human Resources Professional Association—but there is no Sponsorship Management Institute to define and guide the role of the sponsor.

What this book tries to do is to solve a problem with the role of the sponsor, and when trying to systematically solve a problem, there is a need to conduct an analysis and break down the problem before trying to provide a solution. The way to systematically approach problem-solving includes the following:

1. *Identify the root cause of the problem*—where it comes from and what underlying factors contribute to the problem or lead to it
2. *Recognize the symptoms of the problem*—how it appears, in other words, what is seen and heard as signs of the problem
3. *Look at challenges*—the things that sponsors face
4. *Learn about the impact of the problem*—what it causes throughout the organization
5. *Search for a fix*—it might be a short-term fix to minimize the damage and find a remedy
6. *Explore a long-term solution*—one that changes course in the long run, most likely by circling back to address the root cause(s) of the problem; this is also the main ingredient in being proactive and preventing a problem from occurring, or rather reoccurring, in the future

This chapter focuses on the challenges with sponsorship, the symptoms of these challenges, and the impact that these challenges have on an organization's bottom line—opening up the discussion for subsequent chapters to tackle root causes and solutions.

When referring to challenges with the role of the sponsor, keep in mind that the impact is far-reaching throughout the organization (and at times, beyond—thereby impacting the customer), and it may have significant (and often negative) impact on an organization's performance and bottom line. Although, for the most part, the roles and characteristics of project and change sponsors can be paired up—the discussion here about the challenges is broken down into project sponsorship and change sponsorship challenges.

After looking at the common challenges that project and change sponsors face, those challenges need to be sorted into respective categories of project and change initiatives. These categories help break down the challenges by type and by life-cycle phase.

## Common Challenges with Project Sponsorship

Table 1.2 reviews common challenges surrounding project sponsorship, along with a short explanation for each challenge and, depending on the initiative, these challenges may also be applicable to change-related projects. Project-related challenges for sponsors include a lack of definition of the actual role of the sponsor, a lack of awareness about the importance of the sponsor's role, a lack of coordination between the sponsor and the PM, and a failure to understand the organization's capacity to take on the initiative. Then the common challenges should be discussed by project phase and category.

For projects, there are six categories for sponsorship challenges: one is organizational change and governance, and the remaining five are aligned with PMI's five process groups:

**Table 1.2**   Common challenges with project sponsorship

| Project Sponsorship Challenge | What It Means |
|---|---|
| No clear role definition | Sponsorship is often a side job that pairs with other managerial responsibilities in the organization and, as such, there is little understanding as to what it really means to be a sponsor. It is basically up to the individual who acts as a sponsor. There is also no clear definition of the boundaries between the sponsor and the PM—leading to coordination issues, gaps, and overlapping efforts (i.e., redundancies). |
| No job description/unclear mandate for the sponsor | Sponsorship is not a title and therefore it does not have a job description associated with it. |
| Lack of awareness around the importance of sponsorship | Senior stakeholders in organizations often tend to think that sponsorship is a hands-off item and that whoever is appointed or installed as a sponsor will perform their role effectively and as expected. There is no training on what to do or how to do it effectively. |
| Lack of time/capacity | (Almost) everyone is overworked, and this includes sponsors. Sponsors have no time or capacity to perform their role and dedicate sufficient effort toward overseeing their respective projects. Sponsors also lack visibility into whether the performing organizations, or the teams, have the capacity to take on initiatives. |
| Poor resource planning | The sponsor's primary role is to secure funding and resources for projects, but in reality, sponsors rarely provide sufficient support for their project when it comes to resource allocation. Resource availability is one of the main causes of project failures. |

Many challenges with project sponsorship have a lot to do with a lack of sufficient focus and clarity on the role of the sponsor by the organization.

1. *Organizational change and governance*—anything that is related to the project management organization, including the impact of the organization on the project, reporting, escalations, governance, the decision-making process, culture, leadership, and the link between the project and the higher-level organizational objectives and strategy. The sponsor is the one who *owns* the initiative and he/she either sets up or articulates the reporting, governance, and structure of the engagement. Table 1.3 provides a look at a few common challenges that fall under this category.

2. *Pre-project, business case, initiation, and start-up*—anything that is leading to or at the start of the project, including the process of realizing and identifying needs, opportunities, and problems that need to be addressed; selecting projects; kickstarting and initiating projects; as well as setting up a solid and clear foundation. Some of the things under this category are addressed outright prior to the establishment of the project organization and is done by someone in the organization, while other things need to take place as part of initiating the setting up of the project. The fact that these activities are performed by different organizations within the

**Table 1.3** Common challenges associated with the organizational governance and change category

| | Organizational Governance and Change |
|------|------|
| a. | Executive leadership is not involved or engaged in understanding capacity, priorities, or urgencies. |
| b. | Ideas, needs, problems, and initiatives are all stand-alone categories and are reviewed and discussed as silos. |
| c. | There is little to no cross-project coordination. |
| d. | Sponsors do not have a clear understanding of the direction of cross-project priorities. Projects keep getting pushed out to allow other initiatives across the organization to move forward. This applies significant pressure on PMs. |
| e. | Too much red tape blocks the sponsor from providing timely and effective support to the PMs. |
| f. | Project sponsorship is inconsistent and depends on the individual sponsor. There is no global or consistent overview of all sponsorship activities, best practices, or ways to assess sponsor effectiveness. |
| g. | Deadlines keep shifting with a few projects peaking around the same time, creating fierce competition for resources. |

In many organizations, sponsorship is almost taken for granted. There is little guidance as to the role of the sponsor and, correspondingly, limited focus on the performance of the individual who fills the role of the sponsor. There is an expectation of project performance and the sponsor is also expected to deliver on their *day job*, which is typically part of senior management. Unfortunately, the sponsor's capacity as a sponsor is often overlooked.

organization may introduce challenges around handoff, alignment, and coordination. Further, many of these activities are less structured or do not produce tangible deliverables—therefore they may not end up being performed properly or to a sufficient extent. Nevertheless, this is the time where the foundation and the health of the upcoming projects are set and determined. Since in most cases there is no PM yet in place, most of the responsibilities under this category fall under the sponsor's role, with one specific and important deliverable—producing a clear mandate for the project. Table 1.4 lists common challenges associated with the events throughout the time frames.

**Table 1.4**  Common challenges associated with the pre-project and initiation stages

|    | Pre-project, Business Case, and Initiation |
|----|--------------------------------------------|
| a. | There is little to no process in place to circle back at the end of or even after the project to check the original intent behind it. This could provide an important insight into the project selection process. |
| b. | The project charter is generally viewed as a chore, and PMs focus on filling out the sections instead of benefiting from the information that is associated with this important document. Sponsors often do not get involved (or sufficiently involved) in the charter process (many times the sponsor is to blame for not providing sufficient support for this process). |
| c. | Information in the charter is sometimes obtained arbitrarily and unrealistic assumptions are made with no documentation of a validation process. |
| d. | The sponsor's role in the various stages within this category is often not clearly defined. |
| e. | Feasibility analysis is often not done properly, if at all. PMs know how to do this, but do not know if they have the capacity to handle it right now. |
| f. | The vision of the initiatives is often not clear and hard to articulate; most people are not even aware of it. Further, success criteria for projects are not clear, not articulated, and contain gaps. |
| g. | Sponsors are having a hard time building trust and rapport and with establishing rules of engagement with the PM. |
| h. | There is insufficient effort to identify and analyze stakeholders and to align objectives with stakeholders' needs. |
| i. | It is hard to find a common thread or proper continuity from the pre-project and the business case stage to the project. |

Many organizations suffer from various levels of disconnect between the business case and the project once it is formally initiated. This limits the sponsor's and the PM's ability to align needs and objectives and to articulate a clear mandate. Further, project initiation activities are often not clearly defined and since many of these activities are nontangible, it is hard to find time to perform them properly.

3. *Planning*—a lot has been said about planning and how important planning is. It is necessary to create project plans and employ the components of a good plan. Planning is primarily the role of the PM, although an important part of the mandate and the tone about the planning process comes from the sponsor. In most cases, however, it is impossible to know the exact mix of things or responsibilities that make a plan a good one under a specific context. Further, it is also important to note that planning is virtually never considered fun or desired and there is typically a significant push to move forward from the planning stage to actually start *doing* something. Unfortunately, there are many things that can go wrong with planning. It is possible to end up with: a good plan for the wrong thing, an ineffective plan, a rushed plan that misses key information, a plan that is too detailed, an incomplete plan, an unrealistic plan, or a plan that is based on the wrong assumption. Table 1.5 provides insight into common areas that may lead to problems during this stage of the project.

4. *Throughout the project*—this stage is commonly referred to as implementation and execution. From the role of the PM, the intent is to ensure that work is getting done, as well as to enable team members to perform their work by handling issues, risks, and challenges as they emerge or preventing

**Table 1.5** Common challenges associated with project planning

| | **Project Planning** |
|---|---|
| a. | Of all the project constraints, resources (human and other) are, for the most part, the most overlooked and *volatile* element. The PM needs the sponsor to mandate and provide support regarding resource planning and utilization. In many project environments, this area becomes a major source of problems. |
| b. | A lack of cross-project planning and prioritization leads to difficulties for functional area managers in matching resources to project needs. PMs almost systematically complain that they either do not get enough of the resources they need (skills and experience), they are not on time, or they are not available for the right duration. |
| c. | Sponsors and PMs interfere with the team's functionality and estimating process. |
| d. | Customers cannot seem to lock down their actual requirements and there is pressure on the PM to move forward with unclear requirements. |
| e. | Stakeholders (and various teams) claim that they are brought to the table too late. |
| f. | It is unclear which decisions the sponsor is in charge of and which the PM can handle (including risks). |
| g. | Sponsors lack the ability to determine *whether/to what extent* the plans are realistic. |

Although the planning process is led by the PM, it is important for the sponsor to provide an effective mandate for the planning process. In addition, the sponsor needs to oversee and support the planning process and its result. Unfortunately, many sponsors apply undue pressure on teams during the planning process to compress estimates.

them beforehand. The sponsor here is not hands-off and he/she needs to keep an eye on performance, on issues, and on the thresholds—both through the *lenses* of the PM, as well as independently. There are typically a lot of moving parts and many things can go wrong. It is possible to misunderstand actions or results and perhaps take things out of context. Table 1.6 lists some challenges that typically take place during the project execution and implementation phase.

5. *Project controls and reporting*—this stage is not a stand-alone time frame, but rather it happens in parallel to the planning and the implementation stages, following the Deming cycle[1] of plan-do-check-act. The PM leads the effort of checking performance, reporting, adjusting, and handling changes, while ensuring that everyone is on track, aligned with the needs, and continuing to produce and realize value for the stakeholders. The PM has the authority to work within the mandate given by the sponsor, and here too, a lot can be misunderstood and reports may not properly reflect the actual performance. Also, it is the role of the sponsor to make decisions that are outside of the scope, mandate, or authority of the PMs regarding project events, deliverables, risk changes, and other things that require signoff. Table 1.7 provides a look into common challenges during this part of the project.

**Table 1.6**  Common challenges that take place throughout the project

|   | **Throughout the Project** |
|---|---|
| a. | Competing priorities and initiatives in the organization impede the sponsor's ability to support the project and the PMs. |
| b. | There is lack of user support or involvement because the client does not understand the importance of involving users. |
| c. | PMs focus on the critical path and are constantly pushing out non-critical-path activities. It makes the projects look as if they are on schedule until there is no more room to push non-critical-path activities out. |
| d. | Everyone in and around the project is consistently overallocated and pressed for time, compromising the ability to make informed decisions. |
| e. | There is widespread confusion about accounting for time contingencies, where on the schedule to place them, or how to account for them. |
| f. | Project resources are spread too thin, leading to stress, communication breakdowns, conflict, confusion, lack of attention to detail, lack of focus on risks and problems, rushed estimates, and quality problems. |
| g. | Sponsors are often spread too thin, failing to be sufficiently available for their projects' needs. |

When project work is taking place, there is an ongoing need to provide oversight and support for the PM and the team. Sponsors should not allow projects to move forward "hands free." They need to be present beyond the needs around reporting and escalations.

**Table 1.7**  Common challenges through monitoring, controlling, and reporting

|  | **Project Monitoring, Controlling, and Reporting** |
|---|---|
| a. | Projects report status regularly and appear to be in good shape until later in the project (i.e., about the 70% point) when problems start to surface. |
| b. | The information that sponsors get is solely based on what PMs tell them. |
| c. | The PM does not know what information to give the sponsor and the sponsor keeps overstepping boundaries with the PM. |
| d. | Sponsors sit in on too many project meetings. They are not sure why they are there and it is consuming their schedules. |
| e. | Changes are assessed inconsistently and in silos. No full impact is assessed—especially when the change impact is compounded by other changes. Change estimates are based on best-case scenarios and change-related risks are overlooked. |
| f. | Escalation procedures are loose, unclear, and not followed. When there is a problem, no one knows who to go to and confusion ensues. |
| g. | Status reports and their meanings are often open for interpretation—depending on the PM's *flavor*. The inconsistency makes it hard to compare projects in an apples-to-apples manner. |

Monitoring and controlling do not represent a distinct time frame, but rather these activities, along with reporting, take place throughout the project during execution and implementation. The controlling and reporting activities are critical in gaining an understanding of the project status and ensuring that it is under control.

6.  *End of project and post project*—this category spans over the late stages of the project and into the post project. The role of the sponsor is not to perform the closing activities, but to provide the signoffs and acceptance that lead to the closure, as well as oversee many elements of the closing process. The PM and the team will perform most of the project closure work, but things like acceptance, payments, contracts, resource releases, and hand-offs need to be overseen or at least approved by the sponsor. The lessons learned process is also performed predominantly by the PM, but the sponsor needs to review and accept the findings, along with decision making on the application of the lessons. The part that spans beyond the project life cycle and into the post project involves warranties and potentially some late hand-off aspects, along with the option for post-implementation review (PIR). Unlike the lessons learned process, which focuses predominantly on team performance and processes, the PIR is about product delivery and will typically be performed around three to six months after the end of the project, to allow the product's performance to settle into a routine. While the sponsor is not likely to perform these things, there may no longer be an associated PM or even a cost center to handle these

items. Regardless of who drives these activities, it is the sponsor's mandate that matters most here, especially when it comes to the PIR. The PIR does not need to take place in every project (depending on the nature of the product), but it takes place in significantly fewer instances than it should.

One additional possibility is for the sponsor to look into a more strategic lessons learned process that reviews the project's outcomes and benefits with those stated in the business case and the charter in order to check whether it was a good idea to begin with and whether the right approach was taken. This type of a lessons learned exercise is rare and blurs the line between the project and the change sponsor's role. With that said, it is perhaps the most effective way for organizations to strategically examine their project selection process. Table 1.8 reviews the common challenges associated with these late stages of the project life cycle.

In later chapters we cover what is expected of the sponsor in any of these life-cycle phases by reviewing what the sponsor should look for, measure, ask about, or do in any of these stages. While the sponsor's role is to oversee the project, protect the project and the team, promote the project, and serve as an accountable decision maker and escalation point, each life-cycle phase requires different areas of focus, things to measure, and characteristics.

**Table 1.8**   Common challenges with the end of the project and post project

|   | End of Project and Post Project |
|---|---|
| a. | Projects and products are successful, but it is occasionally due to people pulling superhuman acts and saving the day. This is not a sustainable way to operate. |
| b. | Project benefits that are under consideration are mostly tangible and financial. Other benefits are overlooked. |
| c. | There is no mechanism to measure benefits beyond project completion. |
| d. | As projects reach their end, sponsors are unsure of the appropriate time to bow out. |
| e. | PMs focus on a project's considerations within its life cycle with little regard to post project benefits or impact. |
| f. | The lessons learned process does not provide sufficient or meaningful lessons for the organization. |
| g. | No PIR takes place. |
| h. | The lessons learned are mostly tactical and do not provide insight into project selection or approach. |

There are fewer challenges with the end of project and post-project category as there are fewer activities associated with these stages. However, beyond the administrative chores that take place at the end of the project, most of the challenges are associated with identifying the lessons learned from the project, the degree of success achieved, and the benefits associated with the product.

## Common Challenges with Change Sponsorship

Table 1.9 provides an overview of common challenges associated with change initiatives. These include the failure to create a clear and compelling vision, the failure to frame the scope of the change, and the failure to manage the transition. Similar to the project sponsorship discussion, this is followed with a breakdown of the challenges by change *stage*. Although categorized under *change sponsorship*, these challenges may also impact projects. Table 1.10 provides context for some of the more significant change sponsorship challenges.

For the change categories, the U-Curve has been used, based on the Kübler-Ross 5-Stage Model[2] for change that can be seen in Figure 1.1. It has been tweaked a little—as an *interpretation* of the model—by renaming the five primary stages, as they appear in Figure 1.2.

**Table 1.9**   Common challenges with change sponsorship

| Change Sponsorship Challenges |
| --- |
| Failure to define the scope of the change |
| Failure to set coalitions |
| Failure to create a sense of urgency |
| Failure to manage the transition |
| Failure to finish |
| Promising an easy, cheap, and quick change |
| Leaving it up to the PM to lead |
| Not communicating the reason for the change |
| Undermining the status quo |
| Moving at the wrong pace |
| Treating all those who are involved as one, instead of tailoring the messages |
| Failing to set clear expectations |
| Failing to connect with the project(s) |
| Being reactive |
| Failing to prioritize |
| Failing to realize constraints and capacities |
| Fear of making decisions or taking action |
| Failing to coordinate within the initiative and across organizational boundaries |
| Letting exceptions slide and become the norm |
| Weak leadership |
| Unclear communication |
| Allowing political considerations, territories, silos, egos, and emotions to drive decisions |
| Poor time management |

1. *The introduction of the change (where shock ensues)*—this is when the change is announced or introduced, and where the sponsor's focus needs to be on ensuring that there is a clear and compelling vision. For some stakeholders this may come as a surprise, while for others the change could not come soon enough. Some are happy about the change and that it is finally going to take place, while others do not want to change. Once the vision is in place and the message is out, the sponsor needs to start the process of mapping out who might support the change, who might resist, and

**Table 1.10** The meaning of common and significant change sponsorship challenges

| Change Sponsorship Challenge | What It Means |
| --- | --- |
| Failure to identify and communicate a compelling vision | The vision of the change is often poorly defined or unclear to most stakeholders who are not at the senior level of the organization. At times, there is no clear vision altogether, which introduces the question of why the change is even taking place. A lack of consistent understanding of the vision also leads to inconsistencies with decision making and with setting the right level of urgency and prioritization. |
| Failure to frame the scope of the change | We often fail to realize the true magnitude of the change—believing and leading others to believe that the change is going to be smaller, faster, and lower in cost than it actually ends up being. This gap in expectations may lead to performance issues and increase resistance when people realize that benefits are not realized in full, or on time. |
| Failure to manage the transition | From the time an announcement is made about an upcoming change (unfreezing or ending the current status quo) until we reach the destination (the refreezing or the beginning of the new desired state), there is a transition period. This involves uncertainty, resistance, frustration, changing realities, confusion, and disillusionment. It is paramount to manage the transition by ensuring that expectations are managed and that people feel that the change stakeholders care about them and handle their needs properly and with transparency. |
| Failure to effectively deal with resistance | During the transition, it is virtually a guarantee that some (or more than some) stakeholders will express resistance. This could be the result of frustration with the pace or the nature of the transition or due to a lack of knowledge about what it takes to handle the change, a lack of information about the change, or a lack of willingness to change. Either way, the handling of the resistance may spell the difference between the success or failure of the initiative—and it is driven by the change sponsor. |

While the types of challenges that change and project sponsors face may overlap, there are some unique challenges that change sponsors face when dealing with a change initiative; presented here along with their meanings.

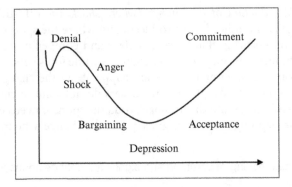

Call it the Kübler-Ross Model, change curve, or the U-Curve—it refers to the stages people go through during the change. Note that the *uptick* at the beginning may take place either because people are happy that the change is finally here and they improve their performance or they try to prove that the current state is fine, so they (temporarily) perform better until they realize that the change is not going away. *Source*: https://www.researchgate.net/figure/Change-curve-Source-Kuebler-Ross-1969_fig1_309816280

**Figure 1.1**    Kübler-Ross 5-Stage Model

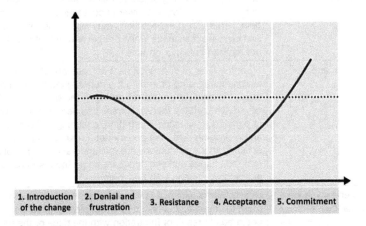

The first stage is the introduction (or announcement) of the change; the second stage is where people realize the status quo is going to be no more; the third stage is where anger and fear trigger resistance; the fourth stage is where exploration is leading to acceptance; and the fifth stage is where we gain commitment and rebuilding—toward the next change.

**Figure 1.2**    Interpretation of the U-Curve

who is unsure or noncommittal. This is the first step in drafting a road-map and the start of what will be an action plan on how to go through the change, at what pace, and what needs to take place at any point. Figure 1.3 provides an overview of the challenges that take place in the introduction of the change stage.

2. *Denial and frustration (early stages of the change, sliding down the U-Curve)*— this is when some stakeholders do not accept that the change is moving forward, while others do not like the direction or the pace of the change. This stage is characterized by stakeholders who *hear and see* different things about the change; there are growing gaps in expectations and misunderstandings about the change and its impact. The sponsor needs to focus on creating alignment and maximizing communication, and if this stage is not handled well, some stakeholders may be lost in the process and the sponsor may never regain their support or trust. Depending on the extent of the dip that stakeholders go through, they may later check out or even leave the organization. Figure 1.4 provides an overview of the challenges that take place during the second stage of the change—the denial stage.

| Leadership | Communication | Planning | Vision |
|---|---|---|---|
| Absence of leadership consensus | Insufficient communication planning | Insufficient, unrealistic, optimistic planning | Lack of clear, compelling, or communicated vision |
| Lack of accountability | Promising a quick, cheap, pain-free transition | No proper resource needs identification | Disconnected/ unrealistic vision |
| Failing to establish a sense of urgency | Failing to assign ownership of the pieces | No planning for resistance | No defined outcomes |
| Assuming people will simply enroll in the change | Lack of organizational agility | Failing to realize the challenges of the transition | Failing to realize the extent of interlocking with other initiatives |
| Failing to recognize or address paradigms | Not establishing clear communication ownership and escalation lines | Disconnect between the change initiative and the project | Failing to frame the change scope |
| | Making the announcement without following up or continuity | Poor risk planning (i.e., tactical, optimistic) | Failing to realize it will be a sail, rather than a straight line toward the vision |
| | | Failing to properly identify, manage, or communicate assumptions | |

Breaking down the challenges during the first stage of the change—the introduction of the change—into four main categories: challenges with leadership, communication, planning, and vision.

**Figure 1.3**   Common challenges during the introduction of the change

| Leadership | Communication | Resistance |
|---|---|---|
| Failure to maintain focus on the vision | Missing or unclear feedback | Attempting to suppress resistance instead of honoring it |
| Disjointed team | Unrealistic expectations and mismanaged | Reactiveness as a result of a lack of planning for resistance and *side effects* |
| Failure to measure and show progress | | |
| Panic: trying to force the change (too strong, too fast) | Insufficient communication leading to rumors and frustration | One size fits all— mishandling those that are unaware, unable, or unwilling |
| Failure to articulate the difference between the change and the pain associated with it | Engaging in meaningless forms of communication | Over-focus on dealing with resisters |

Denial stage challenges are broken into three main categories: challenges with leadership, communication, and resistance handling.

**Figure 1.4**    Common challenges during the denial stage

3. *Resistance (unfreezing of the current state, where depression and experiments are common, essentially at the bottom of the U-Curve, with some movement to the right and eventually slightly upward)*—there may still be gaps in perceptions and expectations and it is normal and expected for some stakeholders to demonstrate resistance. The focus should be on sparking motivation and starting the process of developing capabilities. The sponsor needs to lead the effort and set the tone to handle the resistance effectively, so that more stakeholders will begin the experimentation process toward achieving buy-in. Resistance may show itself in different forms and for various reasons: some want to maintain the status quo while others may not like the direction that the change is moving in, how the change is being executed, or that it is taking too

long or is too painful for them. Some may be concerned about what will happen to their roles or their performance once the change is complete. The sponsor needs to honor the resistance and handle it effectively and efficiently. Chapter 5 deals with change sponsorship in more detail and breaks down the source of the resistance into three primary types: a lack of awareness about the change; a lack of knowledge about what it takes to do the work past the change; and a lack of willingness to change altogether. Figure 1.5 provides a glance into the challenges that are introduced during this stage.

| Organizational | Communication | Resistance | Leadership |
|---|---|---|---|
| Lack of resilience | Failing to reinforce the message in different ways | Failing to handle resistance/ignoring it | Focusing on lost battles and on persistent resisters |
| Focusing on symbols, politics, structure, and appearances—rather than on people and culture | Failing to address different communication needs and styles | Focusing on fighting resistance and on suppressing it, instead of on learning where it comes from | Failing to manage the transition |
| Failing to address the change saturation/ fatigue | | Sending a message that it is better to resist | Failing to lead/lead by example |
| Failing to handle interlocking change initiatives | | Caving to resistance: changing course, slowing down, calling things off | Failing to realize what change stage people are at and that different people are in different stages |
| | | | Allowing people to check out |
| | | | Panicking and allowing panic to ensue |
| | | | Focusing on tactical elements and losing sight of the vision |

Resistance stage challenges are broken into four main categories: organizational, communication, resistance, and leadership.

**Figure 1.5** Common challenges with the resistance stage

4. *Acceptance* (*transitioning through the neutral zone and upward by way of more experiments and decisions*)—there is a chance that the change initiative may never make it to this stage if the initiative is not successful or if it is stopped prematurely. However, reaching the stage of acceptance is a sign that things are moving in the right direction and that they are starting to fall into place. Stakeholders start moving up the right side of the U-Curve. The sponsor needs to make sure that expectations are aligned, benefits and value are beginning to be realized, and that the results are starting to *stick* and become second nature, or a new normal. The sponsor should also see that there is further development in capabilities and that knowledge is shared. Figure 1.6 lists the challenges that are introduced during the acceptance stage.

| Leadership | Organizational | Vision |
|---|---|---|
| Insufficient reinforcement | Failure to check for side effects and organizational impact | Thinking we are done |
| Failure to engrain the change | | Failure to see the big picture |
| Failure to think product, rather than project | Failure to realize that some people have not moved up to this stage | Failure to articulate and show the benefits |
| Letting go too early | Failure to communicate achievements | Failure to check progress against the vision and to revisit the original intent |
| Failure to celebrate success | | |
| | Failure to address anxieties that are triggered by the change | |

Acceptance stage challenges are broken into three main categories: leadership, organizational, and vision.

**Figure 1.6**    Common challenges with the acceptance stage

5. *Commitment* (*integration and refreezing the new state*)—the new or desired state is achieved, and stakeholders are now stabilizing at the top right corner of the curve. It is good to celebrate, but it is more important to ensure that the change sticks and also to check on the results and show the extent to which the goals have been achieved. The new reality is also the new status quo, and it is important to review both the past and the future. For the past: look back at the business case and determine to what extent the objectives were achieved. For the future: assess the new position (status quo), what the upcoming needs are, and whether it is possible to begin the next change. Figure 1.7 discusses challenges that appear at this stage.

| Leadership | Organizational | Vision |
|---|---|---|
| Failure to emphasize mutual accountability | Rushing into the next initiative prematurely | Lack of understanding of the full extent of what we have just achieved |
| Focusing on functions instead of on common goals | Failing to establish a plan to reinforce the achievements | Lack of understanding of the new position, needs, and capabilities |
| Failure to realize that some people have not reached this stage | Lack of preparation for the next change | Failure to understand the true state of the new status quo |
| | Lack of realization of new capabilities | Failure to end properly and redefine the current state |
| | Failure to realize lessons, or to apply learning from lessons | Failure to finish |
| | Failure to realize the full extent of impact on other areas | Failure to accept that the results may not be fully aligned with the original mandate |
| | | Failure to realize *economies of scope*: originally unintended benefits |

Commitment stage challenges are broken into three main categories: leadership, organizational, and vision.

**Figure 1.7**   Common challenges with the commitment stage

## THE IMPACT OF CHALLENGES WITH SPONSORSHIP

The impact that challenges with sponsorship have can be highly damaging to organizations. When project sponsors are not effective, it may lead to performance issues with the project, and often to project failure. Depending on the nature of the project, failures can be damaging and expensive. Clearly, not all project failures are because of sponsorship problems, but many failures do originate from poor sponsorship. This may involve an unclear mandate, failure to envision the project and the team, insufficient support, untimely decision making, or flawed decisions. Unclear or unrealistic expectations, optimistic timelines, poor risk management, or issues around project change control can also be associated with poor sponsorship. Following the principles that *fish rot from their heads*—many project problems can be traced back to challenges with project sponsorship.

When it comes to change sponsorship, although the impact of challenges may be even more severe than that of project sponsorship, it is often hard to measure or articulate the full impact that challenges with change sponsorship may introduce. The change sponsor may be referred to or viewed as the change initiator or the change leader—and as such, he/she oversees the change initiative. In a similar fashion to the role of the project sponsor, the change sponsor provides a mandate, sets expectations, and gives a direction. However, the change initiative may include one or more projects, and naturally it may span over a longer time frame.

Either way, when the sponsor (project or change) does not perform his/her role properly, it has a lasting and often significant impact on whatever they oversee.

## THE REASON FOR SPONSORSHIP-RELATED CHALLENGES

A common theme throughout the book is about the need for sponsors to realize the significant, if not critical, impact they have on the success of their areas of responsibility—be it a project, a program, or a change initiative. While many of those who become sponsors are familiar with the type of work they need to perform, relatively few do it effectively and there is a wide range of reasons behind it:

- A lack of awareness regarding the nature of the sponsor's role or the importance of the sponsor to organizational success
- The sponsor's limited ability to integrate multiple factors into a cohesive big picture
- The sponsor's ineffective collaboration with the PM and other stakeholders
- A lack of time since sponsors are typically also senior officers in their respective organizations and usually focus first and foremost on their day jobs, whereas the sponsorship *hat* they wear is secondary

- Poor portfolio management in the organization with unclear capacity management and inconsistent and insufficient prioritization (both across and within projects) causing sponsors to struggle to focus on what matters most
- A lack of organizational agility (i.e., timely and effective handling of the changing circumstances)
- A lack of clear communication protocols, as well as a lack of clear norms and ground rules, which can lead to confusion and misunderstandings
- The failure of sponsors to draw clear *boundaries* between their role and that of the PM, with clear roles and responsibilities
- No adherence to best practices resulting in poor resource management and almost a complete lack of assumption management, which delays the discussion and surfacing of challenges causing a delay in handling these challenges
- Not seeing the big picture; a lack of clear links between project/initiatives and strategic objectives causes frequent and unnecessary changes to priorities and areas of focus, and with that, comes also a lack of focus on risks that are bigger than and span beyond merely project risks

It is clear that most sponsors (as well as other roles within organizations) suffer from a chronic shortage of time and are consistently overworked. This time shortage means a lack of ability to invest sufficient time and capacity in what they do—leading to poor decision making that involves hasty decisions, misinformed actions, and a constant feeling of being overwhelmed by the continuous barrage of issues and challenges that are thrown at people.

Most of the underlying reasons for challenges with sponsorship are about awareness, role definition, and prioritization. These are all familiar areas that can be improved. None of these areas are in the range of *unchartered territory*; yet, it is unclear why people continually struggle to improve on the area of sponsorship.

*Fixing* project and change sponsorship will not magically make all associated problems go away, but it can significantly improve the way project and change success are delivered. In a way, it is safe to associate project and change sponsorship with the 80:20 Pareto Principle:[3] fixing sponsorship can pave the way to substantial improvement in projects and in change initiatives performance.

## PROJECT VERSUS CHANGE SPONSORSHIP: SIMILARITIES AND DIFFERENCES BETWEEN THEM

Let's take a look at the key differences between project and change management and at why the role of the sponsor, when it comes to these two areas, is surprisingly similar. Project management and change management are intertwined with each other, and while they are two distinct areas and disciplines, many of the roles of the sponsor in these two disciplines are similar. In both disciplines, the sponsor initiates, leads, drives, mandates, supports, oversees, articulates success, enables and serves as an escalation point, accepts, and signs off.

It is safe to say that almost all projects introduce an element of change in them. Any product or result that a project produces may lead to a change in the way things gets done in the organization and in the way people do their work. For that, each project needs to have the basic elements of change management, which include the handoff from the project to operations, any transition requirements, training, and communication. Any PM who does their work properly performs some change management elements in their project management work. It is safe to say that project management and change management were combined in the past, before the awareness for distinct change management needs emerged.

With that said, when referring these days to change management, it is different than project management—and change management goes significantly beyond the scope of the project. In fact, the change management life cycle is expected to be longer than that of the project and potentially entails multiple projects within it—as illustrated by Figure 1.8. Therefore, change management involves a larger initiative, possibly of a more strategic nature, that transitions, moves, or transforms the organization or parts of it into something else. A change initiative may include multiple projects and, as a result, one could ask what the difference is between change and a program. After all, a program is a group of related projects that are managed in a coordinated way. The main difference is that programs, like projects, are tactical and the change may have a more strategic impact. The comparison between change and a program also brings us back to the comparison between the roles of the sponsors and the many similarities between the change sponsor and the project sponsor.

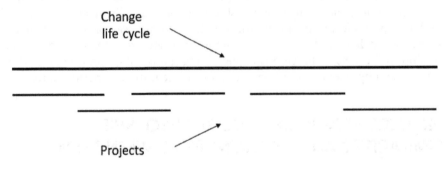

The change life cycle is longer than that of a project and may include multiple projects within it. Changes are different than programs.

**Figure 1.8**    Project and change life cycles

Although project and change management are considered different disciplines, it is important to see how these two areas get closer to each other and perhaps start to converge into one, as they are both intertwined.

## Connecting Change and Project

It is nothing short of critical for organizations to ensure that there is a connection between change and projects. Now that it has been established that change is typically bigger than projects, it is through project management that organizations manage to do things, make changes, implement solutions, and deliver on their objectives. It is therefore important to articulate the needs and success criteria of the change initiative, which is often of a strategic nature, to define and measure what needs to get done in order to fulfill the change and deliver on its vision.

With no proper coordination and connection between change and projects, great ideas might end up failing, and projects may deliver on budget and on time but not deliver value. Chapter 5 further discusses change management and the need to ensure proper connection to project management, including considerations such as the charter, risk management, definition of success, and communication.

## Change and Project Sponsor

When it comes to change and projects—there is often confusion, as many organizations "install" a change manager to work alongside the PM. If these two individuals do not coordinate their roles and responsibilities with each other, it may lead to confusion regarding who is in charge of what, the touchpoints between the two roles, and where one role's scope ends and the other's begins.

The mix of change and project management roles is also confusing at the sponsorship level. If there is both a project sponsor and a change sponsor, it is hard to distinguish who is in charge of what, and it introduces confusion when it comes to separating the product development (i.e., project) from the impact that the same will have on the organization (change management). When these two roles are separate, it may also lead to turf wars, as part of the too widespread siloed thinking.

Although change and project sponsors look at different areas within the organization, have different impacts, and explore different considerations, their roles are similar. That is the thought behind this book: to introduce more knowledge, context, and understanding of how to become a more effective sponsor—change or project. Table 1.11 provides a high-level comparison between project and change sponsorship and their respective roles; showing that many of the roles and the responsibilities of the two positions are similar to each other.

**Table 1.11**   Project and change sponsorship

| Project Sponsorship | Change Sponsorship |
|---|---|
| Charter the project and articulate the business case | Be visionary, build a coalition |
| Promotion, authorization, scoping, funding, and resourcing | Manage, combat, and handle resistance and attitudes |
| Promote this project and provide prioritization within/across/against other projects | Prioritize the projects within the initiative |
| Ensure alignment to strategic objectives | Create alignment to strategic objectives |
| Benefit realization beyond the project | Ensure sustainable change (the change is sticking and is coordinated with organizational needs) |
| Represent the user of the project's product | Represent the organization's needs that may include products and other elements |
| Set priorities within and across the project/initiative ||
| Advocate for assigning the right resources ||
| Ensure funding/budget is in place ||
| Set goals and success criteria ||
| Approve; serve as an escalation point and sign off ||
| Check completion of key deliverables and milestones ||
| Protect the initiative and the team ||
| Engage other stakeholders ||
| Lead certain communications ||
| Promote the needs of the initiative ||
| Be visible and sufficiently involved ||
| Be proactive about the role ||
| Gatekeeper ||
| Leader ||

There are many similarities between the roles of the project and change sponsor.

## Project Management

Projects are tactical by nature; they serve as a means for organizations to introduce new products, services, or results, as part of the effort to grow, improve processes, expand, or achieve strategic goals. As tactical processes, projects are not unimportant, but rather they deal with day-to-day activities toward their defined objectives. Typically, the main focus of projects has been on goals, performance, tasks, and results, in the context of introducing a new product, capability, or process. As a result, PMs are installed to lead projects, with a heavy focus on performance, benefit realization, and capabilities. Unfortunately, the focus on performance has tilted organizations away from managing capacities and effectively handling the human aspect, along with understanding the full range of impact that the project's result will have on the organization and its customers.

Project management has gone through major growth in the past quarter century, since around the time PMI first introduced *A Guide to the Project Management Body of Knowledge (PMBOK® Guide)* in 1996. This practice contributed to the significant increase in awareness around the importance of project management, along with a spike in learning and professional development. Through the years, hundreds of thousands of practitioners have obtained certificates and organizations have pursued alignment with the PMBOK's principles and practices.

## Change Management

Change management is not a new discipline, but rather a newly realized element that is a key factor for performance and success. Change is an integral part of every organization and is about understanding the impact that the project's product will have on the organization, its customers, and its users. Further, while projects typically introduce products and measurable results, change is about managing the attitudes of people and, as a result, of the new reality that the change introduces. Change can come in multiple forms, but overall, it is about how people will respond to new or different things and how to minimize the negative impact of these responses, including side effects, resistance, and getting out of the comfort zone.

There are a few truths about change: it tends to be longer, more expensive, and bigger than it is initially thought to be. Also, although it is called organizational change, organizations do not change, but people do—and the main components, drivers, and keys to success in organizations are *people*. It is Dofasco[4] that since 1970 has used the same corporate slogan: "Our product is steel. Our strength is people."

It is safe to say that change is typically *bigger* than projects. That is, an organizational change may be comprised of more than one project, and it will take longer to commit to the new reality that projects introduce than to implement the project's product. This brings us back to the sponsorship element; a project sponsor is someone who oversees a project, owns it, funds it, and who, most likely, is in charge of defining the objectives and success criteria. In most environments, project sponsors are senior stakeholders in the organization who have a day job within the organization, and in addition, they oversee the project, commonly as part of a portfolio of projects under their umbrella.

Then what, or rather, who is a change sponsor? The change sponsor may be a program sponsor who oversees a group of related projects or initiatives. Alternately, the change sponsor may oversee the areas of accepting, committing, and adapting to a new reality that is introduced in the organization. The sponsor needs to ensure that it is not only the product that is delivered, but that there is also a plan to ensure that the new way of doing things is accepted, is handled effectively, and is in the context of the organizational needs. Change sponsors are senior stakeholders who look at the people, attitudes, and the organizational impact of the change. Either way, the role of the change sponsor is similar to that of the project sponsor—and the two are often related. Further, the two roles may be performed by the same individual.

## Additional Sponsorship Interactions

### Agile

Although many would not agree, agile is an *extension* of project management since it offers a different way to slice the project life cycle and it introduces practices that serve to reduce risk, effectively handle change, and introduce efficiencies. Since the time agile was coined in the context that it is currently known (2001), it has taken a few years to grow and gain significant traction. Around 2010 agile started to take over as a new methodology, offering a new promise to improve project performance. In the process, Scrum has become a household name and multiple organizations have attempted to pursue capabilities in managing agile projects; in many cases, stating that they intend to replace traditional project management approaches with agile.

Unfortunately, although agile is based on very effective concepts, for the most part, agile has not managed to bring with it the full extent of the desired benefits that proponents thought it would. A leading reason that many organizations have fallen short of fully realizing the potential of agile has been due to applying the agile concepts the wrong way, in the wrong context, or for the wrong reason. Another common challenge in agile environments is no other than sponsorship because there is often confusion between the role of the project sponsor or the executive sponsor and that of the product owner. The latter is intended by agile methods to act as a hands-on sponsor, to call the shots, and accept and make decisions. It is common, however, for an organization to *layer up* the role of the sponsor with that of the product owner, introducing a lack of clarity, duplication of effort, confusion, and ultimately friction between the two roles.

The product owner is a distinct agile role who, with the lack of a better term, serves as *the single wringable neck* in a project. He/she sets and defines objectives, articulates success criteria, calls the shots, accepts deliverables, and determines what will happen next (if anything) and what will change.

In addition to the seams between the sponsor and the product owner, in some agile environments, the business analyst (BA) may also be the *acting* product owner when there is no individual to fulfill the product owner role or when the product owner is not sufficiently available or involved. This introduces more challenges to the project's success due to the BA's lack of context and seniority to perform the product owner's role effectively. Having the BA support the product owner can be very helpful, but having the BA outright replace the product owner often backfires.

Around 2014, Gartner introduced the *bimodal approach* that called for an organization to maintain two types of operating systems for managing projects—maintaining abilities in traditional or *waterfall* approaches, while also developing agile capabilities. From this book's perspective, this approach further reinforces the need for an effective sponsor, whatever the life-cycle approach may be.

## Sponsorship and Effective Management

Another aspect of sponsorship that this book covers is the need to develop the ability to become an effective manager. Since most project and change sponsors also serve in different capacities in their organizations (e.g., senior managers, directors, division heads, or executives), it is critical that they develop the right skills and awareness of how to become effective managers and leaders, beyond their product and organizational knowledge, along with the ability to foster, coach, and support their direct reports toward becoming effective managers. These items include the ability to actually manage people (i.e., their teams), as opposed to only managing performance and objectives.

## The PMO and Governance

Sponsorship, like any other function in an organization, cannot be performed in a silo and it must understand its place in relation to other parts of the organization—especially when it comes to bodies that work closely together or those that may impact the ability to deliver success.

Project management offices (PMOs) have had an important role in supporting projects, but when the PMO's involvement is not right (i.e., too much or too little), it may be detrimental to project success. Regardless of the type and mandate of the PMO, the sponsor needs to establish rules of engagement with it so that both sides know their respective and their counterparts' level of involvement, timing, decision-making authority, and all of the associated touchpoints.

It is also important to engage project and organizational governance to ensure understanding of their structure and process. It is necessary to learn how the project/change initiative can benefit from the governance structure and best practices, as well as what vital information to be aware of, or anything that may pose constraints and risks on what is being done. Governance is key in ensuring accountability and process adherence, and it provides transparency and proof to stakeholders of that transparency and final product value. Governance processes cannot be ignored, and it is wrong to think that bypassing these processes will help initiatives in the long run. Therefore, it is necessary to accept, embrace, and work with the governance structure that is in place. When there is a need for a change, the sponsor should pursue the right channel to update the governance structure or processes as required.

## SPONSORSHIP—KEYS FOR SUCCESS

Overall, if organizations fail to improve on the area of sponsorship in both projects and change initiatives, the struggle to maximize benefits and achieve results will continue to persist. Addressing change management alone will not yield the desired outcome because doing so will provide a fix for one area, but it will not be a holistic fix that trickles through the organization. Focusing only on change management will also cause a repeat of the same types of mistakes that have been committed by the "flavor-of-the-month" focus on project management, business analysis, portfolio management, maturity models, PMOs, and agile.

When all of these attempts fell short of delivering success, it was not a result of these areas missing the mark, being irrelevant, or being ineffective, but rather it was the implementation of the concepts around them and treating them as silos that led to the *lukewarm* results. It also was the failure to realize the impact that these respective areas had on the people, and improperly gauging how the people would react to them. Many ideas that look good on paper end up delivering less-than-stellar results in reality.

### Feedback Loops

Establishing and maintaining a strong, clear, and timely feedback loop is crucial for effective sponsorship. A feedback loop is a checkpoint in the experience that helps ensure that whatever has to be done is taking place and that information is flowing from the stakeholders back to the decision makers in the project or the change initiative. Project and change sponsors need to ensure that their teams have the ability to collect and understand information quickly and in turn, the sponsor needs to make decisions with limited amounts of information. This is why creating a strong and effective feedback loop is critical for success. The feedback loop must include formal and informal channels, and it needs to involve pre-identified individuals, along with a definition of their role and a mechanism to allow both ongoing, as well as ad hoc communication. There is also a need for a set of signs, signals, and escalation procedures to enable any side in the loop to initiate communication with minimal effort and red tape. Finally, those involved in this loop must have clear norms and the maturity to retain focus and to avoid drama and overacting.

Feedback loops, as illustrated in Figure 1.9, are about keeping in touch and knowing at any given point what is going on pertaining to any key aspect of the engagement. It does not imply micromanagement; in fact, if the feedback loop works effectively, it is exactly the opposite of micromanagement. A significant part of that loop takes place as part of the training and communication aspects of the engagement, but there is a lot to be said about the informal and ad hoc portions that allow an ongoing flow of information and the ability to effectively manage by exception.

It is common to find project and change practitioners who explain that they do not have time to engage stakeholders, strengthen the communication with team members, improve relationships within or outside of the organization, or enhance the way they manage expectations. In response, the question that should be asked is: "Then what is it you *have* been doing?" PMI found long ago that PMs spend around 80–90% of their time communicating and performing stakeholder engagement activities. In change management it is similar; many of the activities that take

While most of the activities associated with collecting and analyzing feedback take place within our teams (project or change, respectively), it is the role of the sponsor to oversee the establishment of those loops, the collection of feedback, and the analysis. The sponsor then is responsible for authorizing or making the decision based on the feedback and the situation on hand.

**Figure 1.9**  Feedback loop

place as part of a change management plan are related to various forms of training and communication. It is therefore critical to allow sufficient capacity and the level of focus to perform these activities effectively and on an ongoing basis. This is why it is essential to maintain that feedback loop and ensure that it is possible to see how things are progressing and at what rate, and to have as clear a picture as possible of the stakeholders' needs, reactions, concerns, and messages.

The *flow* within the feedback loop needs to provide awareness of what occurs and that it all has meaning that can be informative. Figure 1.10 shows us how the cycle works.

Establishing an effective feedback loop may sound trivial, but such a loop will not fulfill its role unless it is set up properly, maintained, adjusted as needed, and action is taken on the signals that are received. Part of the effort takes place

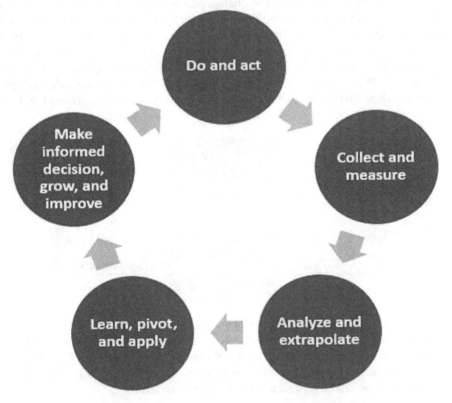

When the terms *context*, *awareness*, and *learning* are used, they mean that there is a need for a mechanism that captures, measures, and analyzes relevant information to further learning, growth, and improvement.

**Figure 1.10**   The feedback loop process

through formal communication and reporting mechanisms, but most of the timely and meaningful information is obtained through a web of informal communications that takes place on an ongoing basis. Due to the structure and frequency of the informal communication, some may view it as quasi-formal; but either way, it is time consuming and complex to set up and manage. Here are several items to consider when trying to establish a meaningful feedback loop:

- *Speed*—determine the speed that is required for communication to flow and for feedback to arrive. It is imperative to ensure that those in need of feedback have access to the effect of actions, simulations, or options that pertain to their needs. Establish who will address their needs, what level of knowledge and experience is required, and what format to use for the feedback.
- *The stakeholder*—the feedback must connect and relate to the needs of the stakeholder and be based on the motivations and the drivers of whoever is involved. This reverts back to the stakeholder analysis and to the importance of understanding people's needs.
- *Measurable*—provide meaningful, actionable, and as much as possible—measurable feedback. Ensure that the feedback is not vague and that it involves action that is in context—relevant and applicable to the specific circumstances.
- *Goals and objectives*—ensure that the feedback provides a solution, or at least a path that is aligned with the stakeholder's goals and objectives.
- *Measurements*—Establish a mechanism to measure the quality and the feedback loop success. The outcomes of the actions and the initiatives need to be collected and understood through a set of quantitative measurements and analytics that will help to identify trends and perform cause-effect analysis.
- *Transparency and ethics*—provide genuine feedback and call for action, then ensure that it focuses on win-win situations and on ensuring that any actions that are taken will work toward constructive results that are in line with all applicable context and rules.
- *People*—make sure that the right people (skills, experience, style, and knowledge) are placed on both (or all) sides of the loop and that everyone in the loop (the provider of feedback and those who receive it) is aware of his/her role.
- *What the loop is about*—set the right expectations about the role of the loop, its mechanisms, the expected turnaround times, and the expected results. The feedback loop may not provide the final solution or, for that matter, any solution, depending on its role.
- *Data and information*—make sure everyone involved knows what data to provide and in what format; and correspondingly, equip those who receive and analyze the feedback with what it takes to convert the data into meaningful information that is a base for decision support. Key performance

indicators may need to be established, researched, or articulated as a benchmark and for decision criteria.

## Back to the Definitions: What Is Sponsorship?

"Project sponsor: A person or group who provides resources and support for the project, program or portfolio and is accountable for enabling success."[5] As for the change sponsor, there is no clear definition. The change sponsor may be referred to as the change initiator, change champion, or even the change leader. The change sponsor leads the change within the organization, and he/she needs to lead by example and be the first person to articulate and work toward the change. While there is no clear and short definition of the role of the change sponsor, according to Procsi,[6] the sponsor has to participate visibly throughout the project, communicate support and promote the change, and build a coalition of leaders to support the change.

## RECAP

This chapter looked into the basics of what change and project management are, what change and project sponsorship are, and the challenges associated with the respective roles. It examined generic challenges, as well as challenges associated with different stages throughout the project and the change.

The need to connect between change and projects was reiterated by ensuring that the projects that are within the change initiative are aligned with the bigger picture and that they produce value toward the intent of the change. This chapter also touched on the notion that although every project introduces a level of change to the organization, change management is about a more strategic type of change to the organization. Recalling the days when project and change management were one, it was discovered that good project management involves elements of change management, and extrapolated that in the near future project and change management will have to converge back into one.

An interesting question was raised in this chapter: what is it that change and project managers or sponsors do if they do not communicate? It is puzzling that many individuals who lead or sponsor projects and change do not find the time to properly communicate with and engage their stakeholders and team members. In fact, there is nothing that is more important than communicating and engaging effectively.

Overall, it is clear that there is a problem with sponsorship when it comes to both projects and change initiatives. The problem is with both the definition of the sponsor's role as well as with the expectations and the performance of sponsors—and the result is poor sponsorship. What does poor sponsorship mean? It appears in many forms, but the end result is the same: failure to deliver on the intended set of values and benefits for the organization, along with all of the negative symptoms that are associated with costs and schedule overruns, unhappy customers and stakeholders, and other performance issues for the organization.

This chapter poses many questions and no real answers as to what it takes to become an effective project or change sponsor. Chapter 2 takes us through the process of looking into the root causes of problems with sponsorship, and it provides actions and concepts that can help improve both project and change sponsorship.

## NOTES

1. https://asq.org/quality-resources/pdca-cycle.
2. Kübler-Ross 5-Stage Model for change https://www.change-management -coach.com/kubler-ross.html; https://www.researchgate.net/figure/Change -curve-Source-Kuebler-Ross-1969_fig1_309816280.
3. https://www.juran.com/blog/a-guide-to-the-pareto-principle-80-20-rule-pareto -analysis/.
4. ArcelorMittal Dofasco is a steel company based in Hamilton, Ontario, Canada. Dofasco is a stand-alone subsidiary of ArcelorMittal, the world's largest integrated steel producer. https://en.wikipedia.org/wiki/Dofasco.
5. Project Management Institute (PMI). *Project Management Body of Knowledge (PMBOK® Guide)—Sixth Edition*. PMI, 2017.
6. https://www.prosci.com/resources/articles/importance-and-role-of-executive -sponsor.

# 2

---

# ACTIONS REQUIRED TO *FIX* SPONSORSHIP

---

After looking into the main challenges with project and change sponsorship in Chapter 1, there will be a review of the main reasons why sponsorship is broken and what it takes to improve it in Chapter 2. Similar to what was done in Chapter 1, the discussion will highlight generic types of actions that can be taken to improve sponsorship in general, and then focus on both project and change sponsorship.

## ROOT CAUSES FOR SPONSORSHIP PROBLEMS

There are only a handful of underlying reasons for sponsorship problems and they are all related to each other. Further, these underlying reasons trigger the large majority of problems that are demonstrated by sponsors; problems that end up putting a major strain on organizational performance: awareness, the sponsorship role, focus, capacity, and time/prioritization. There will be a review of these cause categories, along with how they appear in organizations and what can be done about them. Note that all categories are related to each other and that they partially overlap:

1. *Awareness*—there may be a lack of awareness of the importance of the sponsor's role and involvement; and even if the awareness is there, there may be limited realization and recognition of the need for a hands-on sponsor who makes timely decisions and is sufficiently involved in the project. The same goes for change sponsors. Organizations often fail to have a clear sponsor and there is often confusion between those who initiate the change and the sponsor who is supposed to direct it. It is not that people walk around thinking that sponsors are not important or knowledgeable, but there is a widespread misconception as to what the

sponsor actually does or the criticality of the sponsor's role and involvement to the initiative's success.

2. *Role*—no clear sponsor role definition; sponsors often do not know exactly what is expected of them or what they need to do on a day-to-day basis when it comes to the sponsorship *hat* they are wearing. Further, project managers (PMs), change managers, team members, and other stakeholders also have unclear and inconsistent levels of understanding of the sponsor's role. This leads to a one-two punch of a problem that involves both the gap in expectations and the sponsor's responsibility. For example, the gap is created when the sponsor believes that the PM can handle things on his/her own, leaving him/her to roam and make key project decisions. It is also common to see that the sponsor's responsibility is undefined and unclear. This means that sponsors do not know what they need to do in order to help the project or the initiative. Compounding the role definition with the gap in expectations exacerbates the problem that often leads to significant performance issues.

3. *Focus*—in the majority of cases, the role of the sponsor is *part-time* for members of senior management with no specific role or job title. This often leads to problems related to the amount of focus that the role of the sponsor gets from the individual who performs it. Besides the lack of focus on the sponsor's role, when roles are not defined and there are no clear and tangible deliverables associated with the role, it is easy to lose track of what needs to be done; especially when there are more pressing issues that are more specific and tangible. Living in an era in which most people are overworked or busy beyond their actual work capacity, when people do not have time to complete their work, they look for shortcuts and for things they can drop so they can finish their *more important things*. Like most people, sponsors have a *day job* and since it requires more tangible attention (reports and deliverables) than their role as a sponsor, it is easy to drop things that belong under the sponsorship role. The problem is also prevalent with PMs who focus on more tangible tasks and deliverables (i.e., scope, schedules, budgets, and reports) and often fail to pay sufficient attention to things like defining and managing assumptions, realizing constraints, understanding stakeholder needs, and managing expectations. By focusing on the tangible blocks of time on their schedules, sponsors often fail to address their responsibilities as sponsors.

4. *Capacity*—although the previous item covering focus in the sponsorship role alluded to capacity issues, there is a need to specifically address problems related to sponsors' capacity. Sponsors (like everyone else in the organization) are busy individuals and they rarely have the required capacity to give appropriate attention to the project and the initiatives they oversee. They commonly view the PM or the change manager as the person who owns the initiative. Further, sponsors often believe that their involvement should be on an exception and escalation basis, as opposed

to the actual need for their ongoing involvement. In addition, people do not know their own (or their teams') capacity and, as such, they take on too much work. It is rare to find individuals who are aware of their own capacity; let alone when it comes to teams. The majority of people tend to be overly optimistic about their capacity, thinking that they are stronger and faster than their actual ability to perform. For the most part, people have little awareness of their own capacity; that is, how much time they actually have when it comes to producing value. It is common that people fail to realize how much of their time is wasted or spent on non-value-add activities (both at work and in their personal lives), such as administrative chores, meetings, overhead, waiting, misunderstandings, technical issues, handoffs, duplication of effort, corrective action, and other types of waste. The time spent on these items ends up to be significantly more than what was expected and it adds up to be a large chunk of time. Sponsors also suffer from this gap between expectations and reality when it comes to their own capacity: even though they may think they spend less of their time on non-value-add activities, although their capacity may not be consumed by pure waste as previously listed—there are many tasks and activities that they should delegate so they can find the time to perform their sponsorship role. Figure 2.1 compares activities that consume most of a sponsor's time versus the things that actually need attention. Note that a sponsor needs to spend more of their time on the items below the water level; this iceberg describes the desired way to spend time.

5. *Time and prioritization*—here too, this item has some overlap with capacity: yes, it has already been established that people are overworked, yet being busy is often confused with productivity. This confusion is driven in part by people's fundamental lack of understanding of how to effectively manage their own time and reduce the amount of waste that is riddled throughout their schedule. Time management is also related to prioritization. Everyone has a limited capacity and once that capacity is reached or nearly reached, it is necessary to prioritize what needs to be done within that capacity. People do not only scramble to define priorities among the things they need to do, but it is also a chronic problem in organizations where prioritization is not clear (across the board, within projects, and across initiatives). As a result, managers (at all levels) give work assignments to their direct reports, but they do not provide context for prioritization, thus, transferring the onus to prioritize onto the individuals doing the work. With no clear guidelines as to how to sequence the work, people pick and choose what they like to do, which is often based on convenience and personal preference, as opposed to actual needs. The result is often a failure to deliver on what the managers wanted, and this subsequently leads to conflict and a failure to meet objectives. Figure 2.2 provides insights into the tangible things the sponsor does versus the hidden items that consume disproportionately large portions of our time.

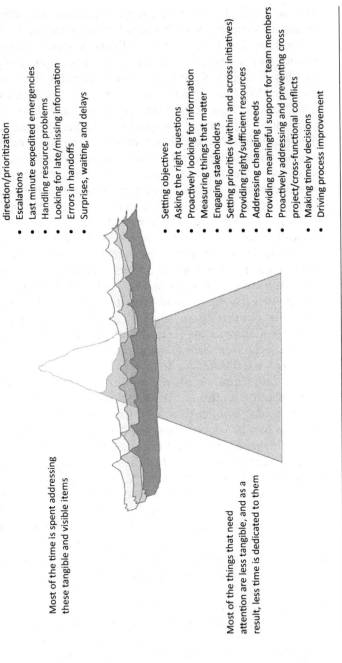

- Meetings
- Misunderstandings
- Clarifications
- Unnecessary conflicts due to lack of clear direction/prioritization
- Escalations
- Last minute expedited emergencies
- Handling resource problems
- Looking for late/missing information
- Errors in handoffs
- Surprises, waiting, and delays

Most of the time is spent addressing these tangible and visible items

- Setting objectives
- Asking the right questions
- Proactively looking for information
- Measuring things that matter
- Engaging stakeholders
- Setting priorities (within and across initiatives)
- Providing right/sufficient resources
- Addressing changing needs
- Providing meaningful support for team members
- Proactively addressing and preventing cross project/cross-functional conflicts
- Making timely decisions
- Driving process improvement

Most of the things that need attention are less tangible, and as a result, less time is dedicated to them

**Figure 2.1**    Capacity: where should the time be focused?

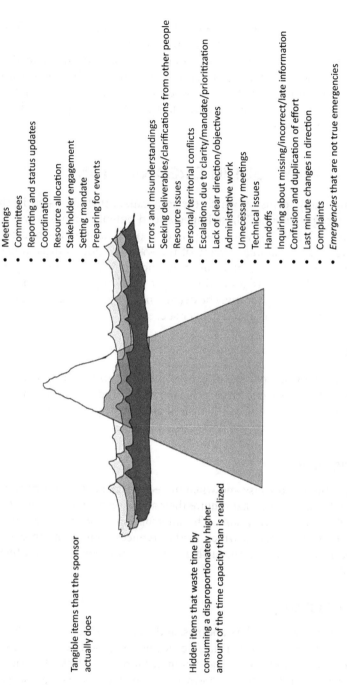

Tangible items that the sponsor actually does

- Day job (which may not be directly related to the sponsorship role: e.g., director, senior manager)
- Meetings
- Committees
- Reporting and status updates
- Coordination
- Resource allocation
- Stakeholder engagement
- Setting mandate
- Preparing for events

Hidden items that waste time by consuming a disproportionately higher amount of the time capacity than is realized

- Errors and misunderstandings
- Seeking deliverables/clarifications from other people
- Resource issues
- Personal/territorial conflicts
- Escalations due to clarity/mandate/prioritization
- Lack of clear direction/objectives
- Administrative work
- Unnecessary meetings
- Technical issues
- Handoffs
- Inquiring about missing/incorrect/late information
- Confusion and duplication of effort
- Last minute changes in direction
- Complaints
- *Emergencies* that are not true emergencies

**Figure 2.2**   Time: where does it go? Unfortunately, most of it is hard to account for.

Unlike the previous iceberg in Figure 2.1 which portrays a desired state of splitting the sponsor's time, this iceberg shows a common breakdown of the sponsor's time, where most of the time is consumed by the items that are below the surface. These are items that are hard to quantify and are more ad hoc in nature. They add up to a large chunk of time and many of them add no value besides fixing and undoing previously made errors and mistakes.

# HOW IT PLAYS OUT IN ORGANIZATIONS

There are many forms by which the root causes that are listed in this chapter appear in organizations. These impacts send potential shock waves that end up consuming a lot of time and energy and, at times, demoralize and confuse team members and stakeholders. Many of the ways to address these impacts will be discussed later in this chapter under the sponsor's leadership competencies, but some approaches toward a solution are provided as part of the impacts' descriptions. Overall, the impacts may be detrimental to projects' and change initiatives' ability to maximize value and deliver success.

## Stress

Sponsors usually do not have time to attend to important matters or enough time to perform their jobs effectively. This inevitably leads to stress that compromises people's effectiveness, makes them less pleasant to be around, and reduces the quality of their guidance and decisions.

## Distractions

When people are too busy and when there is a lack of clear prioritization, people's ability to focus on tasks that require their attention is hindered because their days are riddled with interruptions. The interruptions distract people from focusing on the things that matter, which further reduces their ability to deliver on their commitments. This, in turn, further enhances people's stress and their ability to perform.

## Lack of Clarity

With escalations, misunderstandings, and constantly increasing volumes of work, the stress, distractions, and a chronic lack of time lead to clarity issues with mandates, decisions, and even basic communication. The lack of clarity sends confusing signals and messages downstream, further escalating the gap between expectations and reality. A lack of clarity is directly related to the process of decision making, the transparency around decisions, and the timeliness of decisions.

Unfortunately, many decisions that sponsors make are not clear or not in line with objectives and the full extent of the situation at hand. Further, one of the most common complaints that PMs make is that many problems are not due to performance issues, but rather because of decisions, approvals, and sign-offs that are stalled and delayed on the sponsors' side. Sponsors do not deliberately delay decisions, but time constraints, a lack of full understanding of the associated sense of urgency, along with a reality where most sponsors are overworked, produce the unfavorable bottom line where decisions are delayed or made in a rush and are based on partial or erroneous information—potentially introducing problems and performance issues that will be felt later.

There is one additional problem with regard to decisions: many organizations are plagued by a culture of fear to make them and being overworked and overwhelmed compounds the problem. And with insufficient time to spend on looking into the decision, they often feel that they do not have enough information to make an informed decision. This, in turn, leads them to stall and avoid making a decision—failing to realize that not making a decision (or even a timely decision) is equivalent to making a decision to do nothing—with all of the potential consequences. When decisions are stalled or not made, time becomes a factor that, in most cases, works against the issue on hand.

## Conflict (Not the Good Type)

Although the modern view of conflict is that it is good for team building, growth, and innovation, not all conflict is good. When people are stressed and overworked, and when communication does not flow in an effective fashion, the misunderstandings and the performance issues that ensue often lead to conflict. While some conflict is about opportunities, growth, and new ideas, most of it is of the less-desired kind, such as conflict about performance issues and misunderstandings that surfaces as a result of the lack of guidance and unclear objectives and priorities. In addition, with increasing levels of stress, being overworked and consistently short on time, and with a general lack of clarity, many people default to personal conflict that is about egos, territories, and styles, rather than merits and the actual issues at stake. This latter type of conflict is the negative type—it adds no value and, in fact, has a negative impact on relationships, trust, and performance. With unnecessary conflict, productivity goes down and frustration grows, thereby creating a vicious cycle that fuels more conflict, misunderstandings, and performance issues.

Nevertheless, it is normal to have conflict when engaging in project and change initiatives. It is normal, expected, and even encouraged, when it comes to the *good* type of conflict. However, it is not only up to the PM to manage conflict effectively, but rather it is the responsibility of the sponsor to set up the right type of culture, atmosphere, and process to encourage people to engage in effective conflict. In addition, the sponsor is a point of escalation for conflicts that cannot be resolved at the lower levels, namely by the PM and change manager.

## A Lack of Support

With no time to engage and support the PMs, change managers, middle managers, supervisors, and team members, the sponsors leave them to make their own decisions about prioritization and issues, leading to even more performance problems. Further, sponsors' lack of capacity makes them increasingly unavailable to provide help and support to their teams, leading to an increasing number of urgent matters that need escalations, emergencies, and overall reactive approaches. People no longer proactively address issues and are forced to wait until the size of their crisis warrants action. The cycle feeds itself, as people at all levels become reactive and where organizations neglect to offer training and improvement opportunities.

## Managers and Team Members Lack Key Competencies—Partially Due to Ineffective Training

Most efforts around training are about technical skills and job performance, followed by supporting skills training—such as project management, business analysis, and agile. However, there are a few types of training and supporting activities that are not underutilized:

- *Sponsorship training*—relatively few organizations engage in improving the specific skills and competencies that can help their senior managers become more effective project and change sponsors. It is still believed that sponsorship skills and competencies come with seniority or the job, not realizing that a conscious effort needs to be made to increase awareness of these competencies and ensure that these senior stakeholders manage their time and prioritize in such a way that provides them with sufficient capacity to look after the sponsorship portion of their role.
- *Manager's training (leadership, people)*—the majority of managers (team leads and supervisors) in organizations are appointed or promoted to their role almost exclusively based on their technical skills and abilities to support their teams' subject matters. There is little awareness about how managers need to improve on their interpersonal and leadership skills. With the authority that typically comes with their roles, many organizations do not see a necessity to provide managers with interpersonal training (known as *soft skills*) since they already have the authority to give direction and provide mandate. However, due to the constant increase in cross-functional,

cross-project, and cross-initiative activities, there is also a growing need for managers to exercise more interpersonal skills that include motivation, influence, negotiation, and active listening. It is common to see organizations that struggle in the area of team members' satisfaction with their managers and it is a growing, increasingly urgent need to improve managers' interpersonal and leadership skills. This would help not only in the managers' performance and their teams' satisfaction, but also in the managers' ability to add more value in their engagements with PMs, change practitioners, and sponsors.

- *Coaching*—since organizations constantly look for cost efficiencies, it is important to change the way that training is viewed. Currently, many organizations arrange for their teams to receive training, but there is typically little follow-up action, reinforcement of the learning, or any attempt to check for a return on investment (ROI). While it is hard to provide a measurable ROI, supporting and reinforcing that training through ad hoc coaching and support sessions for team members can clarify issues and help the team to improve performance in the related areas. Designing these coaching sessions and circling back with findings and with sessions that support challenging areas can provide a model that improves competencies at all levels of the organization—improving the quality of work in support of the sponsor's initiatives overall.

## A Lack of Direction: Vision, Mandate, and Success Criteria (Either Unclear or Poorly Communicated Vision)

Project and change charters become increasingly common in many organizations in an effort to lay out the knowledge and understanding of an upcoming initiative. However, it is still common to see misalignments or a lack of understanding of the success criteria of a project or an initiative. Even if the success is well understood at the sponsorship level, it is often not shared with sufficient focus and clarity throughout the working levels of the initiative. Further, when there is a lack of clarity or missing information about success criteria, conflicting and misaligned needs tend to fill that void—creating confusion and undermining the leadership of the sponsor and his/her mandate. Defining and articulating a clear vision, a direction, and a set of success criteria is not easy; it is time consuming and involves tough conversations and engaging with multiple stakeholders early on. However, the alternative is moving forward without a clear direction or sufficient understanding and buy-in for the initiative's objectives—leading to performance problems, challenges, and the need for multiple changes in direction throughout the initiative.

## Capacity and Prioritization Issues

These two aspects of portfolio management are both important and commonly underserved. Sponsors and other senior stakeholders—all the way through the organization to the managers and team levels—have little knowledge of their own (i.e., respectively, organization, team, and individual) capacity. This means that most people, including sponsors, believe that they have more time and bandwidth to do the work than they actually have. With that said, most people have less capacity than they realize, but when they do not know their own capacity, they tend to overcommit and take on more work than they can handle. As listed previously, this results in taking shortcuts and failing to spend sufficient time doing the required work—leading to stress, problems, misunderstandings, and, ultimately, a failure to perform.

Further, since everyone has a limited capacity, it is not only important to identify capacity, but also to prioritize the work within it. A large portion of the prioritization effort has to be performed from the top: sponsors, managers, and team leads need to provide a clear set of guidelines and mandates for the people who work for them, so that the work can be prioritized. Providing such priorities is not only about picking our battles, but also about accountability.

It is unlikely that all organizations will address the capacity issues they all suffer from; and the future, in this sense, looks dark and gloomy—meaning that the capacity problem will get worse with time and employees will continue to be increasingly overworked. It therefore leaves the sponsor with the critical responsibilities of making everyone aware of the need to measure and define their capacity and, in turn, to provide the guidance and the means for the teams to prioritize their work and pick their battles. In short, they need to work with what they have—but it also means that they need to address the constraints and the challenges they introduce, which starts with the sponsor providing a clear mandate and a set of priorities to those they work with.

## Time Management Problems

Time management is an extension of prioritization. When there is a lack of clarity as to what needs to take place first, which items are more important than others, or when it is okay to not attempt or complete certain items, it is typical to try to do everything that is on the plate without having the ability to *pick our battles*. The result is equivalent to trying to juggle multiple balls in the air—sometimes trying to complete that one additional item may spell the difference between succeeding and failing on all other items. If I were to juggle a few balls in the air and then someone passes an additional ball, the result may not only be that I fail to handle that one additional ball, but that in the attempt to catch it, I will drop all of the others.

Further, most people fail to distinguish between value-added and non-value-added activities, the latter consuming a large chunk of their time (think administrative work) to create inefficiencies that could have been easily delegated. The chronic lack of time further prevents them from looking into efficiencies and opportunities to delegate and better match the resources to the tasks.

For the sponsor, a lack of time directly translates into a failure to be there proactively in order to attend to the initiative's needs, and then failing to be there for escalations, problems, and issues. The result often leads to further escalation of the situations at hand, creating more work, more waste, and more performance problems. The sponsor needs to provide mechanisms for team members to become more aware of their time, along with the means for people to better prioritize and manage their time.

## Lack of Accountability

One definition of accountability is: "The obligation of an individual or organization to account for its activities, accept responsibility for them, and to disclose the results in a transparent manner. It also includes the responsibility for money or other entrusted property."[1] The word *sponsorship* is therefore synonymous with accountability; however, many people have a hard time defining what accountability is. In a recent project, I was asked to provide a senior executive with an overview, including a slide deck, of what accountability really meant.

Accountability starts at the top of the organization; the message and actions must be clear and consistent and they need to trickle down throughout. An important precondition to establishing a culture of accountability is through stability and continuity of top leadership, which in turn establishes trust. Here are a few steps that help establish accountability:

- *Role definition and ownership*—this starts with the sponsor, and specific roles and responsibilities need to be defined throughout the project or the engagement. It involves setting expectations through early engagement and role definitions. Without clear role definitions, there will be gaps, duplication of effort, redundancies, confusion, and, subsequently, frustration and failure.
- *Establish a sense of ownership*—focusing on both the process of delivering benefits and on results. This includes the need to establish a clear mandate for governing bodies to follow (along with the right level of authority or *teeth*). Governing processes are in place to protect stakeholders' needs and to ensure that projects and initiatives will deliver according to their objectives or they will not move forward. As the buck ultimately stops with the sponsor, it is important to set clear standards so that situations do not arise where projects and initiatives appear to get to their final stages, only for the sponsor to realize that they are far from completion. Another contributor to establishing a sense of ownership is the introduction of performance scorecards for project and change teams and managers, as well as for their respective sponsors. These scorecards need to be based on process adherence and delivery of benefits. In support of delivery of value, there is

a need to provide guidance, training, coaching, and development opportunities where required, and in the event of failing to adhere to processes, the sponsor needs to consider shifting roles and installing a PM or a change manager who will follow the process.

- *Issue management*—it may be hard for many to make a clear connection between issue management and accountability, but accountability is very much about dealing with, managing, and handling issues. Although most issues should be dealt with at the initiative level, there are things that need to be brought to the attention of the sponsor; and good sponsors address issues effectively and in a timely manner. The sponsor needs to ensure (even if not directly) that the organization has the ability to look back at issues and learn from their findings, challenges, opportunities, and associated ideas. Without the ability to look back at issues, the organization will not become a learning organization and this will hinder growth, improvement, and future performance. Part of effective issues management is also the sponsor's ability to incorporate a constructive feedback loop, in context, that enables a genuine look at the root cause(s) of the issue, the process of handling the issue, the time it took, and the overall result.
- *People and goals*—the sponsor needs to make sure there is a clear definition of goals for teams (i.e., performance measures) and in the process, consider people's feelings and their ways to cope with the direction of the initiative. It is the sponsor's responsibility to oversee the creation of mechanisms for team members and stakeholders to revisit events and ensure that people understand the impact of their actions and behaviors. These goals connect back to the need to articulate and reiterate the vision, reinforce the sense of urgency, and set the standards that will be upheld throughout the process. The sponsor also needs to guide and facilitate the process of establishing specifics regarding end results, time frames, and expected levels of effort.

## Chronic Lack of Resources or Resource Constraints

This item circles back to time management and capacity issues; and similar to these items, it should be expected that resource constraints are not only going to continue plaguing projects and initiatives, but that they are likely to continue to get worse. The sponsor needs to be the engine behind establishing a process for resource allocation and management across projects and initiatives. In Chapter 4, the discussion will include how to establish such a process that allows for an effective collaboration across projects and initiatives when it comes to resource management, and to allocate resources proactively based on actual needs and the circumstances of each project and initiative.

## Turf Wars Due to a Lack of Direction

With the reality presented in this chapter, it is no surprise that most sponsors, PMs, change managers, team members, and other stakeholders put themselves and their needs first and commonly end up in turf wars, battles of ego, and siloed thinking. Time and resource constraints, along with the lack of clear direction and the growing pace of change, put us in a defensive and reactive mode and push us toward thinking about survival, instead of growth, collaboration, and partnerships. It is the responsibility of the sponsor (who is at the top of the initiative) to instill a culture of collaboration and partnership. This takes us to the importance of accountability and the sponsor's leadership competencies. The sponsor needs to establish a clear picture of prioritization, along with escalation procedures that support these priorities, success criteria, and means to achieve these goals.

## Poor Lessons Learned

Most PMs know that the process of capturing and applying lessons learned is one of the most frustrating things they go through and that this process is often ineffective, if it is done at all. Lessons are often not recognized, and even if they are documented, it is very hard to apply them or benefit from that knowledge moving forward. While the lessons learned process is mostly performed by the PM, it is up to the sponsor to enable it and provide the awareness around it and the resources to perform it. Agile methods have made significant progress in the real-time capture and application of lessons throughout the project, but it is important to continue this motion of improvement.

Beyond the need to keep the lessons learned process meaningful, the sponsor needs to ensure that the following two additional aspects of lessons are captured and learned from:

1. *Tie lessons to the business case and charter*—while important, it is not enough to capture only lessons about the process (e.g., communication, conflict, processes, risks, interactions). The sponsor needs to make sure that the organization gets the chance to review the project's/initiative's results against the mandate that was produced in the business case and charter. The extent of this exercise is beyond the scope or context that the PM has, but it is important for the organization to go through this exercise in order to improve project selection criteria, definition of success, and to properly measure the extent of the success achieved. This process is time consuming and requires focus—two things that are typically in short supply at the end of an initiative, where most people are focused on moving on to the next thing.

2. *Post-implementation review* (PIR)—the concept of a PIR is not new, but organizations that perform this exercise are few and far between. The idea behind the PIR is not the same as that of lessons learned. While lessons

learned are about the process and the way the work was done, the PIR is about the product and it essentially checks to what extent success has been delivered, or how much *glue* was delivered for the success to stick. The time to do lessons learned is both at the end of milestones (even small ones) and at the end of the project (likely about three to six months after project completion). The time period that passes after the end of the project gives the opportunity to review the extent of the product's success and whether the change management portion of the project was successful. By this time, people (the users of the project's product) tend to default back to their old behaviors, and it may mean that they are no longer using the new product as intended. The PIR requires capacity, money, time, resources, and, above all, a mandate. It is the sponsor who is supposed to set this up and identify the resources and the way to revisit the project's product. One of the challenges is that by this point, the project team and the PM are no longer in place and are often dispersed. Without the awareness and mandate by the sponsor, a PIR will be very hard to perform.

## Unclear Scope Definition and Boundaries

Whether it is called a project or a change initiative, the sponsor is the one who defines and clarifies what is in scope and out of scope. Any conversation about scope, especially early on in the life cycle of the initiative, appears to be straightforward and many find these conversations to be borderline redundant; it appears to be obvious what is in and out of scope. However, later on in the life cycle is when confusion ensues and the gaps start to appear between the expectations of what was to be included and the reality of what was actually included, which is usually less than previously thought.

When discussing scope and the boundaries of our initiatives, there is a need to further clarify the scope. When referring to *out-of-scope* items, it is important to differentiate between two types:

1. Things that are completely out of scope and therefore will not be part of what will be delivered.
2. Things that are out of scope for the project/initiative but still need to get done. These could range from deliverables that other parties (e.g., vendor, other projects, or operations) produce that are depended on, to items that are part of the product/solution/end result but are not to be performed by us. Either way, there has to be some level of coordination in place to ensure that the necessary tasks can be performed, or that all parts will be integrated at the end.

There is no confusion as to what these two types of deliverables mean, but rather there is a tendency to overlook things that are out of sight. Anything that is beyond the focus and the scope of work for the PM or the change manager needs to be addressed, coordinated, or escalated by the sponsor. There are too many cases where projects and initiatives do their part of the work, but a lack of big-picture considerations leads to issues related to external dependencies, handoffs, or integration with external factors.

## The Impact on Performance

Now that the problems with sponsorship and the extent of the impact that they have on the organization and on performance are expressed, it is easier to see the importance of articulating and addressing the problems and challenges with project and change sponsorship.

# HAVING THE RIGHT SPONSOR IN PLACE

Appointing the right person as the PM or the change manager is a challenge because the skills and competencies necessary are not always available and the right person with the right level of experience, style, or personality is not always accessible. When it comes to the sponsor's role, it may get even more challenging. With no clear and consistent definition of the sponsor's role, it is hard to identify the right person to lead the initiative. Further, the sponsor is usually a member of senior management or leadership of the organization; they are not typically picked for the role, but rather they end up as the sponsor because the initiative is either their own or it falls under their umbrella/portfolio.

Either way, when selecting a PM or a change manager, it is the sponsor's decision as to who will fulfill these roles, and it is the sponsor who needs to identify criteria for the role—including finding an individual with the right personality, leadership competencies, and style for the job. However, when it comes to *installing* a sponsor, it is not about selecting or handpicking members of senior management, but rather it is about the territory and the portfolio that the initiative under consideration falls under. Chapter 4 includes a discussion on what happens when the sponsor ends up leaving their role and what it means to the future of the project/initiative.

With that said, it is necessary to pay more attention to who ends up being the sponsor and whether or not that individual is the right person at the right place. Beyond being able to address the list of symptoms discussed earlier in this chapter, the sponsor needs to be of the right seniority and caliber to lead and oversee the initiative. This means that a champion is needed—someone who can continuously promote the needs of the initiative and ensure funding, resources, ongoing justification, bandwidth, and attention for the initiative at the organizational level. This is not an easy task to perform since there are constant shifts in the needs and the direction of organizations, and other initiatives are in a constant and fierce competition for the limited resources and capacity of the organization. A champion is an advocate who works both at the forefront and behind the scenes to promote the initiative, its cause, and its priorities and to keep its sense of urgency at the right level. While a lot of the championing takes place in committees, boardrooms, and status meetings, a large portion is done through relationships, stakeholder engagement, navigating the political landscape, and demonstrating a variety of leadership competencies.

## Managing the Constraints, Risks, Assumptions, Issues, and Dependencies (CRAIDs)

Before discussing a few leadership competencies and concepts that are applicable to project sponsors, there is a need to review a series of items that may not be very clear or measurable. They may appear to be tactical by nature, but they drive the success of our projects and initiatives. In short, they are called CRAIDs, and although they are usually associated with the responsibilities of the PM, the sponsor has a significant and important role in overseeing the process of identifying, managing, addressing, and validating these items, along with ensuring that the team focuses on managing them.

### Constraints

Constraints are limitations that are present and not going anywhere. Constraints are also major components in defining the success of what is done. Time, money, features, capabilities, quality and performance standards, and contract obligations are all constraints—and the success of the initiative will be measured based on the ability to, and the extent of, meeting or adhering to these constraints. Due to the important part that constraints have in defining success, and since it is the responsibility of the sponsor to define, articulate, and communicate success criteria, it is important that the sponsor focuses on understanding the constraints and ensuring that what is done is in line with them.

### Risks

It is primarily the PM who needs to look at project risks, but the sponsor needs to provide the context around risks. Risks are not just events, but rather they are events that may impact the ability to meet objectives and deliver success. The sponsor—who *owns* the objectives and success criteria—must ensure that these risks are properly addressed. Once these criteria and guidelines are in place, the PM is responsible for the risks, and he/she needs to involve the sponsor as required when there is a danger of failing to deliver on the objectives or when the risk may *spill over* beyond the project's objectives. When it comes to business/operational risks, PMs often do not pay sufficient attention to those risks that may impact the organization beyond the project/initiative objectives. Therefore, the sponsor needs to ensure that there is a mechanism for the PM/change manager to reach out when needed. Further, the sponsor needs to be available and provide a timely response for these escalations and inquiries. It is important that sponsors create the right conditions for the PM to look at risks beyond just the project risks.

## Assumptions

Assumptions have a bad reputation. This is mostly because, as one definition makes light of, when you "assume," you make an *ass* out of *u* and *me*. However, the true definition of an assumption is "something taken for granted" and an "accepted cause and effect relationship, or estimate of the existence of a fact from the known existence of other fact(s)."[2] With this definition comes a word of caution that, while assumptions provide a foundation for understanding certain situations, they must go through a thorough examination process before accepting them as reality. When considering assumptions, the PM wants to keep the project constraints in mind because under certain conditions, the constraints will limit the project's planned performance. Assumptions are also associated with risks because in certain situations, they may change from the time people initially plan for them and, thus, pose a threat to the project objectives.

All assumptions go through a similar path throughout their life cycles—but with changing timelines and implications. At first, nothing happens with them up until a certain point. For example, an assumption that a vendor will deliver its goods or services on time will remain an assumption until the time of the planned delivery or until there is a clear indication that may change the premise of the planning. At that point, one of two things will happen:

1. The delivery is made on time and as planned (after all, somewhere in the universe there is a vendor who delivers what is needed, on time, and to specifications). If the delivery is made as planned, the assumption(s) about it is no longer valid so it is removed from the assumptions log and it is business as usual according to the project plan.
2. Alternately, in the event that anything does not go as planned with the delivery (e.g., the wrong product or a defective product was delivered, it was not on time, it was incomplete, or there was no delivery altogether), it means that the assumption did not turn out as expected and the project is now facing a risk that has materialized.

Similar to risks, here too the bulk of the effort in managing assumptions is on the PM, but the sponsor needs to be the enabler of the process and ensure that the PM has the capacity and awareness to manage assumptions—and above all, that the PM has the means to validate the assumptions and to handle them as they turn into risks. Further, the first places for making assumptions are the business case and project charter, which are documents that are owned by the sponsor (even if the PM partially writes the charter).

Since most people do not like assumptions (including PMs and sponsors), they tend not to talk about assumptions (until it is too late). It is therefore important to identify, track, manage, and validate the assumptions, and to do so in a timely fashion. Table 2.1 provides a simple way to manage and validate assumptions by tracking each assumption using these four elements:

1. *Category/related objective*—what the assumption is about or what will be impacted by it should it not end up as expected.
2. *Necessary information*—what information is required to manage or resolve this assumption.
3. *Who should provide the necessary information*—which stakeholder (often the sponsor) can provide us with relevant information or a decision about the condition behind the assumption.
4. *When the information must be provided*—we need to identify at what time it is necessary to have the information in order to make an informed decision or take meaningful action. This should not be an arbitrary date, but rather a date after which the assumption will *expire* and hence be treated as a risk that materialized or an issue to address.

We should note that, similar to risks, assumptions are about the future and that most assumptions on the project level tend to be related to resource availability.

I have managed assumptions for close to 20 years in my projects. In the early days, I did it with the help of a sticky note, where I wrote the assumptions on these notes. But since the notes had the tendency to quickly deteriorate due to the adhesive, I subsequently started using the *assumptions log* that is mentioned in this chapter—and this was perhaps that single most impactful thing I did to improve my project management work. I first used the log close to 15 years prior to when the Project Management Institute introduced it as a document that is part of the *Guide to the Project Management Body of Knowledge (PMBOK® Guide)*. When I managed to incorporate it into my work, I noticed the value in the assumption for both the PM and the sponsor, and it directly contributed to our ability to

**Table 2.1**   The assumptions log

| Category/Related Objective | What We Need to Know | Whom We Need to Know It From | By When We Need an Answer |
|---|---|---|---|
|  |  |  |  |
|  |  |  |  |
|  |  |  |  |

Managing assumptions is important because assumptions also serve as a precursor for risks. Many risk events can be traced back to assumptions and by managing the assumptions, it is possible to get a head start in looking into the risks. It is important to keep the assumptions real, that is, as realistic as possible, and to base them on as much valid and likely information as possible. By tracking the assumptions, it helps with focusing on what information to look for, who can provide us with the information, and when the deadline is for obtaining information before the assumptions *expire* or turn into risks. A more elaborate table can be created with more information in it, but for the most part this should be enough to effectively manage assumptions.

proactively handle situations, avoid problems, manage risks, and deliver success for our organizations.

### Issues

Issues are also associated with PMs—more so than with sponsors—but once again, the sponsor is a common point of escalation. There is some confusion when it comes to issues since different people refer to them in different ways, so in order to give it some structure: issues are a matter of stakeholder engagement and expectations management because many issues are things, concerns, or problems that are brought up by stakeholders. It is important that the PM logs, assigns, and addresses the issues before they get out of hand. Naturally, many of the issues end up being escalated to the sponsor due to their nature or potential impact. Sometimes risks that have materialized are treated as issues. An issues log is a good way to manage issues, but sponsors need to enable the process and be available to address issues that are escalated to them. Figure 2.3 shows a generic *flow*-issues escalation process.

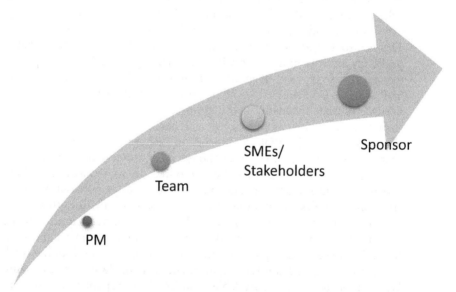

After a concern is raised, the PM determines if it is an issue; and once it is logged as an issue, the PM facilitates the handling or escalation of the matter. If the PM does not have the ability to resolve this issue, he/she should then escalate the issue appropriately—to a team member, subject matter expert, or any other stakeholder who can help with the matter. If the issue is still not resolved, or when whoever is involved does not have the ability to resolve it, the PM escalates the matter to the sponsor for action or decisions.

**Figure 2.3**   Issues escalation process

## *Dependencies*

Dependencies are a form of constraints (therefore, present conditions) and for the most part, the PM handles them within his/her level of authority. There may be risks and assumptions associated with dependencies, and when they are beyond the authority or scope level of the PM, dependencies need to be addressed by the sponsor. In addition, contingent on the type of dependency, the sponsor might be the person to articulate the dependency, address it, or be the one to deal with it once it has escalated. The word *dependency* or the term *it depends* are used often, but many people have a hard time articulating what dependency really means or exactly what to depend on.

Dependencies can be listed under four categories and they are not the types that are learned about when trying to plan and manage project schedules (i.e., mandatory, discretionary, internal and external, or the likes of finish to start):

1. *Deliverable*—this is when the project/initiative depends on a deliverable. These are fairly easy dependencies to identify and manage because the item being sought is known, along with who needs to provide the deliverable. The individual/team can be approached in order to inquire, manage expectations, and learn about whether they are going to deliver on time. This is also a product-related dependency since this is something that is necessary in order to move on with what is being done. The PM typically manages these types of dependencies, and when he/she realizes that the item will not be delivered (at all, on time, or in the right way), the PM needs to escalate the matter to the sponsor.

2. *Resources*—this is a dependency that is harder to identify and manage. Many projects and initiatives depend on resources that are external or shared with other initiatives. Even though *other* projects may have nothing to do with *ours*, the minute that those resources are shared with something else, it introduces this type of dependency. Depending on shared resources essentially doubles the amount of risk because not only does this initiative's problems have to be dealt with, but also whatever happens in the *other* initiative that is currently utilizing the resource becomes important. It requires the PM to inquire into the progress and the status of the work in other projects; and this type of information is not always easy to obtain. When information is not available or favorable, the sponsor serves as an escalation point to handle the situation and make an informed decision. At this point, emotions and stakes are high, an active conflict has already occurred, and the consequences may lead to the derailing of at least one of the initiatives involved. Further, the resource most likely also reports to a functional manager (or a supervisor, department manager, team lead, or resource manager) so there are more stakeholders' needs to consider.

3. *Sign-off*—this dependency is not about a product or a deliverable, but rather about a decision. It may be anyone's decision, but in many cases, it

is a sign-off or a decision that the sponsor needs to make. One of the most common complaints by PMs is that decisions are not made (or at least not made in a timely fashion) and the target of this frustration is often the sponsor. Since sponsors are busy and they have other things to look after, it is common to have situations where decisions, sign-offs, or mandates are delayed, and many times are the reason for project problems and schedule overruns. The solution to this problem starts with the realization that it takes two to tango: the PM needs to set expectations and articulate the needs he/she has of the sponsor, as well as to clearly approach the sponsor with specific and measurable criteria for decisions and sign-offs. The sponsor needs to work with the PM and to be there and available, in a timely manner, to address the PM's needs. Establishing rules of engagements and working norms with the PM is discussed in Chapter 6.

4. *External*—external dependencies can fall under any of the other three categories mentioned previously, but when it comes to external dependencies, the PM needs to identify and articulate them so that the sponsor can step in when and as required. External dependencies are ones that refer to elements, teams, and stakeholders from outside of the organization—and they can be related to deliverables, resources, or decisions. Keep in mind that external dependencies are most likely associated with contracts and, therefore, are of a more binding nature. Accordingly, it may require the involvement of other groups in addition to the sponsor (e.g., legal, procurement, or vendor management).

## The Ori Manifesto

As part of focusing on the things that matter, it is necessary to compare what the things are that consume most of the PM's time and draw most of the focus of the sponsor *against* the things the sponsor and the PM need to focus on in order to maximize the value they deliver. Table 2.2 helps articulate the areas that need to be scrutinized. Inspired by the Agile Manifesto, the Ori Manifesto values the items on the left of Table 2.2, but finds more value in the items on the right. Further, the items on the left are more tangible, and therefore easier to find help with: scope and requirements—with the help of a business analyst; schedule—with help from project team members and coordinators; and budget—with help from the finance team. However, the items on the right are less tangible, therefore, there are less reports and related artifacts to produce and, by nature, they draw less focus and attention across the board. These are also the factors that make it more important for the PM to focus on these items, as he/she is not likely to find anyone else who can provide reliable support in these areas with the exception of the sponsor, who needs to provide guidance and ongoing support for the PM.

**Table 2.2**   The Ori Manifesto

| Things That Matter in Projects | Things That Matter More |
|---|---|
| Scope | CRAIDs |
| Schedule | Quality |
| Budget | Communication and stakeholder engagement |
| | Change |
| | Resource management |
| | Cross-initiative coordination |

Managing what matters means that we need to focus more of our efforts on items on the right side of Table 2.2. Beyond the CRAIDs, the sponsor needs to ensure that there is sufficient capacity to articulate quality standards, manage stakeholder expectations, handle the change to the organization, and ensure resource availability through cross-initiative coordination.

## Quality

There is a significant disconnect between what people and organizations say about quality and what they actually do about it. As one of the four competing demands that serves as project success criteria (along with scope, time, and cost), it is clear that quality standards should be met, but in many circumstances, time and cost considerations get priority over quality. One way in which quality standards get compromised is by delivering to a lower, yet acceptable standard. For example, if it is acceptable, and with the permission of the sponsor, the choice may be made to meet a silver standard instead of a gold standard—but that standard must be acceptable by whomever is in charge of defining the success of the engagement. One way to measure project quality is to look at the number of errors, defects, and warranty calls that users need to contend with and at the cost that is associated with them.

The gap between words and actions illustrates that values about quality cannot only be expressed in words, they must also be evident in the actions and conduct of the organization and its employees.

## Management Responsibility—the 85:15 Rule

In 1945, Joseph Juran said, "It is most important that top management be quality-minded. In the absence of sincere manifestation of interest at the top, little will happen below."[3] If management has the aptitude for it, a passion for quality will eventually spread like a domino effect to the entire team and throughout the organization. There are, however, plenty of examples of large organizations that are not only failing to follow this concept but are acting exactly in the opposite way.

To achieve quality, there is a need for people skills (leadership) first and project management and technical skills (management) second. In fact, leadership starts with the sponsor, who should act as the overall leader of the project, ensure the project vision is accurately articulated, and translate it into actions that inspire and motivate the team. It is not only about the goal of producing deliverables, but also about the means of getting there (accomplishing success for the customer together). This kind of healthy environment instills trust within the team and encourages them to share ideas and challenge processes without fear.

When the atmosphere is not conducive to building relationships, trust, and collaboration, team members' innovation and ideas for improvement are stifled, causing them to shirk responsibility, refrain from sharing feedback and ideas, and hide mistakes. This inevitably leads to team members who fail to learn from previous mistakes and who avoid making decisions altogether. Quality is misunderstood by many who think it only relates to the end product or final deliverable and do not realize that it also involves processes, efficiencies, innovation, and continuous improvement. Ensuring that these are done correctly requires a quality management culture in all levels of the organization from senior management through to the project team members.

There are many reasons why organizational improvements often do not manage to sustain themselves, but one common reason is because team members often try to avoid pointing out problems and challenges so that they are not associated with them and are not assigned to fix them. It is easy to blame employees for this, but the management responsibility concept, along with the 85:15 rule, show that it results from management's propensity toward quality. The 85:15 rule (introduced by Edwards Deming[4]) states that 85% of the problems in any organization are system related and hence are under the control of management, while only 15% are worker related. This concept speaks directly to the sponsor's need to articulate quality standards and establish the right context, setup, atmosphere, and capacity to enable the activities that support quality. It is up to the sponsor to enable the team to do their work and to evaluate it, so they can deliver on the desired results.

Meeting quality standards is closely related to defining benefit measurements and establishing a benefit management plan; once again, these are areas that are under the responsibility of the sponsor to mandate and oversee since they extend beyond the project's or initiative's focus, scope, and time frame.

## Cost of Quality

With most initiatives not having their own quality management plan, it is the sponsor's responsibility to enable and allow for time, money, resources, skills, and supporting activities to take place as part of the effort to deliver quality. If left to the PMs, they will not be able to stand on their own under the pressure from other stakeholders and the results may veer away from the set standards.

Similar to any good thing in life, quality comes with a cost, and as articulated by Phillip Crosby[5] in his book *Quality Is Free*, it is not a gift, but conceptually, it is free. The actual cost of quality[6] was first articulated by Joseph Juran as the cost of poor quality: any cost that would not have been expended if quality were perfect contributes to the cost of quality. Quality costs are the sum total of: the costs incurred by investing in the prevention of nonconformance to requirements, appraising a product or service for conformance to requirements, and failing to meet requirements.

Multiple pieces of research and observations indicate that the cost of poor quality can reach as high as 20–30% of sales, but also that most businesses are not even aware of their actual spending on quality because they do not keep track of it properly. Many people believe that their organizations spend no more than five percent of their total sales on quality. There is a notion that the cost that an organization incurs in an effort to obtain a new customer is by far higher than the cost to retain an existing one. Similarly, the cost to eliminate a failure once the customer gets the product (a.k.a. external failures) is significantly higher than it is at the development phase. Effective quality management is about early detection of errors in an effort to reduce costs.

Cost of quality consists of four elements that are presented in Figure 2.4: prevention, appraisal, internal failure, and external failure. The total cost of quality comprises the cost of conformance (including prevention and appraisal) and the

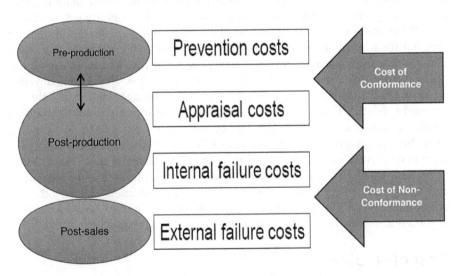

The categories of quality costs are shown in reference to a timeline and broken down into cost of conformance (including pre-production prevention costs and post-production appraisal costs); and cost of nonconformance (including post-production internal failure costs and post-sales external failure costs).

**Figure 2.4**   Quality cost components and timing[8]

cost of nonconformance (including both types of failure costs). The measure of the cost of quality is not the actual price that the organization pays for building a quality product, but rather the cost of failing to create one.[7] Figure 2.4 also shows us the rough timing of when each quality cost category takes place in the product or service sales cycle.

## Project Health

Beyond the many measures proposed through a variety of quality tools and concepts, there are ways for projects and initiatives to measure their project health through *proprietary* measures. These are indicators that the team can collect for tracking progress, but since they are situation-specific and organization-specific, any data that they provide is meaningless on its own unless this is done over a period of time so that the data can be benchmarked and compared against other projects within the organization for trends and for context. Pursuing these types of measures cannot be done only by the PM since it requires capacity and mandate that only the sponsor can provide.

Conducting periodic project health checks provides the PM with real-time findings about areas for potential improvements along with a chance to review ideas for improvement of processes and deliverables. Although the collection and interpretation of the data consumes time and resources, the investment pays off by engaging the team and providing an opportunity for exchanging information and expertise. The project sponsor, other stakeholders, and the organization as a whole benefit with a real-time option to mitigate risk and an ability to quickly address findings about the project management practices in the event that organizational level action is needed.[9]

## Readiness and Complexity Assessments

When organizations take on projects and initiatives, there is usually a sense of urgency associated with them and once there is a decision in place to go ahead, there is a tendency to not question the necessity of these initiatives. However, many organizations tend to confuse the need and the sense of urgency with readiness. The fact that there is a need, a desire, or even a decision to do something does not mean that the necessary components exist to do it. This is the time to look into two types of assessments that can help: readiness and complexity assessments.

These two assessments need to be overseen, initiated, and performed before actually starting the initiative; not only because at this point there may not be a PM as of yet, but also because the assessments can help the sponsor set a direction and make decisions about the upcoming initiative:

- *Readiness assessment*—this is about checking if the organization and the team have what it takes to go ahead with the initiative. It includes an examination of the conditions, support mechanisms, funding, resources, and approach. Additional questions that are necessary to ask concern the alignment of the initiative with strategic objectives, the success criteria, the leadership that is in place to lead it (yes, also that of the sponsor), the organization's track record in this area, and the associated change management considerations. At the end of an effective readiness assessment process, the ability to articulate the organization's readiness for the project should be confirmed and, in turn, the readiness to manage or change the expectations and the risks associated with the undertaking. If the findings indicate that the organization is not ready, it does not mean that the initiative needs to be called off, but rather that measures need to be put in place so that it is possible to move forward. By the time there is a PM in place, the extent of our readiness should be known. In the event that the organization is not ready (and note that there is never *full* readiness for anything), it introduces more complexities and risks that should be identified and recognized.

- *Complexity assessment*—regardless of the level of readiness, the sponsor should examine the amount of complexity that the organization will be up against. Complexity does not only come from the nature of work, the product, the technology, or the circumstances; it also comes from a combination of factors that although none of them may be of a specific high level of complexity, when compounding all factors around it, it adds up to a complex situation. In today's reality, it is hard to find a project that does not have any element of complexity in it, and even if things appear to be straightforward, time and money constraints, resource availability, and stakeholders' expectations are almost always going to introduce a layer of complexity. There are a handful of criteria to look at when considering complexity: (a) technical and the product; (b) organizational; (c) environmental; (d) people; and (e) general complexity (i.e., constraints, project size, and dependencies). The sponsor should arrange for the complexity assessment, and the outcome should give the PM an understanding as to what he/she is up against. Similar to the readiness assessment, do not call things off, but rather, re-tool and move forward with an approach that is appropriate for the level of complexity.

Enabling the readiness and complexity assessment is the responsibility of the sponsor and is certainly in the sponsor's best interest. However, not all sponsors see the importance in these assessments. In addition, the assessments require time and resources (albeit not much time and not too many resources) and, therefore, may slow things down at times when we cannot afford to do so. Further, the assessments may shed new light on the opportunity and the initiative that may reopen questions about the selected approach, or even about the need itself. These questions may act as political headwinds that can work against the cause and the interests of the sponsor. It is important to recognize these elements and, at the same time, be candid about the situation ahead while realizing that it is the sponsor's responsibility and decision to make.

## LEADERSHIP CONCEPTS FOR SPONSORS

Sponsors are leaders. Or rather, sponsors are suppose to be leaders—not because they are senior members in the organization or due to their authority, but because they need to demonstrate leadership characteristics that will inspire, motivate, and lead their teams and stakeholders. In Chapter 3, specific leadership competencies that are necessary for becoming an effective sponsor will be discussed, while in this chapter the discussion will center on what leadership is as it pertains to project and change sponsors.

The sponsor, as a leader, has an important role in making or keeping the organization agile. The term *agile* here does not refer here to agile methodologies and project life cycles, but rather to organizational agility. Table 2.3 shows a list of criteria and practices that characterize an agile organization.

**Table 2.3**    Trademarks of agile organizations[10]

|  | Trademark | Organizational Agility Practices |
|---|---|---|
| **Strategy** | North Star embodied across the organization | • Shared purpose and vision<br>• Sensing and seizing opportunities<br>• Flexible resource allocation |
| **Structure** | Network of empowered teams | • Clear flat structure<br>• Clear accountable roles<br>• Hands-on governance<br>• Robust communities of practice<br>• Active partnerships and ecosystem |
| **Process** | Rapid decision and learning cycles | • Rapid iteration and experimentation<br>• Performance orientation<br>• Information transparency<br>• Continuous learning |
| **People** | Dynamic people model that ignites passion | • Cohesive community<br>• Entrepreneurial drive<br>• Role mobility |
| **Technology** | Next-generation enabling technology | • Evolving technical architecture, systems, and tools |

Organizational agility is not about agile methodologies and project life-cycle type. Of course, to be able to support agile projects, organizations need to become agile, but organizational agility is something we should strive for regardless of project life-cycle types.

## The Role of the Sponsor in Helping to Achieve Organizational Agility

When it comes to achieving organizational agility, the mandate needs to come from the very top, but a mandate alone is not enough, and it will help if senior managers take the initiative on their own, even without an official mandate. It may be challenging to pursue such a tall order of enabling or introducing organizational agility, especially when it may not be part of an official mandate or part of a specific job description.

## Strategy

The sponsor needs to articulate and communicate a clear vision that will guide the organization through the initiative. Chapter 5 covers the process of creating a vision, along with the associated benefits. A good vision is compelling, motivating, realistic, and measurable—but it should not be too detailed. With one overarching vision for the organization, it is easier to articulate the vision of the initiatives and ideas in support of the high-level direction. With a clear vision in mind, the drive to capture opportunities and the process of resource allocation and utilization will be aligned with the objectives and easier to follow.

## Structure

It is not easy to change the organizational structure, and even if the existing structure is not fully aligned with the trademarks of an agile organization, that does not mean it is a losing battle. Focusing on accountability, empowerment, role definition, and a clear and meaningful governance process makes up a significant part of maximizing the benefits from any existing organizational structure. Every sponsor can authorize and establish a governance process, accountability, and empowerment that are aligned with the existing organizational structure and start achieving these benefits *organically*—and if done properly, they will soon become best practices. If these items fail, it is usually not due to a lack of knowledge or awareness, but rather a lack of time to follow and enforce them, along with pressures from across the organization to allow exceptions for quicker delivery of value (i.e., bypassing governance gates and processes). With a clear vision, a strong sponsor will not cave under these pressures.

## Process

The need for quick decision making is important regardless of the level of agility being pursued. It was previously covered in this chapter that decision making and sign-off (timeliness, clarity, transparency, and effectiveness) are major areas of concern among project practitioners since sponsors and other senior stakeholders fail to make timely decisions on a widespread basis. Improving on decision making and sign-offs will provide a significant boost for the effectiveness of any organization, and adding to that the ability for a quick and effective turnaround for lessons learned will further help. Following processes (including governance and escalations) should be ingrained and consistent. Processes are in place for a reason, and if they are a hindrance, there should be a mechanism to adjust them. Regardless, sponsors (and other practitioners) should draw clear lines and not allow for exceptions to take over. Exceptions include when there is permission to bypass or override a process—but they should be done only as necessary, with clear guidelines as to why there is a need to bypass the process. Exceptions must not become the new norm—too often they slowly creep their way in to override processes on a regular basis.

## People

For most organizations, the practices presented under the people category for organizational agility are difficult to apply—especially in the short term. With that said, trust, clear boundaries, and accountability are critical for fostering motivation and inspiring people—and from there, the path to organizational agility is clear. Leadership style and the other trademarks of an agile organization are major inputs to the *people* part.

## Technology

This can also be expanded to *tools*, which include technology, as well as processes, templates, and best practices. This trademark concerns the ability to benefit from tools and technology, as well as the transferable skills associated with adapting to new tools and techniques. With that said, this is possibly the least important and easiest-to-apply trademark of an agile organization.

## Leadership versus Management and Challenges

Managers are often confused with leaders, but it is important to distinguish between managers' attributes (that are typically associated with seniority and authority) and leadership attributes. Table 2.4 shows the key differences between leaders and managers; however, leadership and management should be viewed as two ends on a continuum and the sponsor most likely needs to deliver on both ends:

- Set a direction and ensure there is proper planning
- Align people with the vision and oversee the process of organizing and staffing
- Ensure effectiveness and efficiency

**Table 2.4**  Leadership versus management[11]

| Subject | Manager | Leader |
|---------|---------|--------|
| Makeup of role | Stability | Change |
| Decision making | Makes | Facilitates |
| Approach | Plans detail around constraints | Sets and leads direction |
| Vision | Short-term: today | Long-term: horizon |
| Control | Formal influence | Personal charm |
| Appeals to | The head | The heart |
| Culture | Endorses | Shapes |
| Action | Reactive | Proactive |
| Risk | Minimizes | Takes |
| Rules | Makes | Breaks |
| Direction | Existing direction/keeps the status quo | New direction/challenges the norm |
| Values | Results | Achievement |
| Concern | Doing the thing right | Doing the right thing |
| Focus | Managing work | Leading people |
| Human resource | Subordinates | Followers |

- Focus on problems that are difficult to resolve (challenges) and on ongoing needs (operations)
- Motivate and inspire, while also controlling and solving problems

In many environments it is common to find confusion between leaders and managers; further, there is more value shown toward management than leadership. This is in part due to the responsibilities and authority that come with management, which are more tangible, but it also has to do with the ease of articulating managerial roles and, subsequently, to measure the extent to which a manager performs. Leaders may not be formally appointed to the role. He/she needs to emerge as a leader and step up to lead on a more ad hoc and less formal basis. There is a tendency to miss clear criteria as to how to measure a leader's performance and what specific actions a leader needs to take in order to lead. This means organizations tilt their focus toward the management aspect, which ultimately leads to neglecting to develop leaders.

Another result is a reality where most managers are appointed to their roles based on their technical and organizational skills with little to no focus on leadership skills or on the intangible attributes and experience that are relevant to delivering performance. With less focus on these leadership skills, most employees eventually become unhappy with their managers, which gradually leads to job dissatisfaction, poor performance, and turnover. Multiple surveys have shown that only around 30% of employees are satisfied with their supervisor or manager. With that in mind, while leadership is one of the most studied aspects of business, knowledge of what makes an effective leader is no better than when this subject was first studied around 100 years ago. Figure 2.5 gives an effective meaning for leadership that goes well beyond performance and concerns making our organizations a better place.

There is another distinction to consider when trying to differentiate between a leader and a manager; it is about asking whether one works *in* the business, rather than *on* the business.[13] Working *in* the business is about fixing and fine-tuning the current system in an effort to stay the course, while working *on* the business is about creation and transformation—finding the path when faced with problems that require a new system. Figure 2.6 illustrates the two different motions and directions of working *in* versus *on* the business. Organizations need to assess how much employee time is spent *working on* versus *working in* the business: how much time is spent fixing problems, discussing what is going wrong, and looking for missing items versus how much time is spent looking for new opportunities, improving, and growing.

A final thought regarding challenges with the way leaders are viewed and the study of leadership can be attributed to Warren Bennis: "Ironically, probably more has been written and less known about leadership than any other topic in the behavioral sciences. Always, it seems the concept of leadership eludes us or turns up in another form to taunt us again with its slipperiness and complexity."[15]

> "...leadership is not solely about producing results. Success in leadership is not measured only in numbers. Being a leader brings with it a responsibility to do something of significance that makes families, communities, work organizations, nations, the environment, and the world better places than they are today."

It is important for us to articulate what leadership means so we can aim to become better leaders.

**Figure 2.5**    A view of leadership[12]

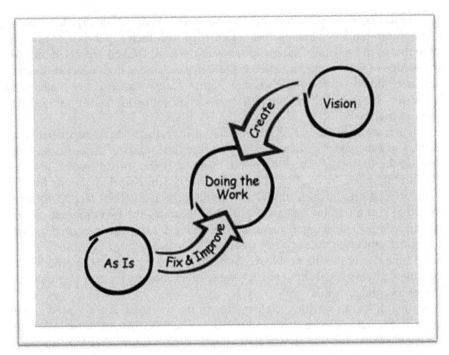

Leaders work *on* the business and managers work *in* the business and *for* the sponsor, it is not a matter of either/or.

**Figure 2.6**   Fixing versus creating[14]

## What Makes a Good Leader?

There are a few elements that can be articulated that are essential to molding anyone into a good leader:

- *Have a vision*—vision is about the future that is being created, and it includes dreams and aspirations. It is not easy to establish and communicate a vision, but having a vision is one of the signature components of leadership. It provides direction, guidance, and something to aspire toward.
- *Identify shared values*—values are the ideas that are believed to be important in the way that things are accomplished. Values help to determine priorities, and they are the underlying measures that are used to determine the right direction in which to move. When what is being done and how it is being done match the organization's values, things appear to be good. However, when *what* and *how* things are done do not align with those values, then trouble is usually brewing. Beyond recognizing the organization's values, it is important to identify and articulate the team's shared values. This helps support the organization's actions and behaviors.

- *Build in integrity*—integrity is an important component in the process of building trust; it involves honesty (ensuring that the answer is yes only when it is truly meant) and promptness (when the product can be delivered). Learn to say no when it is necessary (and provide a rational and alternative course of action) and be credible by doing what was promised and then standing behind it.
- *Create commitment*—building commitment is not only done through leading by example, but also by giving things a meaning. Simon Sinek introduced the Golden Circle, as shown in Figure 2.7, to articulate a way for people and organizations to create meaning. Start with the *why* to give purpose and meaning and then move to the *how* (process) and the *what* (results). Commitment is achieved and loyalty is gained when people realize that their needs are being met. Therefore, to get the commitment, the leader needs to be responsive to their followers' needs.

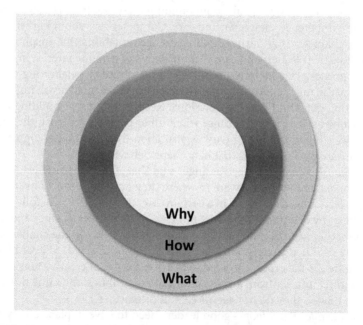

Simon Sinek articulated the need to give meaning and purpose before going into the detail. However, when it comes to projects, the process of the two outer circles should be reversed: after the *why* (business case, vision, and charter), comes the requirements (*what*), and then the project work (*how*). Either way, it starts with purpose and meaning.

**Figure 2.7**    The Golden Circle[16]

- *Build a shared perspective*—in order to develop commitment, it is imperative to have a common outlook and a shared perspective. However, keep in mind that people's biases and perspectives depend on their position within the organization. According to Mile's Law: "Where you stand depends on where you sit."[17] The sponsor needs to drive a genuine effort to engage stakeholders toward having a shared perspective and to achieve diversity in the broader meaning of the word. Diversity is not only about the cultural context, but also about having the ability to discuss, promote, and hold multiple perspectives across multiple levels and functions in the organization.
- *Build trust*—there are several clichés about trust; it is difficult to build, easy to destroy, and next to impossible to recover once it is destroyed. But the question remains, how is trust built? The following list is made of components that are not only about good leaders, but they are also about building trust—two things that go together. Having a vision, communicating, identifying shared values, having integrity, creating commitment, and building a shared perspective are all about building trust. But trust is also about showing competence, character, and care. Competence is about knowing what to do; character is about credibility and accountability that inspire people to follow their leader; and care is about showing genuine interest in the people around us. This includes inquiring about a burden, celebrating with them, empathizing, acknowledging, working together, and involving people in setting goals and making decisions. Keep in mind that building trust also involves taking a risk because when other people gain trust, they also gain power. Finally, building trust is also about rewards and recognition since they are powerful tools that help shape behaviors.
- *Establish a flow*—Henry Kissinger said that "the task of the leader is to get people from where they are to where they have not been." This means that the leader needs to move in a certain direction and have the followers come along, by creating a flow. It is not easy to create a flow since the pace and direction need to maintain a delicate balance between the challenge, which may produce anxiety, and the skills of those involved, to avoid boredom. Figure 2.8 illustrates the need to provide a sense of creative tension so people do not suffer from anxiety and shut down and, at the same time, balance the flow so they do not get bored and disengaged.
- *Create a feedback loop*—good leaders need to have in place a very effective feedback loop, where they can engage, collect, and analyze feedback from their followers, and ensure that their message goes through. Ken Blanchard said that "feedback is the breakfast of champions"[19] and the leader needs to constantly work toward ensuring that the feedback is specific, timely, candid, and actionable.

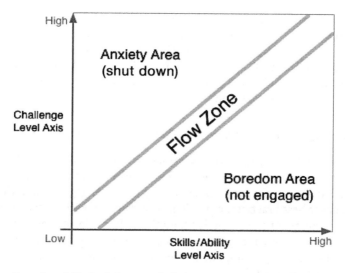

Based on Mihaly Csikzentmihalyi's concept of *flow,* achieving flow—or being in the *flow zone*—indicates someone's state between anxiety and boredom, meeting their own motivational level in that experience.

**Figure 2.8**   Mastering the flow[18]

## Complex versus Complicated

The words *complex* and *complicated* are often interchangeable by nature. Stop for a moment to think about the difference between the two words, then consider the following interpretation:[20]

- *Complicated* is something that is difficult, but the complication is due to the combination of a large number of components. Success depends on the protocols and blueprint that are used through these components, and the components can be broken down into more manageable or even simple pieces. A cockpit is complicated because it is full of knobs, buttons, and switches, but each component has a single specific purpose that can be understood. With that said, even if a person understands all of these components, it does not mean that he/she can fly a plane. Another analogy of *complicated* can be to project management (except for the people part), which is also about breaking something complicated down to more manageable pieces.
- *Complex* is something with rigid protocols that have limited application or are even counterproductive. In complex situations, it is not possible to break down the whole into distinct parts, and even if it could be done,

uncertainty of the outcome remains. Raising a child, or dealing with people, is complex. Every person is unique and must be understood as an individual; for example, success with raising one child does not guarantee success with another. And finally, one more analogy, complex is like making mayonnaise; once it is ready, you cannot really break it back down into its original ingredients. Managing change is definitely complex.

## Governance and Support: PMO and CMO

The sponsor needs to engage and collaborate with anyone who can help and a good candidate is the project management office (PMO). There are many benefits that the sponsor may gain for their initiative by properly engaging the PMO and utilizing whatever best practices, reporting, consistencies, and governance elements it offers. The sponsor needs to understand the PMO's role and the way it operates, and then establish rules of engagement to maximize those benefits. When there is an organizational change component, the sponsor should try to establish a change management office (CMO).

Unlike the PMO, a CMO may not last beyond the initiative since the need for cost savings may not justify it during lulls. Nevertheless, a CMO can be fulfilled by a modified portfolio office, or even under the right settings, a PMO with teeth. The value that a CMO can produce ranges from the selection of initiatives, checking and measuring capacity, helping manage and allocate resources, safeguarding for alignment with strategic objectives, and maintaining the focus on people and attitudes.

Keep in mind that people are the main strength of every organization—and the Dofasco corporate slogan reinforces this notion: "Our product is steel. Our strength is people." This has been Dofasco's slogan since 1970 and it has been referred to as one of the most clearly defined corporate images.

## Critical Thinking

Critical thinking is the ability to perform objective analysis and to evaluate something as part of a problem-solving process. It is safe to say that most sponsors have critical thinking abilities, but this may not be enough for many of the situations that are being faced in organizations today. Critical thinking is probably one of the most popular skills that hiring managers put on job descriptions when they look for new hires; however, in most environments it appears to be one of the least desired things that managers want their direct reports to have. When it comes to moving forward and doing things, once a manager makes a decision, he/she does not want team members to challenge it or to demonstrate any critical thinking capabilities. In fact, many managers prefer team members to just comply and follow them, with no challenge. This is clearly not a call for team members to challenge decisions or the authority of their manager, but sponsors, like other managers, must create and enable a capacity to allow team members to demonstrate critical thinking.

When faced with the challenges around critical thinking, some managers believe they allow it (and few do), others do not have time for it, and the rest just suppress it. Warming up to the notion of critical thinking may be a bigger challenge than previously thought since in many environments, it is perceived to be questioning the managers' authority or just to be a waste of time. Generally, when people are not comfortable with their decision, they do not want others to challenge it, but the opposite is also true—sometimes, when one is comfortable with their decision, they invite constructive criticism. With a chronic lack of capacity and time and with many uninformed decisions, critical thinking is viewed as a nuisance or a pest, rather than an innovation, growth, and improvement tool. Another factor that makes it hard to open up toward critical thinking is corporate culture, which takes us back to the start of the discussion. Those who question and challenge are considered negative or even troublemakers. Corporate culture promotes those who play the game by not challenging decisions, asking questions, or thinking critically, but who demonstrate conformity.

Although it is not easy to reshape or change culture, improvement needs to start somewhere, and a good place to start is for sponsors to encourage critical thinking among their teams by allocating time, capacity, and genuine intent in doing so.

## Circling Back

With leadership as a major component of effective sponsorship, let's recall the main role of the sponsor: provide a mandate, set priorities, establish budget and resources, be active with the project, champion the project, make timely decisions, and help address resistance and the political landscape. The most common mistakes among sponsors are not fulfilling the sponsor's role and failing to proactively be there for the project.

When saying that the sponsor "has to proactively be there," it means not only physically (on an ongoing basis and in regular intervals), but also mentally—beyond being the champion and the advocate of the initiative, the sponsor is also a mentor and a coach who is developing relationships with the team and the stakeholders and working both formally and informally to help build and develop a high-performance machine. Even with the authority the sponsor has, he/she needs to be able to motivate and influence team members and stakeholders, rather than simply exercising his/her authority. The authority will come in handy when it comes to decision making and providing sign-offs (timely, transparent, effective, and based on current information), but even this process needs to be balanced, participative, and inclusive.

But sponsorship is not only about leadership. Another important aspect is for the sponsor to clearly understand the problem/challenge on hand and be able to effectively articulate it, sell it, and build the appropriate sense of urgency around it. Beyond articulating the problem, the sponsor is also in charge of ensuring that the direction and the proposed solution are the right ways to fix the problem. Although the problem may be real and clear, many organizations miss the mark and end up spending time and money applying the wrong solution to the problem. Part of the process of picking the right approach to address or fix the problem is knowing which battles to pick and which areas to focus. Picking the battles is also about accountability and ensuring that things are done in context, in line with organizational objectives, and with the big picture in mind. Accountability starts with the sponsor, but does not end there; the sponsor has to instill a culture of accountability throughout the team that he/she assembles. The makeup of the team has to foster performance, but it also has to ensure cohesiveness and collaboration levels that are in line with the stakes, the sense of urgency, the nature of the work, and the broader organizational context.

Even with accountability, it is easy to lose track of the things that matter and start digging oneself into a rabbit hole that ends up wasting the organization's limited time and resources. It is the sponsor's job to ensure that no matter what is chosen to be fixed or what approach is used to fix it, that value is added, that there are mechanisms to measure the progress and performance, and that he/she will be accountable for results.

Even when there is a PM who leads the project, it is the sponsor's job to keep the team focused all the way through and, at the same time, learn how to start the process of easing out of the project when it comes to an end. When things do not go as planned, a good sponsor must know when to cut losses and cancel the project before that point of no return is crossed, where it is no longer possible to cancel the (failing) project because the repercussions (cost, damage to company, dependencies, etc.) are too great. There are many ways to measure project success, but even projects that do not make it to the finish line can be viewed as a success if a determination can be made as to when to end them before the point of no return, and if there can be lessons learned from the failure for the organization. Whether it is the performance, the circumstances, the changing conditions, or a combination of factors, not all initiatives are able to deliver on their promises and objectives, and it is important to be able to call initiatives off in a timely manner.

## Learning to Articulate Impact and Establishing a Sense of Urgency

The more the role of the sponsor is studied, the more it appears to be challenging. A sponsor is tasked with multiple areas to look at—conflicting priorities, political pressures, people, and leadership challenges—and all that on top of his/her *day job*, which is their job title. There is not enough time in the day to attend to all the needs around sponsors and to engage all stakeholders in a sufficient manner; not to mention to satisfy their needs. Sponsors and managers can blame their organizations (and many do) about the constant cutting of resources and costs. Sponsors can also point at the skills of team members, PMs, and even managers as not being as relevant, suitable, or sufficient as they used to be even five years ago. The surrounding conditions are constantly shifting for the worse, and the bad news is that things are not going to get better. As a matter of fact, these trends are expected to intensify, which brings up the basic conclusion reached earlier in this book that the main problems with sponsorship include the awareness of the role's importance and (obviously, as a result of the lack of awareness) the capacity to perform it effectively. Here are some of the headwinds that are expected to continue and intensify:

a. *Cost cutting and efficiencies*—with organizations continuing their cost cutting initiatives, the pressure on everyone in the organization is going to grow when it comes to work volume, which in turn, will further reduce people's capacity to perform their work and understand the context around them, or in other words, the big picture.

b. *Organizational change*—more *efficiency* initiatives and more cost cutting means more reorganizations and changes to reporting lines, processes, best practices, policies, and comfort zones. More changes will be made on the fly at any given point, more initiatives will be intertwined with each other, more change fatigue will be felt around the organization, and there will be more turnover among staff. This will put additional pressure on the already overwhelmed and overworked sponsor. In addition, the attitude toward cost cutting will continue to focus on the direct cost reduction aspect, instead of the overall value and the impact of the cost. Hiring cheaper resources and cutting costs tend to end up being much more expensive than the direct savings that were expected to be achieved.

c. *Resources*—there are going to be more challenges with resources at multiple levels: allocation (whether initiatives get their resources); timeliness (will resources report on time or for the right amount of time); getting the right resources (skills, experience, personality, style, and fit); and resource conflicts (is it okay to continue to over-allocate resources by planning in silos?).

d. *Capacity and the ability to articulate actual needs*—with an increasing volume of work, the ability to actually measure our own capacity will be lost; and based on that, the ability to set expectations or articulate our needs may also be lost.

e. *Context*—with less capacity and more work on everyone's plates, expect to have less context about the work being done, mandates to continue to be unclear, the ability to prioritize work to continue to diminish, and competing/conflicting demands to increase (as others in the organization also lack context and the ability to prioritize).

f. *Focus on results versus leadership competencies*—with limited resources and pressing constraints, the focus will further shift toward the technical aspects of the work in an effort to improve performance. This comes at a time when more leadership competencies are needed to support increasingly challenged teams.

## RECAP

This chapter started with a list of root causes as to why sponsorship faces so many challenges. It then turned into a series of symptoms that allow the discovery of challenges with sponsorship and the opportunity to learn to recognize them. Along the way, the chapter started to incorporate ideas on how to address these challenges before moving toward a review of some important leadership competencies that sponsors need to have. These competencies are on a high level and serve as a gateway to Chapter 3, where the discussion is about specific leadership attributes that should be looked for, developed, or honed as part of our quest to become an effective sponsor.

The chapter then identified a series of elements that sponsors need to review, but once again, many of them remained at a concept level, as opposed to how to develop these capabilities. Toward the end of the chapter, we circled back to connecting leadership and sponsorship, and then finished with a somewhat gloomier tone that sponsorship is facing an uphill battle due to some growing trends in organizations.

But it is not all negative—this book is dedicated to finding ways to improve awareness and introduce personal efficiencies, competencies, and growth areas that will give the sponsor more time to attend to his/her work, while achieving a better ability to understand the big picture and to align and prioritize what needs attention. Specifically, Chapter 3 looks at ways to address the growing list of challenges that sponsors face.

## NOTES

1. Business Dictionary: http://www.businessdictionary.com/definition/account ability.html.
2. Based on http://www.businessdictionary.com/definition/assumption.html.
3. Juran, J. M. *Juran's Quality Control Handbook*. 4th Edition, McGraw-Hill. 1998
4. *A Brief History of Dr. W. Edwards Deming*. 1992. British Deming Association, SPC Press, Inc.
5. Crosby, Philip. *Quality is Free*. McGraw-Hill, 1979.
6. *Quality Control Handbook, 5th Edition*. McGraw-Hill, 1999.
7. Based on the ASQ Quality Costs Committee *Principles of Quality Costs: Principles, Implementation, and Use, 3rd Ed*, ed. Jack Campanella, ASQ Quality Press, pp. 3–5, 1999.
8. Adapted from *Managing Stakeholder Expectations for Project Success*. J. Ross Publishing, 2013.
9. A detailed discussion of project health measures takes place in Chapter 9 of *Managing Stakeholder Expectations for Project Success*. J. Ross Publishing, 2013.
10. McKinsey Agile Tribe. December 2017.

11. http://www.educational-business-articles.com/leadership-versus-management/.
12. Kouzes, James M. and Barry Z. Posner. *The Leadership Challenge: How to Make Extraordinary Things Happen in Organizations.* Jossey-Bass, 2017.
13. Adapted from *The Primes.* Chris McGoff. John Wiley & Sons, 2012.
14. Adapted from *The Primes.* Chris McGoff. John Wiley & Sons, 2012.
15. Bennis, Warren. *On Becoming a Leader.* Basic Books, 1994.
16. https://simonsinek.com/commit/the-golden-circle.
17. Adapted from https://www.niskanencenter.org/bureaucratic-rigidity-miles-law-and-military-innovation/.
18. https://twobenches.wordpress.com/2012/09/23/flow/.
19. https://cx-journey.com/2012/04/feedback-is-breakfast-of-champions.html, attributed to Ken Blanchard.
20. Adapted from *Getting to Maybe.* Frances Westley, Brenda Zimmerman, and Michael Patton, Random House Canada, 2006.

# 3

# THE EFFECTIVE SPONSOR: THE RIGHT LEVEL OF INVOLVEMENT

## BEHAVIORS AND ACTIVITIES TO ENSURE EFFECTIVE SPONSORSHIP

Chapters 1 and 2 introduced many important questions and anecdotes to consider when trying to understand how to improve sponsorship, so let's go straight into figuring out what it takes to ensure effective sponsorship. This chapter takes us through a set of proposed actions, behaviors, and resolutions for the challenges that were introduced earlier in this book. The next step is to look into a set of leadership competencies, communication activities, escalation processes, and support that need to be in place. The final step will include ideas on how to improve the painful area of resource management and allocation, which seems to be the wild card in most organizations.

## DEALING WITH THE COMMON CHALLENGES OF CHANGE SPONSORSHIP

Earlier in Chapter 1 we discussed a series of common challenges with change sponsorship, along with explanations of their meanings. It is time now to look into some remedies and ideas on how to relieve the impact of these challenges, or overcome them altogether. Most of these challenges also touch on some of the root causes of the problems that were identified, including awareness around the sponsor's role, the role definition, and capacity issues. It is important to note that in no way is this a full list of challenges that organizations face when it comes to change sponsorship, but these are common challenges and they have a common denominator: addressing them can have the Pareto 80:20 effect,[1] because once they are addressed, it will pave the way to overcoming many related smaller and more tactical issues.

Table 3.1 provides some answers to the previously identified common challenges. Overall, the theme of overcoming these challenges is to invest the time and provide sufficient attention to things at the planning stages—including proper visioning and scoping of the change, along with a detailed and realistic plan to go through the transition and deal with the expected resistance.

**Table 3.1** Dealing with change sponsorship challenges

| Change Sponsorship Challenge | Ideas and Proposed Resolutions |
|---|---|
| Failure to identify and communicate a compelling vision | Vision not only provides guidance and direction, it also projects authority and shows leadership. Even if the vision is not clear or articulated at the highest levels of the organization, sponsors must spend the time and effort to put together a clear vision for the initiative, even if the vision is structured iteratively and provides only a high-level direction. |
| Failure to frame the scope of the change | Organizational change resembles a Hoberman sphere. It is hard to see all the layers up front, and a clear scoping process and analysis is necessary in order to realize the true magnitude of the change. Defining the clear scope of the change, its extent, and its boundaries is critical for the process of building an approach and understanding what lies ahead. |
| Failure to manage the transition | Once the old status quo is unfrozen, the change process tends to get a life of its own—until it re-freezes into the new state. Unfortunately, when things get lives of their own, they tend to unravel in undesired ways. It is during the transition when people get lost, disillusioned, and upset—and this is where our focus should be. A solid engagement, communication, training, and coaching plan must be in place. |
| Failure to effectively deal with resistance | Resistance is not futile when it comes to change. Resistance is a fact and if it is recognized and embraced, it can be of benefit. Chapter 6 covers organizational change in detail and provides techniques to identify different types of resistance and how to deal with each type effectively. |

The majority of change initiatives end up being bigger, taking longer, and costing more than was initially thought. This means more pain and reduced chances for success. The sponsor needs to recognize the common challenges that end up plaguing most change initiatives and work toward overcoming them.

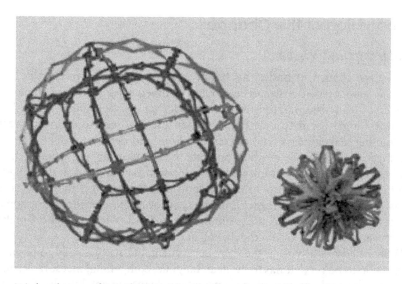

It is hard to see from the outside what goes on inside the change.
Framing and scoping the change involves opening up the sphere,
seeing its true magnitude, and seeing what is inside.

**Figure 3.1**   Hoberman's sphere

Table 3.1 examines a resemblance between the need to frame the scope and a
Hoberman's sphere. Figure 3.1 illustrates the challenges incurred when it comes
to framing and scoping the change. When the sphere is collapsed, there are many
spikes that interfere with the ability to look in and figure out what needs to go on
with the change. These spikes may be constraints, people, or other considerations
that may be in the way of the change. Working on smoothing these spikes is the
act of opening up the scope and realizing its true magnitude. The scope often ends
up being much bigger than was initially thought, but it is better to realize that now
and deal with it, rather than learning about the change's true magnitude midway
through the initiative when the options to address the newly realized problems
become more limited.

# DEALING WITH CHALLENGES THROUGH THE CHANGE U-CURVE CYCLE

In Chapter 1 we reviewed challenges throughout the various stages of change
(along the U-Curve), and now we will propose ways to deal with these challenges.

# Introduction of the Change

## *Leadership and Vision*

Most of the challenges under this broad category can be addressed by ensuring that the sponsor demonstrates leadership competencies. When it comes to an absence-of-leadership consensus, it is the sponsor's responsibility to put his/her foot down and articulate a sense of urgency and the need to define a direction. While other stakeholders tend to stall decisions and default to looking for more information, the sponsor needs to reiterate the need for making a timely decision and help others realize that not making a decision is equivalent to deciding to do nothing. This does not imply that the sponsor needs to rush into a decision or to instill a false sense of urgency, but the sponsor has to consider all options and realize that a bad decision could result in moving in the wrong direction, making a misinformed decision, or not moving at all.

When it comes to vision, there are several conditions that need to be in place for a vision to be *good*: it has to be clear, tangible, compelling, measurable, and realistic for the goal setting and the expectations management, but also for sending a leadership statement that the message of the direction is clear and that there is someone who is in charge. Keeping the vision realistic reduces unnecessary distractions because it helps focus the conversation on the possibilities and it forces the resisters to present valid reasons for their resistance, based on the merits of the vision. A clear vision also allows a roadmap to be identified, making it possible to check whether, or rather *which*, other initiatives may be interlocking with ours for focus and prioritization purposes.

Even with a clear vision, the sponsor must not be misled into thinking that just because they have a great idea or that the need is pressing, that everyone will love it and immediately support it. When trying to move forward in a certain direction, the tendency is to get tunnel vision—and when trying to gain people's buy-in, hope often gets mixed up with strategy. It is important to remember that *hope is not a strategy*. Engaging stakeholders, influencing them, working with them on addressing their needs and concerns, and planning to deal with their pushbacks and resistance are key parts in stepping up one's leadership act and addressing the concerns associated with the sponsor's leadership competencies. The sponsor needs to articulate the need, set the right sense of urgency, understand the underlying needs/concerns of key stakeholders, and work with them to maximize the alignment between everyone's and the initiative's objectives. Needless to say, it will be virtually impossible to fully align all of these needs, but this is when the sponsor gets a sense of what they are up against (not only from the product/process perspective, but also from stakeholders and resistance points of view), and where to focus their efforts.

With a clear vision and realistic expectations about the journey that is ahead, the sponsor needs to set clear expectations that the direction, pace, and flow of progress may not be a straight, linear line, but rather similar to sailing—that it is likely to veer off course based on the tides, winds, and currents that will be encountered.

## Communication

A lot has been said about communication, and most people feel that they are excellent communicators—but reality shows that not only are people not as effective as they believe they are when it comes to communication, but that the results are typically poor. No matter what type of engagement is at hand, communication almost always ends up low on the totem pole. Since many people see communication as a type of necessary evil, they believe that communication will take place virtually on its own. In addition, people tend to focus on more tangible deliverables (e.g., schedules, budgets, reports, and contracts), leaving little to no time to plan for the communication portion of the engagement. And considering that managing change is a lot about managing attitudes, communication is one of the key means to do so.

Until sponsors realize that their change initiative will rise and fall on communication, they will not give it the focus it needs. How to plan for communication is a tough topic to address, but considering the following elements is a step in the right direction:

a. *Own the communication*—the sponsor does not need to manage the details, but he/she needs to own the communication, the flow, and the tone of the conversations. Most of the technical elements of communications can be *outsourced* to the change manager or the project manager (PM), but the sponsor needs to set the tone. How do you own the communication? There is no one, specific, clear action that should be taken to own communication, but many of the concepts introduced in this book will get us closer to owning it: a clear vision, a clear message, one voice, various message styles and formats, and a timely and meaningful feedback loop.

b. *Informal communication*—although there is no way (including desire or ability) to control information communication, this is the place where many problems start or are detected. Understanding the danger starts with simple laws of physics: when there is a vacuum, a stronger force will enter into the vacuum and take over. When there is lack of formal communication (including clarity), rumors, stories, fears, and conversations will infiltrate the communication process and take over the tone and the direction of the engagement. Further, pieces of information that are spread (deliberately or not) will undermine the formal communication and possibly change meanings, symbols, and attitudes. While in many cases the tone of the informal communication simply takes over as a result of defaulting to the void left by the formal communication, astute resisters may take advantage of gaps in the formal communication to shift things in their direction.

   As a result, although it is less tangible and more difficult to articulate what the sponsor needs to do about informal communication, the sponsor needs to start by facilitating a process to establish clear norms and ground rules. Norms and ground rules are effective in maintaining a level of knowledge of the general direction of the informal conversations across the organization. The intent is not to control informal communication, but rather to prevent confusion between formal and informal communication, or the potential for the informal messages to contradict, distort, or take over the tone of the initiative. Knowledge about the informal communication also allows for proactive responses when sensing the tone, temperature, direction of conversations, and people's attitudes. Taking action to adjust, tweak, or retool before the negative impact on the initiative gets out of hand is vital.

Norms and ground rules, although associated with informal communication, also allow us to shape some of the formal communication and to differentiate between formal and informal. There is a wide range of areas to address, including guidelines about meetings and e-mails, differentiating between various communication means and formats, change control, escalations, reporting lines, approval criteria, decision-making processes and authorities, thresholds, and exceptions handling. It also pertains to conflict resolution techniques, protocols to handle disagreements, impact assessment, reporting formats, communication tools and means preferences, and do's and don'ts. In addition, in this day and age, guidelines need to reflect the need for diversity, inclusiveness, and cultural differences for decision-making purposes; and when referring to diversity, that includes a diversity of opinions, views, and styles.

Clear norms help give things a meaning and provide symbolic meanings to others—especially when things get tense, when communication is overwhelming, or when things do not add up. This is when the norms help with a reminder to take a step back and better understand both the clear, as well as the underlying messages.

The sponsor is not responsible for setting all of these norms, nor is he/she responsible for overseeing them at any given point, but as the owner of the initiative, and being ultimately accountable for it, it is the sponsor's territory and he/she needs to have their flavor and mark in place.

c.  *Cover all corners and stakeholders' needs*—it is easy to overlook certain stakeholders (altogether) or stakeholders' needs. Whatever is missed early on tends to haunt people later in the initiative and become detrimental to the cause and the engagement success. The sponsor needs to ensure that all stakeholders are mapped, their needs are known, and that there is a plan in place to address (or at least work around) these needs and expectations. Once again, the sponsor sets the tone, rather than doing all of the associated legwork.

d.  *Address different types/styles/needs of communicators at different times*— this is not easy. There are many people (i.e., stakeholders) involved and they have different communication styles and needs. It is not possible to accommodate all needs at all times, but the messages and interactions must address the multiple groups of needs and styles from the state of mind of the stakeholders. Chapter 4 deals with communication styles and preferences and it incorporates a simple interpretation of DiSC[2] analysis (dominance, influence, steadiness, and conscientiousness) to identify people's communication styles. It is therefore important to plan for engaging people in multiple formats and styles and doing so without too many redundancies—both to reduce waste and to minimize the chance of people checking out due to incoherent, irrelevant, or repeated messages.

e.  *Set up escalation procedures*—escalations, as a part of setting up norms, was touched on already. Setting up clear escalation procedures is important not only for a clear and proper flow of information, but also as part of setting the tone and the leadership style. Defining acceptable performance measures (whether for processes, deliverables, or even communication) is the first step; followed by a clear set of rules on how to address any exceptions, who to engage, what buttons to press, and what tone to attach to the message. It is not enough to leave escalations to if/when they are needed because when things go sideways, people panic and their message may be distorted, taken out of context, and/or fail altogether to reach the right person. Escalation procedures are not only about raising red flags, but also about reducing the number of unnecessary false alarms. Having a framework and a structure around it helps keep things in context in a controlled and consistent way. Reviews, lessons learned, and process improvements also benefit from consistent and controlled escalation procedures.

f.  *Exceptions*—a few years ago, managing by exceptions was a flavor of the day, but unfortunately it was taken out of context. The intent was to identify norms and standards for the things that are routinely done and to establish escalation procedures in the event that there was a performance exception. The intention was to set up guidelines on expected norms and standards as to what to do in the event of an exception (out of norm), as described previously with the escalation procedures. Unfortunately, even with the benefits that this concept has when utilized properly, it is still partially misunderstood. People may focus on performance and deliverables exceptions, but they allow for exceptions in processes and behaviors—and this is when the poor handling of exceptions connects to accountability, or rather a lack of it. The result is that the behavior and process-related exceptions slowly become the norm and overtake the way that things should be done. There is another element to exceptions and it is the double standard—where people expect others to follow the processes and behave within the expected norms, but they themselves do not. This, of course, leads to accountability problems.

To illustrate, the downtown core of a large city—for example, Toronto—can be used. Toronto is the fourth largest metropolitan city in North America, but it is full of people who think they are special and exceptional, or rather, people who think that rules and norms do not apply to them. When a person of this type orders a cup of their favorite coffee drink from their local posh coffee shop through a mobile app, they routinely stop their car in a live traffic lane—just for a minute—to run in and pick up their coffee, thus blocking traffic. This is an example of a behavioral or process exception; they are not supposed to block traffic, even though they are "special," and despite it being for only a minute. However, with no consequences or accountability, their behavior becomes the norm and they will do it again the following day. Further, when other people see that there are no consequences for blocking traffic, they may decide to do the same.

It is impossible to run a successful organization, a city, or even society when there are no consequences to people's actions and when there is no accountability. It is the sponsor's role to set the tone on the norms and expectations and to ensure that there are no exceptions to these norms and that there will be consequences to people's actions. The consequences do not need to be punitive, but they must send a message and establish a sense of ownership and accountability. Setting norms and expectations and holding people accountable for their actions serve as more examples of how setting up and controlling communications can impact accountability, reduce problems due to double standards, and improve the team cohesiveness and performance.

g. *Feedback loop*—feedback is not triggered, collected, provided, or produced on its own. There must be a mechanism to send and collect feedback (along with a way to process, analyze, and act on it). The sponsor needs to set the awareness and provide the means for sending and collecting meaningful feedback and to maintain the feedback loop, or else there will be a chance of losing control over the direction of the engagement.

To recap the communication guidelines: when the wrong thing is pursued, when the right approach is not employed, and when things do not fall into place, communication is unlikely to make a significant difference toward success. However, when barely managing to keep one's head above water, communication is a critical success factor that can make the difference between success and failure.

Communication is a challenge in any type of environment, and the concepts discussed here are applicable for any type of setting, including change and projects.

During the early stages of the change (from the introduction through the denial and the resistance stages), people need to be allowed to express themselves. Effective ways include a lot of one-on-one conversations (does not have to be done with the sponsor), where people can vent and say what is on their minds. It is important to make sure that they get to express themselves; and for change leaders, the job is to remain calm, not become defensive, and not react in haste directly to their concerns. It is not about ignoring their concerns, but rather letting people air them out, legitimizing them, and then letting them know that, in due course, their concerns will be alleviated because the progress being made is not in conflict with their needs. The rationale behind allowing people to vent—and mostly in one-on-one discussions—is to prevent them from falling into *groupthink*, where they feed off each others' comments and concerns into a rabbit hole of negativity that can destroy the initiative.

## Planning

There is no question as to the value of planning, yet failing to plan properly or sufficiently seems to happen on an almost chronic basis. The reasons for the problems with planning range mainly between a lack of time and a lack of clear information to rely on. The problem becomes even more prevalent in change initiatives than in projects since the change initiatives often lack specific or tangible information to work with, the planning horizon is usually longer, and they span multiple areas. More specifically, the sponsor needs to set up the planning process and ensure that enough capacity is in place for the following items (which were identified back in Chapter 1). There will be a deeper discussion of change management in Chapter 5, but for now, the planning activities must address the following:

- *Frame the scope of the change*—the scope and boundaries of change initiatives are often not clearly defined, and even if they are, that level of understanding is not communicated to other stakeholders who need to know. The sponsor needs to look into the organization(s) that will be part of the change, the areas that will be impacted, what will change, and the extent of that change. Also, there is a need to provide clarity about the scope to others and assess the impact on the surrounding areas. How is that accomplished? Start with the vision, define the objectives, clarify what is in and out of scope, and articulate major requirements and deliverables. This makes up the mandate and as the planning moves forward, the breakdown of the deliverables will be refined.
- *Identify key stakeholders and build an engagement plan*—an important part of a change management plan is the communication aspect and managing it effectively. The sponsor needs to know who the key stakeholders are, their needs, their expectations, and their disposition toward the initiative. The stakeholders' engagement and buy-in are key to the success of the initiative, including understanding where stakeholders are on the U-Curve and how to handle them and their needs. Chapter 4 looks into the stakeholder identification, analysis, and engagement process, and it reiterates the importance of not taking any shortcuts when it comes to understanding stakeholders' needs. This process should be treated with the same level of focus and rigor as any other part of the plan.
- *Plan for resistance*—there is no question about it: there will be resistance and the sponsor needs to proactively plan on how to handle it, understand the nature and source of it, work toward reducing it, and engage those stakeholders who resist. Chapter 5 covers the area of change management in detail and it provides an extensive overview of types of resistance and

how to deal with each type. Proper scoping of the change and an effective stakeholder engagement plan will both reduce the resistance and put things in a more proactive position for resistance to be addressed.

- *Plan for handling the transition: the transition refers to the journey, or the time and the place that are in between*—at this point, the initiative has moved away from the status quo, and yet it is far away from the desired future state. The transition is when things happen, but also when things go wrong and when people become disengaged, disillusioned, and frustrated with the progress, the direction, or the initiative as a whole. The mix of hand-holding, engagement, communication, expectations management, and handling problems and gaps in expectations will determine whether it is possible to cross this long chasm.

- *Ensure there is a clear connection between the change and the associated project(s)*—many organizations and sponsors fail to make sure there is a proper connection between the change initiative and the project(s) that drive it. In fact, it turns out to be a much more common cause of failure than was previously realized. The connection is about ensuring proper definitions are in place for the project, articulating success criteria, making sure that the right PM is in place, and ensuring that the project's objectives are connected to the change's objectives. A breakdown of the project at the proper milestones and a meaningful governance process will allow for timely checkpoints that ensure alignment and, ultimately, success.

- *Identify and manage assumptions*—virtually every time there is a conversation about assumptions, gaps and misunderstandings are revealed. Voicing assumptions is the first step in the process of handling them and ensuring that the consequences of their impact are dealt with—but it starts with a conversation. People do not like talking about assumptions; they view it as unpleasant and redundant. While the unpleasant feeling is legitimate, it is better to talk about assumptions early on because later, those assumptions that were not identified or validated become risks, issues, and barriers to delivering success.

Table 3.2 goes over a list of additional items that were identified in Chapter 1 as early challenges to the change initiative, along with remedies and suggestions on how to avoid or overcome these challenges.

## Denial Stage Challenges

The journey along the U-Curve is not the same for everyone. Different people will find themselves moving along the U-curve at different paces; therefore, at any given point, there may be some people in denial, while others may be in the resistance or the acceptance stages. Also, the duration of each stage may change from one individual to another, as well as the fluctuations along the curve. Some people

**Table 3.2**  Additional remedies for change challenges

| Early Change Challenges | Possible Remedies and Actions to Avoid the Challenges |
|---|---|
| Failure to form a coalition | This is an extension of stakeholder analysis. It is necessary to learn the key stakeholders and their expectations. This will provide information about who supports the initiatives and who it is possible to set up alliances with that will help promote the cause and the direction of the initiative. |
| Failure to create a sense of urgency | Many people suffer from *change fatigue*, along with *emergency fatigue*. It is hard to keep people on their toes for too long or for too many reasons. There is therefore a risk of overdoing it and moving from a healthy sense of urgency to the drama territory. However, in most cases, the opposite applies; it is hard to enroll people to share a sufficient level of urgency and hard to keep this intensity going over an extended period of time. Establishing a set of success criteria, clear deliverables, and timely milestones can help manage and even control the ups and downs through the initiative. Meaningful signs of progress along with a sense of achievement should be incorporated into the milestones. |
| Promising an easy, cheap, and quick change | There is no such thing as easy, fast, or low-cost change (at least not a meaningful one). Therefore, it is important to set the correct and realistic expectations. Setting false expectations will cause problems, resistance, and trust issues downstream. |
| Leaving it up to the PM to lead | The PM leads the project, but the sponsor needs to lead the change initiative and set the mandate and tone. The PM lacks sufficient authority and context to lead on his/her own. |
| Not communicating the reason for the change | We cannot assume that people will just buy in to the change. The sponsor needs to communicate the reasoning and rationale for the change. |
| Undermining the status quo | As an attempt to gain support, stakeholders tend to undermine the status quo as bad or negative. This should be avoided since it also undermines those who are associated with creating and maintaining the status quo. Undermining actions appeal to a lower common denominator and it is not a testament of strong leadership. |
| Failing to realize constraints and capacities | Constraints shape the engagement and its success criteria. Failing to realize them will likely lead to a collision course with the constraints, which means failure. Capacity (i.e., time, resources, and bandwidth) is also a form of a constraint, as the people and teams all have limited capacities. |

The early stages of the change—around the time when we introduce the change—is when it is necessary to build a foundation and set up the path toward success. Building a coalition, setting clear expectations, providing drive, and maintaining integrity are key components during the early stages.

will go through a steeper downturn (toward denial) than others, and they may stay there for a longer period of time. It is therefore important for the sponsor to establish a variety of communication styles and engagement activities to address every type of stakeholder, wherever they are on the U-Curve, while effectively communicating with other stakeholders who are at different stages.

The key challenges that the sponsor faces when engaging stakeholders at the denial stage can be broken down primarily into three groups: leadership, communication, and resistance. Table 3.3 looks at the actions needed to address the leadership challenges that sponsors face when addressing stakeholders who are in

**Table 3.3** Leadership challenges and remedies during the denial stage

| Leadership Challenges for Those in the Denial Stage | Possible Remedies and Actions to Avoid Challenges |
|---|---|
| Failure to maintain focus on the vision | The denial stage is when things are starting to happen. However, stakeholders may not be happy with the course of action, the direction, or the pace of events. It is easy to get distracted and lose focus on the big picture. The sponsor needs to reiterate the vision and the link between the actions being taken and the progress toward achieving the vision. |
| Disjointed team | Not only can stakeholders get distracted, disillusioned, or lost—team members do as well. There may be a PM, a change manager, or others who directly lead the team, but the sponsor is the one who needs to set the tone and enable the process of keeping the team focused and engaged. |
| Failure to measure and show progress | The change initiative may be long and progress may not be felt or realized for some time. Milestones and communication are key measures to put in place to ensure that everyone involved is aware of the true status and the meaning of the events that take place. |
| Panic | When things do not go in the expected direction, many people panic. At that point, pushing too hard or moving too fast may be exactly what should *not* be done. At this point, a step back, more hand-holding and support, along with revisiting the vision and the objectives, are the best courses of action. |
| The change vs. the pain | As things get tough, people start confusing the change (along with its goals and benefits) with the pain that they are experiencing as part of the transition. The sponsor needs to ensure that the focus shifts back to the benefits and that things progress in the right direction, as opposed to allowing people to dig themselves into a hole by focusing on the pain. |

The denial stage on the U-Curve is when the curve moves down; it takes place early on during the transition. The sponsor needs to lead the effort to ensure that stakeholders go through the denial stage only in the early stages of the transition, and that they do not stay there throughout.

the denial stage. This needs to take place while keeping in mind that other stakeholders may move faster or slower on the U-Curve.

## Communication Challenges and Remedies During the Denial Stage

Not all stakeholders will need the same style or message; some stakeholders do not necessarily go through this stage, while others may already be further along on the curve (this could be either good or bad for the change initiative). One of the most common communication challenges at this stage is insufficient, unclear, or a lack of communication. When it comes to communication, the sponsor, along with his/her partners in leading the initiative, must gain and maintain control over the communication process because with no control over virtually all aspects of communication, someone else will find a way to fill the void. The tendency of others to default into voids is similar to that of the laws of physics: when a space is not occupied by anyone, someone will find their way in. Unfortunately, those who enter that void usually have their own agenda and they may reset the tone of the communication around the initiative.

Other communication-related challenges are introduced as a result of insufficient or the lack of communication altogether—resulting in unrealistic expectations and the introduction of rumors about where the initiative is heading and at what pace. These rumors often do not match reality and the result can further derail the buy-in efforts and the stakeholder engagement process. Little to no mechanisms to collect and gauge feedback may further contribute to the rumor mill and to the spread of false information. Too much communication can also be a challenge, resulting in communication efforts that are meaningless. These produce noise, confuse people, and make it difficult to distinguish the signal from the noise and the meaningful information from the rumors.

Dealing with communication challenges requires a proactive and preventive effort. Once the communication challenges are in place, it is hard to recover without taking a significant hit to the initiative's objectives. This further reinforces the role of the sponsor in both enabling and taking part in the planning and the establishment of communication lines, forms, and approaches. The term *gaining control over the communication* goes a long way toward illustrating the importance of the communication aspect throughout the change initiative—especially at this stage. The change management plan consists of communication and engagement components where every step of the way must be planned and accounted for.

There is always a question as to what is meaningful communication—and the answer is: checking the needs of the stakeholders and engaging them in multiple ways, at consistent intervals, with ample capacity for feedback; and ensuring that the form, frequency, and style of the communication matches their needs. How to address stakeholder needs is another question (discussed more in Chapter 4) where the main *characteristics* that define the stakeholders' communication style and needs are identified and then the style is matched to where these stakeholders are on the U-Curve. Matching stakeholders' communication needs with where they are on the U-Curve will help to determine the right communication mix, style, and frequency in order to engage them most effectively.

Another factor that casts a shadow on communication during this stage is the hesitation and doubt that are spreading (on many occasions, rapidly), even among those who are supposed to lead the initiative. This not only weakens their message, but it also projects a lack of confidence and a lack of clarity regarding the initiative's direction. While the substance and clarity of the communications must be maintained, this is possibly where *appearances* matter the most—as stakeholders seek reassurances and look for consistency, stability, and clarity. Part of the communication process is to repeat the message; yet it is not about outright repetition, but rather about reinforcing our messages and conveying the same message in different channels and formats. Stakeholders are going to cling to any piece of information and to any clue that indicates that things are moving in the right direction, and it is the sponsor's responsibility to provide them with this sense of direction. And in case it was forgotten—this is not a call for the sponsor to actually perform all of these communication activities, but rather for the sponsor to enable the process and facilitate it.

When communicating with stakeholders during the denial stage, the objective is to provide reassurances, comfort, and signs of stability. Stakeholders should also be shown that everything that is happening is expected and normal, and that it is within predictable and ordinary parameters. It may be helpful to demonstrate that everything is under control (meaning communication, as well as events and direction)—but it is advisable to avoid the appearance of being overconfident.

### Early Resistance Challenges and Remedies During the Denial Stage

When stakeholders go through the denial stage (while at the same time, others may be at different stages), early signs of resistance may be displayed; although most of these early signs will be hard to detect and the resistance at this point is still weaker and maybe even somewhat passive aggressive. It is important to not ignore resistance or to attempt to suppress the signs of it (Chapter 5 will go into this as it relates to change sponsorship). Suppressing resistance is one of the most instinctive and common things (or rather mistakes) that people do. Instead, it is best to recognize and accept that there will be some resistance, and then handle it systematically. Ignoring resistance or attempting to distract others and draw attention away from it (or the signs of resistance) may buy some time, but overall, it will only make things worse. This is because later—when it is no longer possible to ignore, distract from, or contain the signs of resistance—the resistance will be stronger and harder to handle. The first signs of resistance to the change initiative call for a visit to the resistance stage on the U-Curve.

## Resistance Stage Challenges

Resistance is not only expected and normal when change is being introduced, but it can also be beneficial. For the change team and the sponsor, signs of resistance provide a chance to view areas of concern that people have and an opportunity to address them. For those who resist, it is both an opportunity to express their concern (people have a need to *vent*), as well as a way to draw attention to their areas of concern.

When it comes to resistance, it is important to plan for it and strategize about how to handle it, but, with that said, it is somewhat hard to plan for the unknown. It is important to identify the resistance as early as possible, determine the underlying causes for it, decide which stakeholders are likely to show signs of resistance, and try to anticipate their reactions and behaviors. With this information, an action plan can be drafted, the necessary capacity needed for it can be identified, and the roles and responsibilities to address the concerns can be determined. Planning for resistance falls under a similar category as risk management—it is about planning for the unknown and for conditions that may or may not introduce themselves. As a result, some stakeholders may not see the value in planning for resistance that *may not occur*; nevertheless, failing to plan for potential resistance will result in surprises and unpreparedness for the reality and challenges it may introduce.

Resistance may come in different forms and be due to different underlying reasons (i.e., lack of awareness, lack of knowledge, concerns, or lack of desire). Therefore, it is not possible to view the preparation for resistance as a *one-size-fits-all* situation. A large part of the resistance during this stage will likely be due to a lack of awareness of what is happening (discomfort), concerns about the direction things are moving toward, and whether those who are impacted will be able to maintain their comfort, structure, knowledge, and reputation. Planning for resistance is an extension of the change planning process. Having a change management plan, along with a stakeholder engagement plan and a comprehensive communications plan will equip us with better means to handle resistance, address it, and ultimately defuse it; but it will also proactively help reduce the amount of resistance that is introduced to begin with.

There will always be resistance and there will always be stakeholders who are not happy with something (what, how, or where things are changing). With some of the resistance, there is nothing that can be said or done to alleviate these stakeholders' concerns or appease them in any way; but most resistance can be effectively handled or minimized with proper and sufficient planning. It is therefore important to balance our efforts and not disproportionately over-allocate our scarce resources only (or even mostly) toward the resisters because that effort may be partially futile and it will give others the wrong message that resistance will pay off for them.

The appearance of resistance is a sign that stakeholders are moving from denial and disbelief into recognition that things are different or about to be different. Resistance will take over, along with frustration and even anger, that may soon negatively shift people's moods. It may also lead some to demonstrate signs that are similar to depression and low energy.

Let's review the specific challenges that could materialize here, along with the proposed remedies for each of these challenges: organizational, communication, leadership, and the resistance itself.

## *Organizational Challenges During the Resistance Stage*

The first type of challenge to discuss here is organizational challenges; they are bigger than any individual change initiative. Many of these challenges are a result of the gross oversaturation in change initiatives in most project environments. Since this is an already preexisting condition, the change sponsor needs to react to this reality by introducing the initiative's needs and direction to higher-level decision makers and propose ways to *direct traffic* and perform cross-initiative analysis for dependencies, interlocks, and conflicts. The alternative is an organization where all initiatives act as silos and compete with each other, resulting in falling short on meeting most of these initiatives' objectives. More information about the organizational challenges and remedies is explored in Table 3.4.

**Table 3.4**  Organizational challenges and remedies during the resistance stage

| Organizational Challenges When in the Resistance Stage | Details and Possible Remedies and Actions to Address or Avoid the Challenges |
|---|---|
| Lack of resilience | Change saturation and change fatigue are two common ways to describe a reality of too much change in the organization; where people become numb in the face of more change. No one is sure what goes on, changes are intertwined with each other, and people are confused about which change they are a part of. These conditions are a precursor for resilience issues, where there is no more energy or capacity to handle yet another change.  Resilience challenges range from a lack of competence to handle the situation, a lack of coping with the changing reality (due to morale issues during the resistance stage), a lack of confidence, and withdrawals from buy-in and contribution.  Remedies include establishing mechanisms to address stakeholders' concerns, multiple forms of communication on an ongoing basis (not all the time, but in agreed-upon intervals), and maintaining a feedback mechanism to ensure accurate knowledge about what goes on so that it is possible to move forward, recalibrate as needed, and address people's concerns. |
| Failing to address change saturation | This item is related to organizational resilience, but since it is so common and acute, there is a real need to focus on addressing it. The way to do that is to look at the big picture and check what else the organization is currently going through. It is the sponsor's job to explore what other initiatives are taking place in the organization since this initiative (even if very important and high profile) cannot be managed in a disconnected way from organizational context. When there is too much change around, there has to be a strategic decision to stagger some initiatives so they do not interfere with each other. |

*continued*

| Organizational Challenges When in the Resistance Stage | Details and Possible Remedies and Actions to Address or Avoid the Challenges |
|---|---|
| Overfocus on symbolism, politics, structure, and appearance | There is a tendency to over-allocate efforts and capacity toward items that are *above the water*: they are visible, tangible, and easier to articulate. It is tempting to spend more time on these items, but these efforts will not yield a meaningful result, support, or buy-in. For positive and meaningful impact, it is necessary to address people's concerns and monitor the impact that the change has on the organizational culture so the deeper impacts on the organization can be managed and controlled. |

Organizational challenges require the sponsor's focus since they impact the change initiative not only from the outside, but specifically from higher up in the organization.

## Communication Challenges and Remedies During the Resistance Stage

One underlying cause for communication challenges is, in fact, an underlying cause for most problems in today's organizations—the lack of time and capacity. It seems that everyone is overworked and busy, and a lack of time leads to an attempt to cut corners and reduce workloads quickly—and communication is most likely one of the first victims. This is why handling communication starts from the top (the sponsor) with enabling capacity and ensuring the right level of awareness is in place regarding the importance of communication.

There are a few guidelines to follow when it comes to communication. While these are applicable for any type of communication in any situation, now, during the resistance stage of the change, there is a need to further reinforce them:

1. Display clarity in communication by using simple, upfront, and clear language that speaks straight to people and not downward at them
2. Articulate the scope of what is changing and to what extent
3. Consider the outcome of what is changing and how it will impact people in all aspects, including emotionally
4. Provide transparency on the journey and the destination; it is not only where to go, it is how to get there
5. Everyone needs to know what is expected of them; a RACI chart[3] (responsibility assignment matrix) can help, and most likely more than one will be needed
6. Ensure that each piece of information is done in context, as discussed earlier in this chapter; consider the source of each message, its sense of urgency, its format, and the channel it will go through, and also establish a feedback loop
7. Ensure there is reinforcement and that messages go out on an ongoing basis to everyone who is involved

The following is a list of items to address when it comes to communication challenges in general and specifically during the resistance stage:

- *Make sure communication is actually taking place*—some say that there is no such thing as overcommunication during organizational change; but the goal here is not for quantity, but rather for quality communication. Figure 3.2 reviews the basic components to consider when planning for communication.
- *Failure to reinforce the message in different ways*—even with all the communication tools and technology available, it is necessary to try to utilize the most powerful method: face-to-face. Find as many ways as possible to reinforce the message and address different communication needs, including small group discussions, one-on-one meetings, team meetings, information sessions, and focus groups. Additional means should be incorporated, such as hotlines, frequently asked questions, video conferencing, and even discussion boards, in order to allow people to voice their views and seek information. E-mails and memos can also help relay messages, but more as support, rather than as a primary form of sending important messages. These methods will allow the messages to go through in different ways, and

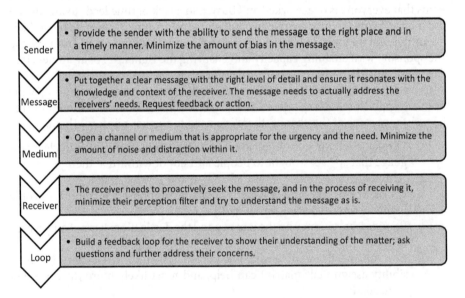

Effective communication is better planned for by breaking down the communication process into distinct components and then planning on how to handle the challenges and the potential breakdown of each component. This process is based on the basic communication model of sender-message-medium-receiver-loop.

**Figure 3.2**   Components of effective communication

they will also allow the collection of feedback and ways to get the general reaction of people to the events that are associated with the change.

- *Failure to address different communication needs and styles*—this item is related to the previous bullet point and deals with reinforcing the message. By conveying the message in multiple forms, it should effectively reach every stakeholder's style and method that resonates with them. Chapter 4 will cover more specifically the area of identifying the needs of people around us and tailoring the message styles to their needs.
- *Failure to establish a feedback loop*—feedback is a key success factor for any type of change. Employees must have a way to send feedback (positive, negative, constructive, or any kind), and there must be a way to capture, process, and act on it effectively and in a timely manner. Even the best ideas cannot move forward successfully without understanding what people think and how to respond to their needs.
- *What needs to be communicated and how*—Table 3.5 provides a look into items that are necessary for good communication and how to utilize them during the resistance stage.

**Table 3.5**   Communication best practices

| Communication Best Practices | Details |
| --- | --- |
| Listen | Do not be defensive; provide thoughtful answers in a timely manner, no excuses. |
| Vision | Reiterate the vision, the stage of achievement, and for whatever is being done—what it means toward reaching the vision. |
| Reasoning | Make sure there is transparency and reasoning for any action and deliverable that is taking place. |
| Be available | Those who lead the change and the sponsor need to be visible and available, potentially on a daily basis. |
| Do not stumble | It may not be possible to have the answers to all questions on the spot. Incorrect information will damage a person's credibility. If an answer is not immediately available, it is best to offer to supply an answer at a later time (and ensure that it is resolved—and in a timely manner). |
| Interactive communication | Engage people in an interactive manner, including workshops and Q&A sessions. Make sure to explore the impact and direction of the change together with the stakeholders. It will not only give them information that they need, it will also go a long way in making them feel included and part of the process. Some resistance will be a direct result of people feeling not included or uncomfortable. |
| Be proactive | The resistance stage is the most common breeding ground for rumors and misinformation. |

*continued*

| Communication Best Practices | Details |
|---|---|
| Multi-channel | Maintain consistency in frequency and direction and do it through multiple channels: speaking, Q&As, one-on-one, writing, videos, training, focus groups, memos, message boards, FAQs, and intranet. |
| Timeliness | Communicate the information that has been gathered in a timely manner so that people do not feel that anything is being withheld. Follow up as required and update if the message changes. |
| Feedback | Encourage people to ask questions, seek feedback, request clarification, express opinions, and provide input. |
| Keep them involved | Provide people with pieces of ownership and updates about what is happening so that they feel part of the change. The involvement will build trust and yield commitment. |
| Informal and networking | Encourage people to network with each other and exchange information in an informal setting. This will help share ideas and reduce misinformation. Ensure there is a clear distinction between formal and informal communication. |
| Status updates | Provide status updates in real time (as much as possible) and allow feedback and questions; even (or especially) if information is less than favorable. |
| Rewards and recognition | Beyond the show of appreciation, an important part of rewards and recognitions is the communication—to show accomplishments and celebrate even small wins. |

These communication best practices are relevant for any situation, but they must especially guide us during the delicate stage of resistance.

## *Resistance Challenges and Remedies During the Resistance Stage*

Resistance does not just happen because people choose to resist, but rather as a result of a range of underlying reasons. Besides addressing the signs of resistance and people's behaviors and actions, there is a need to explore the underlying reasons behind the resistance and provide answers about them. There is a range of potential answers to choose from, based on the nature of the problem:

a. Solve the problem
b. Reduce the impact
c. Alleviate the concerns
d. Provide clarifications
e. Ask for more input
f. Escalate and seek more information
g. Show a level of effort by taking some sort of action
h. Reiterate the situation and the impact, and that there is nothing that can be done

However, it is not advisable to simply hope that resistance will disappear on its own. Ignoring the resistance, focusing on fighting its signs, or suppressing it will not solve the problems that trigger the resistance. On the other hand, being firm and clear in the response is essential, so that any engagement or attempts to handle the situation do not send a message of rewards for the resisters.

The response chosen should be based on the type of resistance (i.e., due to a lack of awareness, a lack of knowledge, or a lack of desire).

## Leadership Challenges and Remedies During the Resistance Stage

When it comes to leadership challenges, it is important to take another look at the communications section; and specifically, the best practices that are listed in Table 3.5. The communication style and its overall effectiveness is in direct relation to the demonstration of leadership competencies, and as discussed earlier in the chapter, it starts with the sponsor. It is clear that the sponsor does not need to lead all communication activities or to be present in every conversation; but the sponsor is an enabler, a facilitator, and a leader who provides the context, tone, and capacity for the communication process. Along with those responsibilities, he/she empowers others to follow the communication processes and guidelines in order to ensure that the messages go through, that the feedback loop is open, and that communication does not hinder the change initiative. Strong leaders provide the needs that enable effective communication.

In addition, the leader needs to determine which battles to engage in and which are not worth the effort. Depending on who demonstrates resistance and to what extent, the sponsor determines if it is worth the effort to engage those stakeholders and to what degree. When resistance persists, depending on whether or not it directly and negatively impacts the initiative, it is sometimes advisable to call it a losing battle and put together a plan as to how to deal with this persistent resistance. Leadership is about making tough decisions and ensuring that time is being spent on resources and efforts efficiently, and therefore, it is necessary to *pick our battles*. Losing a specific resistance battle does not mean that the entire cause is lost and sometimes it creates an opportunity to channel our efforts more efficiently in delivering success. The alternative would be to engage in losing battles and end up endangering the entire initiative as a result.

With that said, it is important to not give freebies by caving in to resistance too easily. Accommodating the needs of the resisters for reasons that do not support the big picture (or giving that impression) will send a message to others that the resistance pays off and that commitments are not always upheld.

Another leadership-related challenge is when sponsors take a step back and fail to lead. There are multiple potential reasons for why it may happen (with the leading one being a lack of time), but the result is the same: when taking a step back, a void is left that will be filled quickly by others. Many times, those who default into that void usually have a specific agenda that they pursue, which is most likely misaligned with the organization's. Failure to lead is not an option. If sponsors feel that they do not have the capacity or the time to provide the change leadership, they should delegate some of it to others who are on the same page and who can help with this very important task.

Even when leading, there is yet another challenge—failure to lead by example. Sponsors must show guidance and strength by applying the same (or even stricter) standards for themselves as leaders than for others—and to faithfully follow those standards. The topic of leading by example may be the primary reason why it is hard to find true leaders in most political systems. Sometimes, those who govern apply more favorable standards for themselves than for their constituents. The resentment and the negative results that a failure to lead by example causes in politics can easily be seen—and it has the same effect in the corporate world. Since people view sponsors as leaders, their actions influence the way others behave, and they will respond to the way that they see their leaders behave.

The phrase *leading by example* can be dissected into a few specific behaviors that include the following:

- *Accountability*—be responsible; do what you say and say what you do, and ensure that you identify and perform your role in the process
- *Apply and adhere to the same standards*—this includes everyone
- *Be proactive*—see trends and look for things you can do to avoid problems and improve outcomes
- *Ensure what you do is in the context of the desired goal*—admit it when you veer from the intended process
- *Own up*—make decisions based on the best interest of those involved and of the business objectives

While in the resistance stage, people look for a leader, for someone who leads by example, and for someone to take ownership of things—especially when things do not necessarily move at the expected pace or direction. Leading is also about realizing what stage on the U-Curve people are and that it is normal to experience what they are going through. A failure to recognize the stage where people reside will result in ignoring, misinterpreting, or mishandling their resistance. Before long, leaders may find themselves with people who are checking out and with an increase in the number of lost-cause resistance battles.

Finally, panic is another serious challenge to leadership. Besides the fact that when someone panics they do not think straight, the message that is sent by panicking is that he/she is not in charge or is not capable of leading, which will open the door for others to step in with their interests and agendas. Panic is a symptom of a lack of leadership. The ability to lead is measured by how you handle a situation when other people panic—confidently lead the initiative, stay focused on the vision, and align stakeholders' needs with that vision.

## Acceptance Stage Challenges

The progression that people go through on the U-curve is normal and it is expected that most stakeholders will go through a resistance stage. If the change is moving in the right direction and at a satisfactory pace, and if the resistance is handled properly, moving into the acceptance stage should be anticipated.

The acceptance stage is where people start experimenting with the new reality that is forming in an attempt to engage with the new situation. With resistance winding down, people are starting to accept the reality that is shaping and forming, and they start tilting toward becoming more positive toward it. However, full acceptance has not been attained yet and there are still several challenges that may introduce themselves and possibly impede the progress that has been made.

## Leadership Challenges and Remedies During the Acceptance Stage

Realizing that we are not there yet is important, and the effort to continuously engage stakeholders must continue. Letting go and failing to provide sufficient reinforcement of the change, the direction, and the necessary assurances is a common mistake that change leaders and sponsors make at this stage. It is not about repeating ourselves, or just reiterating the message, progress, benefits, and wins; it is about ensuring that the perception is maintained that things are moving in the right direction. The acceptance and the waning resistance that are beginning to emerge at this stage are fragile, and this is the time to provide our stakeholders with the reassurances and reaffirmations that they need.

Another common mistake is failing to ingrain the change. This is the time to introduce mechanisms, guidelines, and assurances that processes, practices, and actions become second nature; that people know how to perform their role under the newly shaping reality; and that technical elements, tasks, and handoffs are all in place. It is expected that there will be some challenges since people are now entering a reality that is far from their comfort zone; they need to feel as though things are being looked after and that their leaders are working with them to remove hurdles and soften their landing.

Celebrating wins and showing recognition are also important at this point. These are not ad hoc activities: they must be planned for, budgeted, and some thought must go into the celebrations, rewards, and recognitions, so they are done the right way and send the right message.

Last, but not least, the sponsor needs to maintain and ensure a big-picture view. This means that even though this one change initiative or project is coming to an end, it is still imperative to think product, integration, and organization. The change initiative does not exist in a vacuum; it must be integrated and set up in such a way that considers the next steps, the overall product, or the next entity to deal with our outcome. It may be tempting to focus on achievements, but they must be incorporated in context to that big picture of the organization as a whole. Thinking product or integration and not only project will also send a message of accountability and sustainability to others.

While moving through the acceptance stage, there is a need to focus more on workshops—to show the processes, roles, details, and direction involved with the change. This does not preclude the need for workshops in earlier stages, but the main focus of this stage is to stabilize the change, explore and move toward acceptance, and brainstorm for engagement.

## Organizational Challenges and Remedies During the Acceptance Stage

Thinking big picture is also about determining overall organizational impact. The ability to do so is a function of leadership, and failing to do it properly or sufficiently is an all too common challenge. This is where context comes into play, and even the positive results being introduced need to be properly integrated into the overall context of the organization. If a change initiative is in motion and it is not properly integrated within the context of the organization, it may be deemed as a failure. It is similar to a situation, as illustrated by Figure 3.3, where two gears are not turning at the same speed and when trying to converge, they clash with each other.

In addition to the danger of having the change initiative clash with the organization, the sponsor must check for potential side effects or secondary risks that may be introduced. Trying to solve a problem or introduce a better way of doing things may cause a disruption somewhere else in the organization or to another process. Those side effects are likely to be smaller in their negative impact than the overall value being produced, but there is no guarantee this is the case. Avoid getting trapped into this unforeseen situation by ensuring that all of the handoffs, touchpoints, and interlocking processes are accounted for and that there has been preparation for them.

As some stakeholders are moving up on the U-Curve into the acceptance stage, keep in mind that others may still be in the resistance stage. Failing to acknowledge this may introduce a disconnect because people may think the sponsor is abandoning them in their current state of resistance. Maintaining a mix of addressing the needs of those stakeholders who are still in the resistance stage, while celebrating achievements and communicating progress, will maintain a connection with stakeholders regardless of where they are on the U-Curve.

If the gears of the change cannot mesh together with those of the organization, we may negatively disrupt the work of the organization, while at the same time failing to deliver the promised benefits from the initiative.

**Figure 3.3**    Gears need to mesh together

It is also important to remember that even during the acceptance stage, a stakeholder may demonstrate anxieties that are related to the change and the celebration of achievements can help alleviate those anxieties. Open communication and a feedback loop will help deal with the specific sources or triggers of the anxiety, but it is possible that some stakeholders may slide *backward* on the U-Curve to the resistance or even the denial stage. If sponsors don't handle these anxieties effectively, it is possible to *lose* these stakeholders—they may check out, lose buy-in, abort the initiative, or leave the organization altogether.

### Vision Challenges and Remedies During the Acceptance Stage

Stakeholders must consistently be reminded of the vision of the initiative. For some stakeholders, it may be as simple as a reinforcement of the mandate and the progress that has been made, but for others it may serve as an important reminder of what they are there to accomplish. Although this stage may not be a formal milestone, connecting the progress and achievement back to the reasoning, rationale, and mandate of the intended goal may reintroduce enthusiasm, as well as re-energize some of the stakeholders. Re-emphasizing the vision presents a good opportunity to articulate the benefits and to reinforce (or update) the expectations found in the benefits realization plan. It will remind people that not all benefits are realized at this stage, and that things happen in due course. It will also serve as a reminder that the team is pretty much where they need to be, even though for some it may not feel that way.

## Challenges During the Commitment Stage

The final stage on the U-Curve is the commitment stage, where people are moving beyond acceptance and on to rationalizing the change, problem solving, supporting it—and ultimately getting ready to move on. As stakeholders reach this stage, they learn how to work in the new reality, they feel more positive, and they internalize the change by deciding to commit to it. At this point the change is pretty much integrated and becomes second nature. The team has now come a long way from the initial shock, followed by denial, frustration, and sometimes even depression that was brought on by the acceptance and experimentation process. Some stakeholders may not have gotten to this point since they may have aborted along the way, while others may still abort at any time. However, the project is still not done. The final touches need to be put on the change initiative without dropping the ball at this late stage.

### Leadership Challenges and Remedies During the Commitment Stage

The team is closing in on officially calling the initiative a success, and the sponsor needs to drive it home by ensuring that he/she emphasizes the notion of mutual accountability. Team members are all in it together and will continue to be mutually accountable to each other. It is no coincidence that the U-Curve starts with an ending and ends with a beginning, as the new status quo or desired state is in place and is now moving forward. Although a critical mass of stakeholders are crossing the finish line of the initiative, there might still be some people who demonstrate pockets of resistance or who are not quite there yet. The new reality is still somewhat fragile and it is crucial that sponsors remain present.

Reiterating the need to focus on the big picture, leaders need to steer people's focus away from their functions and technical considerations, and emphasize common goals and mutual accountability. Even at this stage, people may default back and away from realizing the benefits and the common goals. In addition, leaders must scan, once again, for stakeholders who may have stayed behind. While it may not be possible to address all of the underlying issues that stakeholders have and next to impossible to overcome all resistance, it is still necessary to make a genuine effort and show that all stakeholders are being included, even if they are not buying into the success to the same extent.

With the goal to embrace the change and rebuild the way people work at this stage, the main goal here is to find ways to look for the benefits to feed back into the organization, stabilize the situation, and capture learning.

## Organizational Challenges and Remedies During the Commitment Stage

From an organizational perspective, it is important to expand our horizons now and ensure that the view extends on past the current initiative. Even if the current initiative is a success, the leader's job here is not done:

- *Do not rush to the next initiative prematurely*—the pace of change is overwhelming, and with it the need to pursue the next big thing. The dust has not settled yet and it is important to recalibrate, rethink, and carefully consider where to go from here. Do not jeopardize the benefits realization of the just-finished initiative. Sponsors must ensure that the new reality is understood, new capabilities are realized, new capacities are utilized, and that the current state is known before moving to unfreeze it, again.
- *Establish a plan to reinforce the achievements*—with the settling new reality, do not drop the initiative altogether. When entering the long-term phase—post initiative—of benefits realization, there is a need to ensure that there are capacity, processes, and mechanisms to realize these benefits. It would be wise to further question the extent of the benefits being realized along the way and attempt to tweak, adjust, or do anything that can maximize these benefits over time.
- *Set up and prepare for the next change*—this is another angle of looking beyond the current initiative, and comes to address a common mistake many change leaders and sponsors make of failing to properly prepare for the next change. As the next initiative is only a matter of time (and likely a short time if it is not already in progress)—it is imperative to move to stabilize

and refreeze into the new status quo and properly understand our new capabilities in order to get ready for the next change. It is common that by now the teams are exhausted, relationships may be strained, and the organization as a whole may not run in harmony—as a result of the impact, jolt, or events that the most recent or even other initiatives have introduced. It may take some time to recover, but more important, inventory must be taken in order to properly realize what can be done, what capabilities will be necessary for the next step, and whether those capabilities exist to attempt it. Many organizations reach the end of the change in a position that is significantly less than what they think they can do. Further, change saturation or even change exhaustion may weaken the extent of the benefits, along with the organizational capabilities. The sponsor needs to facilitate the process of taking inventory and to present the findings to senior decision makers. The worst thing that could be done after a success is to attempt the next big thing prematurely—or to fail to the deliver the next thing—not because *how* to do it is not clear, but because the team is not ready for it.

- *The need to search for new benefits and new capabilities*—this is another consideration about the benefits realization process that may have been overlooked. This can also relate to economies of scope, where positive and previously unforeseen side effects may be introduced as a result of our change initiative.

- *Lessons learned*—beyond any lessons learned process that takes place within the associated projects, or product lessons in the form of a post-implementation review, the sponsor needs to perform an organizational lessons learned. This type of lessons exercise is an attempt to look back at the original intent, the business case, the charter, and anything else that helped identify the mandate, the proposed benefits, and the approach. The next step would be to check whether it was the right idea and/or the right approach. Performing this type of lessons learned process can yield strong benefits to organizations because it can constructively explore project selection criteria, the approaches taken, and the cost-benefit analysis process. Whether success is achieved or there was a failure to deliver, it is important to take a clear, sober look in hindsight at the entire initiative. This is not the same as *traditional* lessons learned because it is more strategic (big picture) by nature. With the chronic lack of time and with new, emerging pressing needs, it is not surprising that most sponsors do not perform this exercise. The incorporation of the benefits circles back to our readiness for the next initiative.

- *Failing to realize the full extent of the change impact on other areas*—for this the sponsor should introduce an organizational environmental scan. This is not a scan in the context of the environment (i.e., nature, earth), but rather the environment of the organization—including the utilization of familiar tools, as listed and elaborated on in Table 3.6.

**Table 3.6** Tools for organizational scan[4]

| Tools for Organizational Environmental Scan | What It Stands for | Explanation |
|---|---|---|
| SWOT analysis | Strengths, weaknesses, opportunities, threats | Strengths and weaknesses are internal (and mutually exclusive); opportunities and threats are external to the organization:<br>1. Make sure to identify only 3–5 items for each category. For example, a strength is a true core competence or competitive advantage. This will keep the list from becoming trivial.<br>2. Identify four areas of intersection (S-O, S-T, W-O, W-T) and discuss potential strategies in light of these combinations. |
| PEST analysis | Political, economical, social, technological | This technique can help to consider trends that exist in the organization and how they may impact or intersect with upcoming needs or initiatives. |
| ETOP analysis | Environmental threat and opportunity profile | Divides the environment outside of the organization into different sections; analyzes each section's impact on the organization. |
| QUEST analysis | Quick environmental scanning technique | Makes observations of events and trends to check the feasibility of proposed strategies and upcoming initiatives. |
| Readiness assessment | | Chapter 2 of this book covers the importance of performing a readiness assessment before a change initiative, and the main concepts to perform such an assessment. |
| CRAIDs | Constraints, risks, assumptions, issues, dependencies | This scan is necessary for a specific initiative. It provides an overview of a series of factors that must be considered, adhered to, and worked around—or else they will be in the way. The sponsor drives and facilitates, but much of this may be delegated. |

The sponsor needs to gain an understanding of the organizational surroundings in order to fully understand capacity, capabilities, and direction. The organization may be viewed as the company, division, change initiative, project, or team—depending on the scope of the scan.

## Vision Challenges and Remedies During the Commitment Stage

When considering vision-related challenges during the commitment stage, it is important to note the common lack of understanding of the full extent of what has been achieved. As most change initiatives take longer than anticipated and the level of pain associated with them is higher than expected, the team arrives at the final stage of the change initiative tired and frustrated. This may cloud the ability to properly assess or realize the benefits, which may lead to tunnel vision and a failure to see them (or side effects) beyond the most obvious things. Revisiting the vision and conducting the scans discussed in this chapter will help find and realize a wider range of benefits.

A review of the vision will also help attain a position that is based on actual conditions and instill an awareness of new or adjusted capabilities that are now part of the new refrozen status quo. At this point, a proper closure, transition, handoff, or any other required set of activities must take place, to ensure continuity in the organization for benefits realization and for setup for the next initiative. With the danger of failing to finish properly, it is also important for the sponsors not to *overstay their welcome*, even though at some point, there will be a need to move on to the next initiative. The sponsor may need to appoint someone to take over the next steps to avoid overstaying.

## A Different Type of Change Challenge

We have discussed a series of challenges associated with the various stages along the U-Curve. However, there is another type of common challenge, or rather reality, that poses issues—that is, where the sponsor either joins an engagement that is already underway or when the change organization is developing mechanisms for a change initiative that is already in motion. For example, many organizations have efforts underway to adopt agile methods. At some point, someone higher up in the organization realizes that agile is a larger and a more complex undertaking than was previously thought and that it takes an increasing and partially negative toll on the organization. At this point, there is a call to introduce an organizational change initiative that requires planning, containment, and handling of the change that is introduced by the practices, processes, and ceremonies associated with agile. The next step would be to identify a sponsor, put together a change team, and start working toward formulating a plan to go through the change.

However, in many situations, some teams are already practicing agile which creates a mixed reality where some teams are using agile methods effectively, others are struggling with them, others are about to start, and still others are completely in the dark. There may also be groups or teams that have already failed to realize the benefits from agile.

Situations like this are more challenging if there is no consistency across the organization; it is not about a big announcement that will introduce the change, but rather a situation where stakeholders find themselves on opposite ends of the change U-Curve. This is where the sponsor needs to land quickly on his/her feet, map out the conditions, and perform a quick but effective scan of the situation, along with a stakeholder analysis. Since things are already in motion, the sponsor needs to get up to speed rather quickly and draft a plan to set the tone and earn his/her role as a leader. A kickoff meeting, announcement, quick action on visioning, and focused stakeholder engagement activities will help the sponsor frame the change and show ownership. With things already in motion, there are already adversarial stakeholders, some things are already misaligned, and the environment becomes very unforgiving. There is no room for error and the sponsor will get little to no grace period to get up to speed.

When the sponsor is introduced into a change initiative that is already in motion—typically replacing someone else—the set of actions needs to be similar to those previously mentioned, but a slightly longer grace period should be expected and the focus needs to be on reiterating the vision and gaining traction.

## DEALING WITH THE COMMON CHALLENGES OF PROJECT SPONSORSHIP

When talking about sponsorship, the first thing that comes to mind is project management. In recent years, an increasing number of project practitioners and organizations have come to realize that challenges with project sponsorship are common and that these challenges severely impair the project's ability to deliver success, including the PM's ability to perform effectively. In this section, the project sponsorship challenges that were identified in Chapter 1 will be reviewed and addressed, along with a series of proposed remedies for the challenges. The distinction between projects and change initiatives is often blurry; thus, a change sponsor and a project sponsor should review both respective sections regarding the challenges since in many environments, they may be intertwined.

### General Project Sponsorship Challenges and Remedies

a. *No clear role definition*—this challenge is two-tiered in that it involves the challenges related to both the sponsor's role definition as well as role definitions within the project. When it comes to a situation where the sponsor does not have a clear role definition, there needs to be adequate training, communication, and awareness to ensure that whoever is appointed to be the project sponsor knows what it entails. Since *sponsor* is not a job title and the role is secondary in most cases to a primary role that is held by that senior individual, it is important to set expectations as to the needs and capacity that are required for the sponsor's role. Chapter 6 will discuss these items in detail. The second problem—role definition within the project—is even more common and the awareness and discipline about it starts with the sponsor, and is then delegated to the PM.

b. *Sponsor and PM relations, authority, and mandate*—as part of the sponsor realizing his/her own role and the requirements of this role, it is important to set relationships, expectations, and boundaries between the sponsor and the PM. It is also important to articulate the level of authority that each of these individuals has, their decision-making capacity, escalation procedures, and any other rules of engagement. It cannot be assumed that just because people work closely together, the working relations will be seamless.

c. *Time and capacity*—challenges around time and capacity keep haunting us at all levels of the organization and at all types of engagements. It is safe to say that additional capacity will not be gained and more time will not miraculously appear (at least not any time soon); therefore, there is a need to set up norms, rules, processes, and as many efficiencies as possible to maximize the utilization of our time, in order to reduce waste. Not only is this applicable to the role of the sponsor, but it is the sponsor's role to mandate it for any project under their wing. Two additional important challenges that are faced in relation to capacity planning and time management are the prioritization process and resource planning. It is no coincidence that the three most common types of conflicts that are found in project environments are (in no particular order)—schedules, priorities, and resources. These are all closely tied to each other because with the lack of a clear prioritization process (within our capacity), there is a failure to allocate sufficient resources—and the result is schedule overruns. While these are project management specific, capacity, prioritization, and resource management all start with the sponsor.

# CHALLENGES AND THEIR REMEDIES THROUGH THE PROJECT LIFE CYCLE

In Chapter 1, these challenges were grouped into categories that for the most part aligned with the project life cycle. Let's review the challenges for each category, along with a series of techniques to minimize their negative impact or overcome them altogether.

## Organizational Governance and Change

Inherently, many of the problems being faced when it comes to project sponsorship are connected to deeper underlying issues related to governance and to the way the reporting lines, escalations, and senior management style take place in the organization. One of the most common challenges that is related to sponsorship is a lack of involvement by executive leadership in understanding capacity, priorities, or urgencies. In fact, it is not that senior management is not involved, but rather that these areas are little studied or explored and are barely addressed in most organizations.

Fixing these problems will shed new light on an organization's ability to manage projects effectively and will most certainly improve overall performance across the board. These three areas keep coming up as important areas to address, and the lack of clarity around them can be traced back to accountability and to the chronic lack of time at all levels of the organization. Ironically, the challenges that exist around these three areas are also a result of not managing them properly:

- *Capacity management*—ultimately, the responsibility for identifying capacity lies on everyone in the organization. It starts at the individual level, and it goes through teams, departments, and the organization overall. Capacity management is about identifying and articulating aptitudes, bandwidth, and overall ability to deliver work within the known constraints. A large majority of organizations do not have an understanding of their capacity to deliver and the result is a chronic over-allocation of resources. Capacity management involves a cost-benefit analysis where it is necessary to identify what the investment (cost) should be of capacity and the rewards (benefits) from this investment. Measuring and improving organizational capacity is about understanding the combination of the factors listed in Table 3.7.

**Table 3.7**　Organizational capacity

| Organizational Capacity Factors | How to Measure Capacity | Means to Improve Capacity |
|---|---|---|
| Culture | Time management, effort, and duration measurements | Improve communications and engagement |
| Communication | Waste and non-value-added: down time, handoffs, wait times, misunderstandings, breakdowns in communication, errors | Resource planning; allocation, utilization, matching (fit), and tracking |
| Leadership | Overhead and admins | Team building and development |
| Governance | Planning, risks, issues, exceptions, escalations | Productivity |
| Skills and human capital | Cost tracking | Process improvements and efficiencies |
| Strategy | Resource management and reporting | Collaboration and cross-initiative collaboration |
| Accountability | Reporting: plan versus actual Output and throughout (velocity) | Coaching Developing managerial and leadership competencies Ownership and accountability Role definition and escalations Lessons learned Relationships and expectations management Needs assessment Articulating risks, assumptions, and constraints Norms and ground rules |

The focus here is not on the details of how to measure and improve capacity management, but rather to build a foundation that involves the three independent columns here: what capacity is about, how to measure it, and means to improve it. Capacity management is not only about how the time is utilized, but also about everything that boils down to how that time is utilized.

- *Prioritization*—if capacity is about being accountable for what can be done and articulating the limitations of that capacity, prioritization is about accountability for the sequencing of the work within that limited capacity. Sequencing the work is about prioritizing it and realizing the sense of urgency around what has to be done. There are two elements of prioritization—and both are originated by the sponsor: (1) prioritizing the work across projects and initiatives—this is about determining which initiative is more important; this is not necessarily the role of the sponsor, but the sponsor has a role here to represent the needs of the project/initiative in the grand scheme of organizational priorities, considerations, and competition for limited resources; and (2) prioritization within the project—prioritizing the requirement and features and determining which of the competing demands is more important (time, cost, quality, scope, or features within the scope). To sequence the requirements (determining the order by which the scope items will be built), the sponsor needs to provide a breakdown of the requirements by importance (high, medium, or low), driven by business value. Table 3.8 provides a review of the requirement and scope prioritization and sequencing process.

**Table 3.8**   Requirements prioritization and sequencing

| Prioritization Criteria for Sequencing | What It Means | Who |
|---|---|---|
| Business value | Business value (needs, judgment)— by ranking items (that compete with each other) as high/medium/low. | The sponsor may get input from other stakeholders, but the buck stops with the sponsor |
| Technical considerations | Risk, dependencies, and anything that is related to the nature of the work and the product. This will not override the sponsor's call for priority, but if the technical team manages to get the sponsor to agree, it will lead to change in the sequence of the work. | Technical team, with the sponsor |
| Logical groupings | Any considerations related to efficiencies, cost savings, economies of scale, or best practices; including minimal feature set and product viability. | Team members |

Prioritization goes beyond importance; it is about sequencing the work (or requirements) to determine what has to be built first. It is based on the (relative) importance of each item and it helps determine what can be done within the established capacity. Note that not all items compete with each other since the relationship between many of the requirements will not be either/or.

- *Urgency assessment*—this use of the word *urgent* is loose and inconsistent, but if used in the right context, it can provide a valuable mechanism to *break the tie* when it comes to requirements prioritization, cross-project prioritization, or even to determine the sequence of the work being done on a day-to-day basis. When requirements have the same priority (e.g., high) and there is no other consideration that breaks the tie, the urgency of each of the items must be determined. To determine urgency, it is necessary to logically break down the word *urgency* into three elements (in no particular order):

  a. *Time/proximity*—if two things are equally important, then the one that is due first is more urgent (it sounds trivial, but there is often a failure to articulate this).

  b. *Dependencies*—if all are the same, the item that has more significant things depending on it should be done first. The use of the word dependency is done in the broader sense: impact of doing it, what depends on it, areas and visibility of the dependency, cost, impact of not doing something, or the span of the impact.

  c. *Who is asking?*—this criterion is less about the merits of the work because it refers to the stakeholders who are involved with the needs, along with the visibility of the need. For example, if it is the president of my company who needs something from me, I will most likely drop anything else that I need to do and perform that work. Further, it is also important to look at the associated political impact or whether the impact is internal versus external.

When there is doubt about our capacity to do something, the priority of an item, or something's urgency, the sponsor should be able to provide us with answers, or at least with guidance.

There are more challenges that are associated with this category of governance and the organization, and they are listed, along with suggested ways to alleviate them, in Table 3.9.

**Table 3.9**   Organizational and governance challenges and remedies

| Common Organizational and Governance Challenges that Impact Project Sponsorship | Remedies for the Challenges |
|---|---|
| Initiatives and ideas are considered as stand-alones and discussed/handled as silos | A consistent approach to project sponsorship with a set of best practices, a centralized mechanism to handle and oversee sponsorship, and creation of a sponsorship center of excellence will need to take place. In addition, a proper connection to organizational strategy, portfolio management, capacity management, and prioritization will need to improve. |

*continued*

| Common Organizational and Governance Challenges that Impact Project Sponsorship | Remedies for the Challenges |
|---|---|
| Lack of poor/inconsistent cross-project coordination | This area can be significantly improved through addressing capacity, prioritization, and urgency measurement issues (described in this chapter). |
| *Flavor of the day* | There are urgent matters and organizational emergencies to attend to, but a clear strategy and well-defined portfolio management practices can help improve organizational focus and direction so that there are not too many dramatic flip-flops. Cross-project coordination will also help with this area, as when there is a need to push a project over, it is done in a coordinated way and with a consistent and centralized approach. |
| Unclear mandate and guidance by sponsors | This does not only pressure PMs, but also leads to performance problems, stress, and, in a snowball effect, poor decisions by PMs, who make desperate moves and further reduce their collaboration with other PMs and stakeholders. The fixes are ownership, accountability, cross-project prioritization and collaboration—mandated and facilitated by the sponsor. |
| Too much red tape slows down decisions and actions | Red tape is a sign of a mature and risk-averse organization. Sponsors must encourage a process of challenging unnecessary red tape or it will interfere with their project. Continuous improvement must be encouraged and planned for since it does not happen on its own. |
| Sponsors' support for PMs | It takes two to tango. The sponsor and the PM must plan early on and coordinate how to work together—including boundaries, decision making, and escalations. |
| Sponsorship is inconsistent and depends on the individual sponsor | Only a drive for improving sponsorship as an organizational initiative will improve this area. |
| Deadlines keep shifting and multiple projects peak around the same time, creating severe resource constraints | Cross-project coordination requires action beyond just saying that such collaboration is needed. A process and mechanism to perform cross-project coordination is discussed in Chapter 5. |

Many project managers feel that their hands are tied and despite their best efforts, there are organizational issues that prevent them from maximizing the value they deliver. The project sponsor is in a position to address most of these types of issues.

## Challenges and Remedies for the Pre-Project Period, Business Case, and Project Initiation

The period leading up to the project, along with the business case process, are *out of scope* for the PM. These things happen before the project is initiated and chartered, and since PMs are not appointed yet for their role, they are not around to oversee, contribute, or even become aware of the things that take place during this time. Before the project, a series of considerations take place in order to determine which of the needs, problems, ideas, opportunities, and initiatives are under consideration or are in the pipeline that will end up being pursued. This involves using project selection criteria and the business case to determine justification, cost-benefit analysis, and feasibility of each competing priority. While the PM is not (in most cases) part of this process, the sponsor is. In fact, the sponsor may end up driving most of the activities at this pre-project stage.

Once the project is deemed as a go, initiation activities take place and the project gets chartered. Many of the challenges during the initiation stage are associated with the lack of clarity as to who leads the creation of the charter. In short, this project is *owned* by the sponsor. It is the sponsor's budget, mandate, and reputation that are on the line; therefore, it would make sense for the sponsor to be actively involved at this stage. The pendulum of responsibility for the charter has swung back and forth over the years. It used to be that the sponsor had to write the charter, then many, including the Project Management Institute (PMI), pointed out the common practice that the PM usually leads this process. In recent years (along with the significant improvement in awareness around the importance of the project charter), a shift back toward the sponsor is noticeable. The person who writes the charter may be the PM or the sponsor, but the sponsor must be involved and oversee the process. There will be more discussion of these pre-project and initiation elements in Chapter 5.

The lack of consistency and clarity around the sponsor's involvement and his/ her roles and responsibilities in leading and performing these critical activities introduces several challenges that may be exacerbated later in the project if not handled or overcome. The first, and perhaps most common, challenge to discuss concerns the project charter—a formal document that gives birth to the project. It is critical for setting up expectations, expressing what is known, and mandating things for the project. It must not be viewed as a chore and must be given the amount of focus it deserves. The sponsor drives the creation of the charter and both the sponsor and the PM must share the work in putting it together. This is the time to ensure that the information that is being fed into the charter is relevant, clear, and realistic and that the right assumptions are made, along with a process to manage and validate them.

The following is a list of additional challenges and an overview on how to handle and overcome them:

a. *The sponsor's role*—in the various stages within this category, this role is often not clearly defined; this is an organizational challenge. Even if the sponsor's involvement is not hands-on in the pre-project and initiation stages, he/she must oversee the process and own it. There might be other stakeholders, subject matter experts, or business analysts (BAs) who actually do the due diligence, but the sponsor needs to mandate and over-see the process. It is a matter of setting up goals, identifying the capacity required to perform these activities, allocating time and resources, com-municating, and defining roles and responsibilities.

b. *Initiatives' vision*—this is often not clear, hard to articulate, and most peo-ple are not aware of it; resulting in unclear objectives and gaps in the proj-ect success criteria. Although this challenge goes deeper (and higher up) in the organization, the sponsor needs to make a genuine effort to define and articulate the vision for the initiative. The fix starts with awareness around the importance of setting up a vision, goes through allocating resources for the task, and ends with communicating the vision and defining project success criteria.

c. *Feasibility analysis*—this analysis is often done improperly or not at all. Even after an idea or initiative *passes* the business case and is deemed justi-fied to move forward (and becomes a project), the sponsor needs to ensure that the initiative goes through a feasibility analysis. The goal is to perform an environmental/organizational scan (discussed earlier in this chapter) and determine if the organization has what it takes (e.g., cash flow, re-sources, or capacity) to go through the project. It should include checking whether there are other initiatives, projects, or considerations that may cross paths with or interfere with the upcoming project. Even great ideas may be deemed as *not the right thing at this time*. The sponsor has to make sure that the feasibility portion of the business case is performed. It is not a matter of knowing what it is about, but rather—once again—about aware-ness and the capacity to do it.

d. *Thread*—it is hard to find a common thread, or proper continuity, from the pre-project and the business case stage to the project. This common challenge might be a textbook sponsorship problem. The sponsor is the thread and the charter is the most effective mechanism to ensure that the knowledge is transferred to the project.

e. *Sponsor-PM rapport*—the sponsor has the primary responsibility to con-nect with the PM in order to set expectations, develop a rapport, build a relationship, provide a mandate, and establish lines of communication and feedback. There are no shortcuts about it; it requires effort, thinking, plan-ning, and conversations. The time spent now on setting things up properly between the sponsor and the PM serves as an investment and will save (dramatically more) time later and throughout the project.

f. *Stakeholders*—there is insufficient effort to identify and analyze stake-holders and to align objectives with stakeholders' needs. Chapter 4 covers stakeholder analysis. This area is challenging due to a combination of a lack of time (the awareness of its importance is mostly in place) and the lack of tangible actions to perform as part of it. Determining what actions are necessary as part of stakeholder identification and analysis will give the sponsor and the PM a roadmap as to how to gain knowledge about stakeholders' needs and then align this information with the project's objectives.

g. *Lessons*—there is little to no process in place at the end of the project, or even after the project is finished, to check the original intent behind it. This could provide important insight into the project selection process, its objectives, the mandate, and the approach. Sponsors need to circle back at the end or shortly after the initiative is complete to seek more information about the gaps and variances between the original intent and the final outcome and benefits. This is not about eliminating such gaps, but rather to check what happened, why, and how, along with how to do things better the next time by utilizing the power of hindsight.

## Challenges and Remedies Through Project Planning

The planning process for a project is a challenge in and of itself and although focus during planning is on the PM, the setup, context, and oversight of the planning processes are the responsibility of the sponsor. In most organizations, planning is not done sufficiently or in the right way and there is significant inconsistency as to what it takes to perform proper planning. The setup and the tone of the planning process starts with the sponsor, and if there is a lack of awareness and focus from the top, there is little that the PM and the team can do. Time is virtually always pressing because commitments are already in place and there is usually not enough capacity to spend on planning. There is constant pressure to move forward since there is often little appreciation for or attention to the planning process.

The pressure on the PM and the team to produce plans is likely only going to increase, along with a downward pressure on the amount of time, resources, and capacity that can be allocated to planning. In fact, much of the unhealthy pressure to move forward comes from the sponsor, who will also end up taking most of the blame for the problems that will be triggered as a result.

Table 3.10 lists challenges during and around the project planning process, and provides remedies to overcome them. It is important to note that the context and setup for planning needs to be provided by the sponsor and, in turn, enables the PM to proceed with the planning process. Also, although it is hard to quantify the value of effective planning, it has been proven that investing a unit of time in planning leads to an average savings of approximately three units of time downstream. This may not be a scientific number and it should be taken with a grain of salt (after all, it is not about the time spent planning, but primarily about effective and quality planning). Nevertheless, PMs have a limited say on how much planning they can perform, and it is common to see PMs and teams attempting to plan with their hands tied because there is no time or capacity to support it.

**Table 3.10**   Common planning challenges and remedies

| Project Planning Challenges | Potential Remedies |
|---|---|
| Multiple mandates | When there is more than one sponsor, to avoid contradictions or vague messages and mandates, all sponsors must align the mandate and message with each other and provide the PM with a clear direction. The sponsors also need to figure out which sponsor is responsible for which area/deliverable of the project. |
| Sponsor-PM boundaries | The sponsor and the PM need to clarify who is in charge of which areas and to what extent. The sponsor needs to ensure these lines are clear, along with the proper escalation processes and channels for the PM. |
| Unrealistic planning (and sponsor's lack of visibility in the planning process) | The sponsor needs to establish proactive mechanisms to determine to what extent the project plans are realistic. This includes access to historical information, benchmarking, and consultations with SMEs, along with establishing lines of communication with stakeholders and team members for points of view that do not solely rely on that of the PM. In addition, the sponsor needs to perform ad hoc checks and ask questions about the planning and estimating process, rationale, and source of information. These measures will slow things down and require more capacity by the sponsor, which is less costly than the impact of flawed plans and unrealistic estimates. |
| Sponsors/PMs interfere with team's estimating process | Meddling with the planning process interferes with the team's ability to produce realistic estimates. The presence of sponsors (for providing information or answering questions) in estimating sessions or communicating with team members/stakeholders should not be confused with, or turn into, pressure to squeeze estimates. |
| Stakeholders (and various teams) are brought to the table too late | Although it is primarily the PM's job to engage stakeholders, the sponsor needs to support this effort and ensure that stakeholders are brought into the planning process early. Even if their involvement is scheduled for later, it helps set up expectations, perform capacity planning, and ensure that everyone's needs are identified before it is too late. The sponsor must oversee this process. |
| Poor and siloed resource planning | Resource-related challenges are a leading cause of project problems and conflicts in organizations (primarily among PMs and between PMs and functional managers). Chapter 7 further discusses mechanisms for effective resource planning, starting with a realistic identification of resource needs (by the PM) and including a clear prioritization process—led by the sponsor. |
| Pressure to move forward without clear requirements | Pressure to move forward without sufficient information (i.e., unclear requirements, even for the delivery of short-term goals) can come from multiple sources (e.g., sponsor, organization, or customer). Even if the PM is under pressure, he/she must work with the sponsor to ensure that the project does not move forward without sufficient information to do so. |

The mandate, direction, and setup for proper planning are the responsibility of the sponsor. It is the sponsor's job to provide the PM with a balanced path between the pressure to move on and the need to plan for it.

Following a systematic and iterative approach that starts with the sponsor, along with effective communication and feedback loops, are the keys to success. The main components of this approach include the following items:

- Clear vision and mandate
- Definition of success criteria
- Prioritization (for project objectives and across projects)
- Articulating assumptions, risks, and constraints
- Understanding requirements
- Realistic project estimates
- Realizing project resource needs
- Cross project and organizational resource coordination, planning, and collaboration
- Checks and balances for realistic planning and quality of information used
- Sufficient capacity to perform the planning process
- Choosing the right approach for the project life cycle

## Challenges and Remedies Throughout the Project (Execution and Implementation)

Even with realistic plans in place, the implementation stages of the project introduce multiple challenges. Many of these are a result of sponsorship and other challenges that are not directly related to the project sponsor, but may be an indirect result of sponsorship-related challenges. Let's review a series of common sponsorship-related challenges that occur in the execution stages of the project, along with a proposed way to alleviate the resulting negative impact.

### Sponsor Support

Due to competing priorities, as well as changing focus over time throughout the organization, other initiatives may require the sponsor's focus, attention, and time. The word support here does not intend to question whether the sponsor supports the projects (that should go without saying) but rather whether the sponsor is there for the project—for decisions, escalations, sign-offs, and other types of guidance and answers. Sponsors commonly get lost in the myriad of priorities and needs around them, taking their focus and attention away from certain projects and initiatives. The way to overcome this challenge is to ensure structure around the sponsor's involvement in projects and initiatives by articulating the importance of the awareness around the role of the sponsor and by establishing regularly occurring touchpoints and interactions between the sponsor and the PM, as well as with team members, subject matter experts (SMEs), and other stakeholders, as required. In the planning challenges section of this chapter, the need of the sponsor to establish alternative lines of communication and feedback for planning purposes was discussed, and this needs to continue throughout the project. Preset touchpoints will ensure communication continuity for the sponsor, a more proactive approach to handling issues and situations, and a clear escalation process. Even if the sponsor is not available to address all of the items that are brought up in these communications or the sponsor is not available altogether to touch base, it will raise the right type of flags among the other players in and around the project.

## Lack of Sufficient User Involvement

This may not seem like a sponsor problem, but the sponsor needs to ensure that this does not happen. Since user involvement is a leading cause of project failure, there is a need to ensure that users are properly involved from the planning throughout the rest of the project. The sponsor needs to engage the customer, reiterate the need for user involvement, and enable the PM with the capacity and resources to ensure sufficient user involvement.

## The PM's Focus on the Critical Path

The critical path is one of the most important and visible measures of progress for every project. Most sponsors naturally focus heavily on the critical path to get a picture of the project schedule performance. However, whether it is because of the PM's tendency to focus on the critical path or the attention it gets from sponsors and other stakeholders, there is a need to ensure that the PM does not ignore other scheduling measures. Focusing too much on the critical path may lead the PM to push out noncritical path activities—leading to problems downstream in the project. The priorities of activities are not determined solely on whether or not they are on the critical path. Failing to perform activities when they need to be done (on or off the critical path) only kicks the can down the road by making things look like they are on schedule when, in fact, they are consistently falling behind.

## Resource Over-Allocation

Resource conflicts are not only a result of people having too much work. There are several underlying actions that may cause resource over-allocation and it is the sponsor's responsibility to address these factors and minimize the amount of resource conflict and over-allocation across their span of influence. Resource-related problems are a symptom of (often deeper) organizational problems. When everyone is consistently over-allocated and pressed for time, it compromises the ability to make informed decisions. Table 3.11 provides a look into some causes of resource conflicts and over-allocation, the symptoms and impacts of these problems, and a set of techniques to address resource-related challenges. The sponsor cannot fix all of the conflicts that lead to the resource problems, but improving on the areas mentioned will lead to improvement around resource allocation.

**Table 3.11**  Resource conflict and over-allocation

| Causes of Resource Conflicts/ Over-Allocation | Symptoms and Impact | Techniques to Address Resource-Related Challenges |
|---|---|---|
| Poor cross-project prioritization | Conflicting priorities across projects (and projects versus operations), leading to an unclear mandate for resources' needs | Cross-project collaboration to establish a clear mandate; establish and follow a clear strategy |
| Communication breakdowns/ unclear mandates | PMs unaware of decisions or directions; sponsors and decision makers fail to make timely decisions | Clear communication lines; set sponsor's involvement in initiatives, exception management, and escalation paths |
| Unclear objectives/ project priorities | Unclear project success criteria, leading to unrealistic estimates for effort and resource needs | Work with PM to clearly articulate project success criteria and requirements prioritization |
| Inconsistent sense of urgency | Due to lack of organizational prioritization, people are overworked and have conflicting priorities | Articulate what *urgent* means and apply it consistently (i.e., timelines, impact, stakeholders involved) |
| Not enough resources/too much work/a lack of capacity management | This reality is not going to change (definitely not for the better). People are unaware of their own capacity, leading to aggressive estimates, increased stress, and delivery problems | Identify team members' capacity, roll it up to the team level and, subsequently, to the organization level |
| Inefficiencies and low productivity | Waste, handoffs, misunderstandings, gaps, redundancies, duplication of effort, doing the wrong thing, last-minute changes | Before addressing significant waste producers (i.e., prioritization, capacity management, urgency assessment and collaboration), start with easier fixes: streamline communication, meetings, and e-mails through norms and ground rules |
| Leadership, decision making, and escalations | Late decisions, unclear mandates, lack of decision making, siloed decisions | Cross-project coordination to establish accountability, exception management, leading by example |
| *Double dipping* | The matrix organization misleads people to think there are more resources than they actually have | Capacity management, proper project resource planning, cross-project collaboration |
| Failing to follow processes | A lack of process adherence and discipline, including quality/risk management/optimistic planning | Enforce processes, realistic planning, proper risk management |

Resource conflicts, over-allocation, and mismanagement are the leading causes of project problems. Little effort is made to properly address the area of resource management effectively.

### Contingency

There is widespread confusion about accounting for time contingency and where on the project schedule to place it. The sponsor needs to ensure that the risk management activities performed by the PM and the team lead to meaningful contingencies that are properly reflected on both the budget and the schedule, respectively. Ironically, in many organizations the sponsor is the source of pressure to reduce or even eliminate contingencies, while he/she should be the one protecting them.

### The Sponsor's Role

Throughout the project, it is common to see sponsors who are spread too thin and, therefore, fail to be sufficiently available for their projects' needs. This takes us back to the sponsor's leadership and accountability, as well as to the awareness around the role of the sponsor and the role definition. There are no shortcuts to providing sufficient sponsor support throughout the project.

## Challenges and Remedies for Project Monitoring, Controlling, and Reporting

The challenges being covered here do not take place during a distinct period of time in the project because reporting and controls are not a distinct phase. The reporting and controlling activities, including the challenges associated with them, appear at any point in the project (primarily during the execution stage or phases). From a project management perspective, when referring to the activities during the execution stage, the PM takes a more facilitating role (i.e., clearing the way, removing hurdles, handling conflicts, and leading communications), but at the same time, the monitoring, controlling, and reporting activities pick up. A similar pattern also applies to the sponsor—the activities (and challenges) of the execution of the project get intertwined with those of the monitoring and controlling stage. With many activities occurring around multiple deliverables at once, and with various teams involved (internal and external), monitoring, controlling, and reporting activities become challenging. It becomes difficult to paint the right picture and properly understand the status, progress, trends, forecasts, and needs of the project.

While the PM naturally leads most of the activities at this stage, the sponsor, as the primary customer, needs to get a full and clear picture of the progress, including what information to look for in status reports. Further, the sponsor needs to *read between the lines* and develop the ability to identify trends and ask questions that will provide him/her with a realistic picture of the project's status. The following list explores challenges that surface through the controlling/reporting stage (presented as questions), along with approaches to address these challenges (presented as answers):

(A) *Why do problems tend to appear later in the project?*

Many projects will show a "good" status throughout and then in later stages (typically around the 70% mark), problems begin to surface and the project status tends to fall behind. Most problems do not actually appear later in the project; it's just that earlier on, the PM and the team have more means to hide/ defer problems until later. Usually at around the ¾ mark, the PM and the team run out of options and can no longer hide things. The sponsor needs to look for information and ask questions throughout the project, so that a situation like that does not materialize. Chapter 6 gives more detail into specific things the sponsor needs to do throughout the project in order to maintain a sufficient level of knowledge and context. With that said, ongoing updates; meetings with the PM; ad hoc meetings with stakeholders, SMEs, and team members; and informal inquiries and checks are necessary to prevent a runaway project from the sponsor's perspective. The sponsor needs to develop an eye and an ear for project events so that he/she can identify trends and interpret the information that is obtained independent of the official status updates that are being reported regularly. This is not only about experience, but also about engagement, involvement, and maintaining a proactive approach. Previously discussed in the context of communications, the sponsor needs to get information that is not solely from the PM's *lens*.

(B) *What information does the sponsor need?*

On many occasions the PM does not know what information to give their sponsor, and the sponsor may overstep his/her boundaries with the PM. This takes us back, again, to the communication and engagement discussion from earlier in this chapter. The PM and the sponsor need to sit together early in the project and establish their working relationship—including rules of engagement, boundaries, and how to communicate with each other. The PM is usually overwhelmed with information and has a hard time filtering out the noise and what information is truly valuable for the sponsor. Early on in the project, the sponsor may not know what information he/she needs and in what format, so the sponsor and the PM need to have regularly occurring (and frequent) touchpoints. The sponsor's regularly occurring meetings with the PM and with others (stakeholders, team members, and SMEs) will provide the sponsor with different points of view; incorporate different agendas, styles, and sets of information; and if the sponsor is in tune with the information coming in, he/she will be able to put together a realistic picture of the project. There is no need to ask people for information that is out of their scope of work, but with the formal reports flowing in and by applying critical thinking skills, the sponsor can easily connect the dots and sense where things are heading. If the formal information is not in line with the information that the sponsor is picking up, it is time to challenge the PM and check where things really are.

(C) *Why does the sponsor participate in so many project meetings?*

When it comes to sponsor involvement, there are different *types* of sponsors. It is important for the sponsor to be consistently involved, and important for both the sponsor and the PM to realize what *type* of sponsor they are and what it means to the project. The four types include the following:

1. *The meddler*—this is the micromanaging sponsor; too involved, asking too many questions, and attending too many meetings. The meddling sponsor has a *need to know* but also struggles in differentiating between signals and noises, or between valuable information and the volume of the information. From the PM's perspective, it is not a matter of how or what he/she does, or whether it is the PM's fault that the sponsor meddles, but it is a reality that everyone involved needs to deal with. How involved the sponsor is mostly depends on the sponsor's personality but the sponsor must not get in the way. The sponsor should not attend all meetings nor step across the PM's boundaries. By micromanaging, the sponsor not only overlaps with the PM, but also undermines the PM's authority and creates confusion with conflicting messages that lead to the sponsor failing to attend to their actual job (both as a sponsor and as a senior stakeholder in the organization).

2. *The pragmatic/involved*—this is the type of sponsor this book is preaching for: proactive, working with the PM and the team, working *on* the business (as opposed to *in* the business), steering, making decisions, and leading. It is a delicate mix of *too much* versus *not enough* and there is no magic, off-the-shelf formula that applies to all environments in a unified manner.

3. *The missing in action (MIA)*—unfortunately, many (likely the majority of) sponsors are of the MIA type. They believe that by appointing a PM, their role becomes hands-off and they become reactive; they get involved only when they are called in; and they lag on decisions, mandates, direction, or support. The MIA sponsor is busy with his/her regular day job and does not have the capacity to get involved in project(s) beyond the minimum necessary. Without the sponsor's involvement, the project will soon lose focus and start to drift sideways in its performance.

4. *The hawk*—this is a *hybrid* sponsor who is a mix of the MIA and the meddler. This sponsor is generally not around, but from time to time remembers that there is a project to look after and he/she makes sporadic appearances by diving into the project to look for specific information (that is most likely irrelevant) before disappearing again, until the next time. Hawk sponsors are busy with other things (their day job) and try to show that he/she is involved. The inconsistency gives mixed messages and confuses everyone involved.

(D) *Why are project changes assessed in silos?*

With the team typically being overworked, there is little time to properly assess the impact of project changes (scope changes). Due to the rush, impact assessment for the changes is done partially or incorrectly, and the result is that the change ends up costing more (time, money, and resources) and introduces more risks and challenges than previously thought. It is also common that the change has an impact beyond the project—on other parts of the organization. Although this is a project-specific problem, the sponsor needs to be aware of the change impact and to make sure that the impact assessment is realistic. Further, since it is the sponsor's decision to approve the change, he/she must know the true impact of the individual change on the project and on the organization, as well as the impact of the change in light of other changes. Since most changes are assessed individually, the sponsor must engage the team and the PM so that they will check the overall impact of the change in light of other changes outside of a project vacuum. Changes, being risky and expensive as they are, must be evaluated in context, including in light of all other changes that are in the pipeline, and not only one at a time.

(E) *Why are escalation procedures loose, unclear, and not followed?*

When there is a problem, no one knows who to go to and confusion ensues. Even if the lines of communication within the project are clear and effective, when it comes to escalations that need the sponsor's involvement, that may not be the case. This takes us back to the communication process, where the sponsor needs to set up not only an escalation process, but also an exceptions process to ensure that the PM knows when and how to escalate matters to the sponsor, with the right sense of urgency. The effectiveness of the communication and escalations process is measured when things do not go well— when it becomes a matter of not only addressing the issue, but also how it is handled and the turnaround time. A sponsor who is not regularly involved in the project cannot expect escalations to go smoothly and in a timely manner. Escalations and exceptions handling are an extension of effective ongoing communication.

(F) *Why are status reports and their meanings often open for interpretation?*

The information that is in the status report has to be consistent and presented in a way that is not subjective and up to the individual PM. Inconsistency makes it hard for the sponsor to compare projects in an apples-to-apples context. While reporting may typically be the role of a project management office, the sponsor needs to ensure that reports, at least under the sponsor's portfolio of projects, are consistent and as objective as possible. Chapter 6 provides more information on what the sponsor needs to focus on in order to get consistent and realistic information.

## Challenges and Remedies at the End of the Project and Beyond

The end of the project and the period after the project introduce several challenges that, if not handled properly, can be the difference between success and failure. The late stages of the project and many post-project activities are also connected to the change management aspect of the project, including the handover of the project's product and benefits realization. Let's review the challenges and their respective remedies for the end of the project and post-project:

- *Reaching the end*—many projects deliver success (or partial success) not thanks to processes and doing the right things, but rather thanks to people who manage to somehow exhibit *superhuman* capabilities—saving the day despite the processes, team, and roadblocks. This is not a sustainable way to do things and it would be hard to recreate this type of success. The sponsor needs to make sure that processes, practices, communication, the PM, and the makeup of the team point toward delivering success, rather than relying on *heroes* to save the day at the last minute. Setting the tone, managing expectations, leading effectively, and establishing norms help to build a foundation for consistent success.
- *Benefits definition and realization*—financials and other tangible benefits are easy to identify, articulate, measure, and realize but the sponsor needs to make sure that there are additional benefits that are less tangible. These include goodwill, reputation, alignment, experience, team performance, and other benefits that can be captured through key performance indicators. In addition, a project's benefits should not aim to be realized only at the end of the project, but also beyond the project. This is part of thinking big by the sponsor—*big* refers to realizing benefits after the project and ensuring consideration for nontangible benefits. Without this type of mandate, there would be no effort on the project level to track and measure those nontangible benefits.
- *Project versus product thinking*—this also addresses the need to think bigger than the project. It is about ensuring that the project and its product fit into the bigger organizational picture. While it is the PM's job to focus on the project, it is the role of the sponsor to think beyond that—to how the project's product is going to be received and used, handoffs of the product, impact on operations, how long the product can be used, how the product interacts and interfaces with other parts of the organization, and anything else related to the day after the project ends. The time to plan for it is not at the end of the project, but rather in its early stage, yet it is important to maintain the *product thinking* that goes beyond the *project thinking*. Too much project thinking risks that our projects' products will act as silos and patches, instead of building a more sustainable picture that is cohesive and consistent with the strategic direction of the organization. The alignment,

continuity, and thread between organizational needs and the project are areas that the sponsor needs to look after, address, and promote.

- *Lessons learned*—as discussed earlier in the chapter, the sponsor needs to enable the lessons learned process, and ensure that a proper post implementation review process takes place where applicable, as well as facilitating the "strategic" review to check whether the right project was selected, the right approach taken, and if the intended set of benefits were realized.
- *Handoffs*—the handoff of the product created by the project combines the big picture thinking, the product thinking, the benefits realization, and the lessons learned processes. The sponsor needs to make sure there is a proper transition plan and that whatever the project produces is handed off to the next level as intended (where the next level can be operations, maintenance, or an external customer). One could argue that this is the job of the PM, but typically the organizational reward system does not incentivize PMs for handoffs and other considerations that are beyond the project life cycle. It is therefore important for the sponsor to become familiar with the transition and the handoff plan to ensure that these are done properly.
- *Saying goodbye*—there is no one way or one specific time for the sponsor to bow out. Some sponsors are unsure of the appropriate time or way to end their involvement in the project, and this commonly leads to the sponsor's premature departure or to sponsors who do not let go. A premature departure by the sponsor can damage the benefits realization process and may lead to problems with handoffs and coordination between the project and operations. However, sponsors who overstay may lead to waste that prevents that sponsor from moving on to their next engagement, where they are in a greater need. In some situations, the sponsor actually does not step aside since he/she may be the main thread that enables benefits measurement and realization beyond the project. Whatever the situation is, coordination between the sponsor and the PM is crucial, as well as understanding the role and the value that the sponsor brings to the table to ensure that the organizational needs are properly and fully addressed.

## BEHAVIOR AND ACTIVITIES TO ENSURE EFFECTIVE SPONSORSHIP

Whether it is change or a project, the sponsor needs to demonstrate behaviors and perform activities that will ensure effective sponsorship. What does effective sponsorship mean? It means doing things that support the cause and planting the seeds for success by enabling capabilities that will allow the project or the initiative to maximize value delivery for the organization under the current circumstances.

The list of items that describe the responsibility of the sponsor appears straightforward, and our focus needs to be on *how to do it better*. Table 3.12 describes the

**Table 3.12** Fulfilling the role of the sponsor

| *Traditional* Expectations of the Sponsor | Techniques and Behaviors to Achieve it |
| --- | --- |
| Authorization, owning, and empowering | Give a mandate, appoint an appropriate PM, and establish rules of engagement to share responsibilities; ensure team members' fit; maintain proactive involvement throughout, while balancing with the PM |
| Approving/Accepting | Approve the approach and plans; accept deliverables and ensure integration and benefit realization |
| Funding | Secure funding up front and throughout, especially in light of change to the project or changing priorities in the organization |
| Promoting and championing | Ensure the project/initiative gets the right of way, in context, when considered against other competing priorities |
| Reporting, informing, and managing expectations | Get status updates, understand the true state and progress of the project, inform stakeholders, and engage them to manage their expectations |
| Providing methodology and governance | Set up an approach, escalation procedures, lines of reporting and communication, decision support, and decision-making processes, gates, and checkpoints to maximize benefits and make informed and timely decisions |
| Demonstrating leadership | Lead by example; promote transparency, fairness, credibility, confidence, consistency, and accountability; be there for the team |
| Direction during uncertainty | Make timely and clear decisions under ambiguous and uncertain environments and through constantly changing conditions; promote proper assumptions management and risk management processes |
| Charter | No matter what, it is the responsibility of the sponsor to oversee the writing of the charter |
| Scoping | Set up scope and boundaries; approve changes |
| Business case and benefits | Own and maintain justification and feasibility of the project throughout its life cycle; balance between the plan's robustness and the flexibility of delivery |
| Strategic alignment and benefits for the organization | Provide a balancing act between the needs of the project/initiative and operational/business needs; set clear priorities; ensure capacity is in place; manage cross-project priorities, collaboration, and interactions |
| People and communication | Make sure communication is a priority; keep in mind that people are the main strength you have; ensure norms are in place |

This table provides a summary of the key responsibilities of the sponsor, along with a list of techniques and behaviors to help fulfill the sponsor's role.

*traditional* expectations for the sponsor and how to meet those expectations. There are additional competencies, traits, or behaviors that the effective sponsor needs to demonstrate, and they fall mainly under these leadership characteristics:

- *Motivator and influencer*—although the sponsor has authority and is generally the most senior person in the project organization, he/she needs to be a strong motivator. Whether it is when the team encounters difficulties in the project or when individuals go through the change U-Curve, there is an ongoing need to motivate people and to keep them going. Motivation comes in many forms, and it changes based on the needs, circumstances, and people involved. It is about moving people, inspiring them, energizing the situation, prompting them, and providing them with *drive*. The drive will come in various currencies and values, as required, and all of these things are in place to influence people and get them to do things—not because the sponsor tells them what to do from a position of authority, but rather because the sponsor gets them to want to do it.

- *A link and a protector*—the sponsor serves as a link between the project and upper management (in both directions). He/She ensures the mandate is clear, that the project gets the focus and capacity it needs, and that the team is (as much as possible) protected from unnecessary interruptions and distractions.

- *Decision maker*—whatever decisions are not within the authority of the PM to make or are outside of the PM's ability to make (due to lack of knowledge, fear, etc.) are the sponsor's responsibilities. The sponsor needs to make decisions and provide sign-off within agreed-upon turnaround times, along with clarity, transparency, and specific action items. Many organizations suffer from problems with decision making (timeliness, effectiveness, or lack of decision-making ability altogether), and it is imperative that the sponsor perform this role as required. When there is not enough information available, when the direction is unclear, or when there is no clear distinction between the options' benefits, the sponsor needs to step up and make a decision based on the ambiguous information that is at hand. Remember that not making a decision within a given time frame is equivalent to making a decision to do nothing—and it bears consequences.

- *Coach and mentor*—this is not an official job description for the sponsor, but it is definitely an important role that the sponsor needs to fill. Part of the support that the sponsor needs to provide to his/her team is the need to be a coach and mentor—to the PM, team members, and sometimes even stakeholders. Coaching and mentoring are time-consuming. It requires emotional focus and resilience; understanding the situation; being familiar with those involved; providing genuine, clear, and appropriate support that is within the boundaries of maintaining a professional relationship; and maintaining balance (regarding both the time investment and the importance of not singling people out).

- *Seller and negotiator*—with conflicting priorities, unclear objectives, ambiguity, and constantly changing organizational needs, the sponsor must combine expectations-management activities with selling his/her initiatives to upper management and negotiating the best possible teams, resources, and capacity for the initiative's needs. Add these (less visible from the project's perspective) activities to the hands-on activities—in addition to the sponsor's day job—and it is no surprise that sponsors suffer from a chronic time shortage.

- *Resource management*—things always seem to keep going back to the resource management *chore*. This is a responsibility that the sponsor shares with the PM since the PM needs to provide a timely assessment of resource needs so the sponsor can secure those resources. Of all the constraints that will need to be dealt with (specifically time and money), resources are the tightest and most volatile constraint. The resources that end up being allocated to the project/initiative are a reflection of multiple organizational challenges (i.e., prioritization, capacity management, interlocking initiatives, changing priorities, budget cuts, schedule changes, unrealistic estimating, and risk). In addition, with resources shared across multiple initiatives, projects, and departments, there are multiple potential failure points that can compound resource-related problems: (1) not getting the resource at all; (2) not getting the right skills/experience level needed; (3) not getting the resource at the right time (e.g., late); (4) not getting resources for the right duration; or (5) a combination of any of these things. Resource issues can also occur due to project-specific problems, other initiative's problems, operational problems, contract/external issues, or shifting organizational priorities. The PM alone is not enough when it comes to securing resources—the sponsor must provide support and clout to reduce the risks that are associated with resource allocation.

## WHAT MAKES A GOOD SPONSOR?

When looking for a sponsor, the problem is not whether the person who acts like a sponsor is good at what he/she does, but whether this person is going to be good as a sponsor. It has already been established that the senior stakeholders who are appointed to become project or change sponsors are typically good at their day jobs. The challenge is how well they can perform their role as a sponsor, how much time they have for it, and how much capacity they can allocate to this portion of their role. Sponsor capacity is not only about allowing time, but also about *being there*—physically and mentally—asking questions, engaging stakeholders, and promoting the cause of the project or initiative. Awareness and dedication are the key here because, for the most part, it is mostly about paying attention. An effective sponsor should be:

- *Supportive*—the good sponsor needs to be supportive of the cause and of the people (team members and stakeholders). Supportive means that the sponsor is there for the team and is engaged, caring, helpful, and accommodating. The sponsor also needs to encourage and provide reassurances.
- *Authoritative*—along with support, sponsors need to be authoritative, which goes beyond having the right level of seniority and decision-making authority. Being authoritative is also about the style and the clout that sponsors need to have when it comes to putting their foot down, making timely decisions, instilling and showing confidence, and demonstrating firmness, honesty, and reliability. This individual needs to be influential, convincing, and trustworthy, as well as dependable, credible, respected, and willing to commit.
- *Influential*—The sponsor needs to be influential within the organization in order to be able to remove hurdles and handle challenges that may impact his/her initiative or that are introduced as a result of the initiative; while ensuring that the actions align with organizational and strategic objectives. Exerting influence will help the sponsor keep the project/initiative on track and drive it to success.
- *Engaging*—*The PMI Pulse of the Profession® In-Depth Report 2018*[5] mentioned that 26% of organizations reported that the primary cause of failed projects is inadequate sponsor support. In contrast, organizations with a higher percentage of projects that included actively engaged executive sponsors reported 40% more successful projects than those with a lower percentage of projects that had actively engaged sponsors.

The search for a sponsor is not the same as a search for a PM, as in most cases there is no real *search* for the sponsor. Usually, the person in charge of the respective area for the project/initiative, the senior stakeholder who initiates and identifies the need, or the one who provides the funding becomes the sponsor. It should go without saying that the sponsor has to support the cause they lead, but it is not only about supporting it, rather, it is mainly about leading and driving the initiative (meaning that it is not about managing the day-to-day activities, like the PM).

To summarize the search for a good sponsor, remember the words of Walt Disney,[6] who said, "Of all the things I've done, the most vital is coordinating the talents of those who work for us and pointing them toward a certain goal."

## WHAT IF THE SPONSOR LEAVES?

Sponsors own their initiatives and when performing their role effectively, they are an integral part of success. The sponsor is the executive or manager; he/she has the financial authority, provides the political clout, and by definition has a personal commitment toward the initiative. The sponsor is often the initiator or the champion of an initiative, and as such, drives it (even if many times from behind the scenes). Either way, what happens when the sponsor leaves their role? What happens to the continuity, the commitment, the direction, and the overall sense of urgency? It does not make much difference why the sponsor leaves (unless it is directly due to underperforming as a sponsor)—it could be because the sponsor got promoted, moved to a different role, or left the organization altogether. In any case, the sponsor's departure serves as a shock to the initiative and sometimes it is hard to overcome that shock.

Since the initiative is actually the *sponsor's* initiative, one school of thought calls for the initiative to shut down. If the sponsor who championed the project is leaving, it may be necessary to stop what is being done altogether. There is some truth to this approach since without the sponsor, there may be no rationale for the initiative. However, when there is a change of sponsorship, there must be an effort to try to minimize the level of interruption that it brings to the initiative. Here are a few considerations to look at when there is a sponsorship change:

a. *Determine whether or not there is a reason to continue*—sometimes the change in sponsorship is part of a larger change in the organization and this may deem the current project or initiative obsolete. The case may also be that the initiative was closely associated with the sponsor and his/her departure would also spell the end of it.

b. *Ensure continuity*—make sure that the departing sponsor and the new sponsor sit down together with the PM to ensure that the departing sponsor passes the baton properly and that the new sponsor shares the same values and drivers, along with having a similar level of commitment toward the initiative.

c. *Make sure there is a new single "wringable" neck*—the departure of a sponsor should not mean that the initiative proceeds with no sponsor or should be led by a steering committee. A single voice (a single sponsor) is more likely to provide the initiative with the support it needs, and with a higher level of commitment.

d. *Beware if the sponsor is new to the organization*—new sponsors may lack political clout, context, or awareness, and even if they have the experience and relevant knowledge, the time it takes them to become familiar with the task at hand may be too long and be detrimental to the project.

e. *Recalibrate*—the change in sponsorship is no reason to slow down on the team level or to despair. Although there may be a need to put the initiative on hold, stakeholders should be aware of the options and should get quickly back on their feet, go through whatever team forming and building steps are necessary, then refocus on moving forward. It may be a chance for the PM to step up his/her game and cover for whatever deficiencies may be in place.

f. *The new sponsor should not change everything right away*—the new sponsor is likely to have a day job and a new role in senior management. Newly appointed senior members in the organization often bring with them new processes, practices, and priorities. As the new person in the role, they are now in charge, but the new sponsor may want to stop short of changing everything and check around them to see which things work and which require changes. Many new senior stakeholders have a tendency to walk in and shortly afterward make sweeping changes in the way things get done. These changes may translate to canceling certain initiatives, changing directions, updating mandates, modifying the sense of urgency, and rejuggling priorities. Although it is their call, it is important to ensure that they are aware of the impact of their actions and the price to pay, especially if the new direction may undo a significant part of the progress that has been achieved to date.

## RECAP

This chapter began where Chapters 1 and 2 left off. The scenarios and challenges that had been introduced earlier in the book were both addressed on the change level and, subsequently, on the project level. Many of the remedies and suggestions on how to overcome sponsorship-related challenges come down to increasing the awareness of the sponsor's role and identifying the capacity that the sponsor needs in order to provide support and authority, along with a mandate to drive the initiative. There will most likely not be any change for the better in sponsors' availability to perform their roles as sponsors since organizations will continue to try to further squeeze more productivity from them, as well as the PMs, team members, and other stakeholders. With time (or lack thereof) being a significant factor that contributes to sponsorship challenges, sponsors need to better utilize their time and introduce efficiencies in what they do so that they can maintain effectiveness as sponsors and still manage to perform their full range of duties.

If the sponsor carries the dual role of sponsoring both the change initiative and the project that leads or represents the change, he/she will encounter both types of challenges. There is much overlap and it is expected that most change sponsors will encounter many of the challenges that were discussed under the project sponsorship section. However, the opposite may be applicable as well.

We then moved on to review a few key behaviors and activities that ensure effective sponsorship. Due to a sponsor's time and capacity constraints, it is important to be aware and focus on those elements that are truly vital for success. This led to an evaluation of a few vital characteristics that sponsors need to have—namely being supportive, authoritative, and influential.

The last part of the chapter discussed an important question: what if a sponsor leaves? While some initiatives may stop, the reality is that they usually continue, and a few pieces of advice were provided as to what to do and what to avoid in the event of a sponsor's departure.

Next, Chapter 4 covers everything that sponsors need to know about how to effectively handle stakeholders, manage their expectations, engage them, and build relationships.

## NOTES

1. https://www.briantracy.com/blog/personal-success/how-to-use-the-80-20-rule-pareto-principle/.
2. https://www.discprofile.com/what-is-disc/overview/.
3. https://www.projectsmart.co.uk/how-to-do-raci-charting-and-analysis.php.
4. Partially adapted from https://studiousguy.com/techniques-of-environmental-scanning/.
5. https://www.pmi.org/about/press-media/press-releases/pmi-2018-pulse-of-the-profession-in-depth-report.
6. https://www.disneydreamer.com/walt-disney-quotes-3/.

# 4

---

# WORKING WITH STAKEHOLDERS: RELATIONSHIPS, BOUNDARIES, AND COMMUNICATION

---

Stakeholders have a significant impact on our initiatives; and from one engagement to another, it feels that stakeholders have more impact on what is being done than was previously thought. The realization of the increasing role and impact that stakeholders have is partially due to attempts to become more proactive and to deliver a more aggressive set of objectives. As more research is done, there is a greater realization that everything is driven by stakeholders and that one way or another, they determine the extent of the success of the initiative. To make sure that everyone is on the same page, recall the definition of a stakeholder: "An individual, group, or organization that may affect, be affected by, or perceive itself to be affected by a decision, activity, or outcome of a project, program, or portfolio."[1] It may be fairly straightforward to identify, engage, and work with stakeholders who affect what is being done or who gets impacted; but then again, things change, needs change, stakeholders change—and with it comes the need to further engage. In addition, there are those stakeholders who perceive themselves to be affected, and as the number of stakeholders grows, the access to them becomes limited, which then limits the ability to work with them effectively. Further, that layer of stakeholders may have a more adversarial position toward what is being done.

The need to consider stakeholders' needs is due to the reality that projects do not exist in isolation. Everything (including scope, schedule, and budget) is subject to influences from stakeholders who represent different needs, agendas, considerations, and organizations. Further, even if it is possible to manage to articulate the *hard* parameters around what is being done (i.e., scope, time, and costs), different stakeholders will have different needs and views about what is expected. Similar to a group of friends who cannot make up their minds about where to go for dinner because everyone has a different idea, it is hard to align all stakeholders to have the same view on why something needs to be done, what success should look like, and how to get there.

The context around the project or initiative makes up the political landscape, and it is populated by those stakeholders who have a particular stake or interest in the outcome of the initiative. It is not only about what is done, but also about how it is conveyed and how that makes people feel. The needs and expectations of the stakeholders do not only represent their objectives and their view of success, but may also be a significant risk to what is being accomplished. If stakeholders do not view the initiative as adding value to their needs, or if they view it as moving in the wrong direction—depending on what is at stake and the amount of involvement they have—they will act in their own basic interest. This means that they may resort to any measure that they see fit in order to pursue their interest and minimize the amount of downside they face. The downside risk to the project depends on the amount of influence they have on the direction of the initiative, as well as who they know that they could leverage. Stakeholders' needs will turn into pressure and it may lead to changes in what or how things are done. These changes are either changes in direction or the need for more things, which in turn lead to more money, more time, more resources, and more risk and complexity. And although stakeholders' needs are being addressed, more risk and complexity increase the chance of failing to deliver parts of the initiative—or failing to deliver success altogether.

Addressing the needs of one stakeholder can lead to a negative reaction from another stakeholder; and soon enough, the situation seems like a constant pursuit of attempting to put out fires in an effort to manage the competing and conflicting stakeholders' needs. This can feel like a game of Whack-A-Mole, as illustrated in Figure 4.1.

It is important (both for the sponsor and for the project manager (PM)) to strike the right balance with stakeholder involvement, while trying to protect the project/initiative from too much noise and external influence. The only way to understand stakeholders' needs is to perform a stakeholder analysis, and even though this exercise is time-consuming and does not produce a tangible work product, it serves as a critical foundation to delivering success for the organization, the customer, and other stakeholders.

## WHY STAKEHOLDERS MATTER SO MUCH FOR THE SPONSOR

Why talk so much about stakeholders? After all, most of the work that is associated with identifying, analyzing, and engaging stakeholders is associated with the PM,

Managing competing stakeholder priorities and needs feels at time like playing a game of Whack-A-Mole.

**Figure 4.1**   Whack-A-Mole

but whether it is a change initiative or *just* a project, it all starts with the sponsor. First, it is the sponsor's project or initiative and, as such, the sponsor sets up the initial contact and relationships with stakeholders. Also, there are matters that are not within the scope, authority, or reach of the PM—and the sponsor needs to handle these things relating to various stakeholders. In addition, the sponsor with the decision-making capacity may need to shape some of the relationships before handing them over to the PM, and afterwards continue to serve as the escalation and sign-off point. Overall, although the PM ends up handling most of the actual leg work when it comes to managing stakeholder engagement, the tone and the context are set up (and need to be maintained) by the sponsor.

Typically, once the project is chartered, the PM is starting to take over the duties of leading the project. It is important for the sponsor and the PM to sit down together, and as part of setting up their working relationships and norms, divide the workload and areas of responsibility. When it comes to the stakeholders, establish rules of engagement and territories regarding who handles which stakeholder and develop a strategy on how to engage them. It is not enough to leave all of the stakeholder engagement activities in the hands of the PM from a work volume perspective, from a relationship perspective, and from an efficiency perspective—the sharing of the stakeholder engagement responsibilities between the sponsor and the PM will provide benefits, access, and rapport that each alone will not be able to achieve.

## Assumptions About Stakeholders

In Chapter 2 we discussed the importance of managing assumptions and the need to have this process partially managed and enabled by the sponsor. Let's go back to assumptions, but now specifically in the context of stakeholders. The techniques of managing assumptions about stakeholders are essentially the same as managing other assumptions. However, there is a significant need to identify and manage assumptions about stakeholders' involvement, needs, disposition, potential reactions to situations, and even their existence in the project's vicinity altogether. Especially during the early stages of the project, there is going to be limited information about stakeholders and limited access to many of them. These elements are the major drivers for the need to voice and manage assumptions, along with the need to establish context and a common level of knowledge that helps place *everyone* who is involved on the same page.

Identifying and managing assumptions helps voice each individual's knowledge and understanding of the situation, and allows everyone (especially the sponsor and the PM) to understand each other, where they come from, and what their views and context are. Even if much of the assumptions' identification process is about realizing to what extent those who are involved are not on the same page, it is important to go through the process to set expectations and close the gaps in views and levels of understanding of the situation.

Identifying and managing assumptions about stakeholders also comes in handy as part of the effort to identify stakeholders' requirements and map them to business value and technical considerations, and then to manage these requirements as part of the prioritization process. In turn, it is possible to categorize the stakeholders and group them based on their needs and the engagement and communication levels that they require and expect.

It is necessary to be aware of the purpose for making assumptions. For planning purposes, assumptions help identify the "correct" condition or direction, but only until more information is gathered to validate (or refute) the assumption. At that point, if the assumption is not confirmed, it turns into a risk or an issue—and subsequently needs to be handled accordingly. In short, assumptions are temporary conditions that await additional information.

## Grouping Stakeholders

The purpose of categorizing stakeholders is to be able to provide them with focused, relevant, and targeted communication about the project/initiative based on their needs and interest. There is no one consistent criteria to categorize stakeholders, but the stakeholder analysis process provides us with a few considerations to slice and dice the stakeholders into categories that can make it easier to engage them effectively. Table 4.1 provides a look into common grouping categories.

**Table 4.1**  Stakeholder categories

| Stakeholder Category | What It Means |
|---|---|
| Internal versus external | This is the easiest distinction and the most obvious, but it can provide important guidelines about the nature of the information to be exchanged and the level of formality. |
| Users | Those who will use the product or service being created; for the most part, they are benefactors of the results. Can break down further to customers versus users. |
| Contributors and providers | Suppliers and vendors, business partners, internal groups, and departments who provide input (i.e., deliverables, information) or resources. |
| Governance | They have an interest in what is being done (supporters or not) and decision-making powers (could be steering committees, internal or external decision makers, and those with specific areas to look after for quality and performance). |
| Technical | These are subject matter experts and specific technical skills providers (internal and external). |
| Influencers | People or groups who have the power or authority to influence decisions or the direction of what is being done or how it is being done; could include unions, lobbyists, special interest groups, or even internal stakeholders who have a say. |
| Impacted | Other stakeholders who may be (or feel that they are) impacted by what is being done. These auxiliary stakeholders may exert more influence than is initially thought. It can be broken down further to positively versus negatively impacted. |
| Staff and team members | They can be both users or providers. |
| Supporters versus resisters (or on the fence) | This is a subcategory that applies to every stakeholder. At times it may not be possible to know their stance, but at some point, they can be categorized into one side or another. |
| Active versus passive | Another subcategory to help determine how adamantly, or strongly, stakeholders feel about the initiative and to what extent they are willing to go in pursuit of their needs. |
| Sensitivities | Another subcategory that looks at specific sensitivities regarding issues, styles, concerns, or soft spots to consider. |
| Additional areas | Risk tolerance, areas of influence, position, timing, drivers/ motivators, agendas, and transparency. |

Stakeholder grouping categories can help identify areas of commonalities among stakeholders so that the engagement process can be made more efficient and effective. Note that the categories are not mutually exclusive, which means that there may be some overlap. It is very important to not misread any stakeholder or misidentify any of their needs.

## Identifying Potential Flare-Ups

Stakeholder analysis must be done in context and cannot be done in isolation. Even if there is a strong understanding of an individual stakeholder's needs, things must be considered in context; there may be specific areas of sensitivity due to territories, interests, involvement, or even relationships with other stakeholders. There is also the risk that with a combination of elements and agendas, even though each on its own does not appear to stand out as an area of concern, they may compound to something more. Here too, stakeholders' relationships, concerns, and interactions should be examined in order to identify whether there are any stakeholders who may be affected by the presence or involvement of other specific stakeholders. This can apply to both internal and external stakeholders, where the position, style, or interests of one stakeholder may conflict with another. Even if things appear straightforward, relationships between or among various stakeholders may pose specific challenges.

It is not the role of the sponsor to identify all potential areas of conflict, but the sponsor may have specific knowledge or relevant insights for the PM due to the sponsor's clout, familiarity, or previous experience.

# THE STAKEHOLDER ANALYSIS

Stakeholder analysis should take place early on in the project initiation stages, but then repeat itself as needed throughout the process to ensure that our understanding and mapping of the stakeholders is still relevant. Let's review the key steps and considerations of stakeholder analysis from a practical perspective knowing that there is not much capacity or bandwidth to spend on it. Once again, this step is usually led by the PM but it must have the mandate and capacity provided by the sponsor, along with a division of areas of responsibility.

## What to Do with the Information from the Stakeholder Analysis

Most of the findings from the stakeholder analysis must remain confidential. Obviously, the sponsor and the PM need to share information with each other, but most of the analysis should not be communicated beyond that. Even information that is more generic about stakeholders and that is documented in a stakeholder log should not be shared with others or posted on shared drivers. This analysis helps us obtain a realistic view of the stakeholders, but it also deals with the sensitive relationships with these stakeholders and the ability of the sponsor and the PM to interact with them effectively. There can be a backlash from people who feel the results of the stakeholder analysis do not meet their own expectations or their perceived self-importance.

Considering that stakeholder analysis does not involve big planning meetings and that the effort, intensity, and duration will vary significantly from one engagement to another, there is usually no allocation of time or budget to perform it. This makes it even more challenging when trying to establish plans and expectations for the initiative. However, these challenges should not serve as an excuse for not performing a stakeholder analysis.

## The Stakeholder Identification and Analysis Process

The stakeholder identification process essentially starts at the business case stage, when the sponsor is in the process of considering the opportunities (or problems) in the pipeline and their cost-benefit-risk considerations. Stakeholders come along with the opportunities; relationships form and the sponsor makes decisions on how to proceed. Once the initiative is chartered, the PM is introduced and he/she takes over a lot of the stakeholder engagement role, but it is important for the sponsor to provide the PM with a synopsis of the stakeholder landscape. From here, a more systemic process of stakeholder identification needs to take place, where the categories mentioned earlier in this chapter can serve as a partial checklist to help guide where to find stakeholders.

The sponsor and the PM should list potential stakeholders, and depending on the size and scope of the engagement, stakeholders could include performing organizations, communities, government agencies, users and customers, and funding organizations, as well as the employees, vendors and subject matter experts (SMEs) responsible for delivering the work. It is fairly straightforward to identify the more involved and visible stakeholders, but it gets more challenging to find those who are indirectly or passively involved or impacted. With this information, the process proceeds to the analysis stage, which is about understanding stakeholders, learning about their needs, involvement, interests, timing of involvement, drivers, and the ability to influence what is being undertaken, as well as considering how they may respond to various situations and to less than favorable news. The next step is to draft an approach to engage them based on the findings.

## The Tools for Stakeholder Analysis

The stakeholder analysis process includes three distinct layers for the sponsor and the PM to consider and the process to finding answers about these layers includes the utilization of a few simple tools. It is important to incorporate the use of these tools since the stakeholder analysis process involves a lot of nontangible information, and these tools can help us articulate our findings and convert them into meaningful information, direction, and guidelines. The tools involve the following:

1. *A two-by-two grid of influence versus interest*—this is the traditional stakeholder analysis tool and it maps out the stakeholders on two dimensions: interest (or stake) on the X-axis and influence (or power) on the Y-axis.

I am a little leery of using the word *power* here because there are many stakeholders with a strong ability to exert influence on what or how things are done, even though they do not hold a high-power position. Further, it is important not to confuse the use of the word *power* between its formal context (authority) and more informal forms. There is a significant limitation on this grid since it does not consider whether the stakeholder in question supports what is to be done. Figure 4.2 provides a visual representation of the four quadrants, along with a name for each quadrant to represent the stakeholder types that should be seen in it. These four areas appear here in order (from high to lower) of how important it is to closely manage the engagement with these stakeholders, or to put it more bluntly—how *important* these stakeholders are:

- *Principals* (high interest, high influence) are the important stakeholders, with high stakes and a high ability to influence. It is expected that these stakeholders are also supporters of our engagement.
- *Loose Cannons* (low-high) are stakeholders with limited concerns about our engagement, but with a strong ability to influence it. The majority of stakeholders who are identified will end up placed in this quadrant and they will be the most challenging to engage. Many of them will have priorities that are misaligned (different views of organizational priorities), while some will have priorities

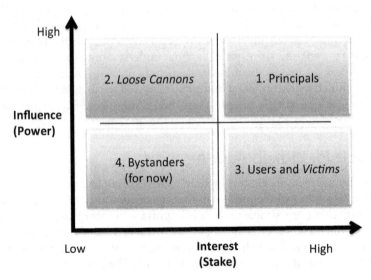

A basic stakeholder analysis tool to check the levels of influence and interest that stakeholders have.

**Figure 4.2**    Stakeholder influence-interest grid[2]

that outright conflict (for example, sponsors and PMs of other initiatives, or resource owners).

- *Users and Victims* (high-low) are those who have to bear the consequences of the initiative. Ideally, these stakeholders should be given more attention, but unfortunately, with a limited ability to influence the direction of the initiative, their voices are rarely heard. The sponsor must ensure that the project team engages these stakeholders, as they will include representation from the users who will need to deal with the final product once delivered. It is usually challenging to deal with the stakeholders in this group since they are typically fragmented and hard to engage, making it difficult for them to properly provide a focused articulation of their needs. Having a strong ability to influence does not imply that these stakeholders are in support of what is being done. Further, their influence can be positive (i.e., ability to give, approve, and reward), negative (i.e., the ability to take, remove, or reject), or both. These stakeholders can be senior, internal, external, team members, SMEs, or anyone with a position of formal or informal power.

- *Bystanders* (low-low) are stakeholders that currently have no specific or known interest or ability to make a significant impact on what is being done. This is almost guaranteed to change as things happen and time passes and most changes will be between the two quadrants on the left, in both directions. Recognizing that there will be movement of stakeholders into and out of this quadrant reinforces the need to revisit the process of stakeholder analysis periodically. The sponsor needs to be the voice behind reiterating this need.

This grid is the first step in performing stakeholder analysis. Although simplified, it provides valuable information about the project's stakeholders.

2. *A two-by-two grid comparing the level of involvement and the level of support/resistance*—most of the stakeholders who are looked at through this tool will come from quadrant number two in the interest-influence grid—the loose cannons. The fact that any given stakeholder has the ability to influence what/how things are done does not imply that they support the project or approach. This grid breaks down the high-influence stakeholders to check whether or not they support us and to what extent. Our two dimensions include support versus resistance to what and how things are being done (on the Y-axis) and the extent of the stakeholder's disposition—active versus passive or strong versus weak (on the X-axis). In this case, the first thing to do is to measure whether a stakeholder is supportive or not (they could be on the fence), and then measure to what extent they are going to demonstrate their support/resistance. Some stakeholders are very adamant about how they feel and will go a long way to exert their influence, while others do not feel as strongly about the matter in question.

Figure 4.3 breaks down the level of support of the stakeholders (support versus resist) and how actively the respective stakeholders pursue their stances. Quadrants will include the following:

- *Active supporters*—mobilize and capitalize, but make sure they remain leading supporters.
- *Passive supporters*—they do not feel strongly about their support and may be on the fence. Leveraging their support would be beneficial, but otherwise, they are good where they are, in general.
- *Passive resisters*—they too, may be on the fence. Once again, it would be nice to get them to support what is being done, but for the most part their resistance is not too much of a concern.
- *Active resisters*—the most challenging. It is necessary to engage them despite the urge to ignore or retaliate. Be careful to not overspend efforts on them since they may be a *lost cause*; that is, a resister who cannot be *converted*. On the other hand, the potential for mutual gains is significant and can be mutually beneficial.

The goal is not to turn everyone into an avid and excited supporter, but rather, it is to map out the stakeholders and check who to engage and to what extent.

After working with our supporters and ensuring alignment, perhaps the most important stakeholders to consider are the *active* resisters. While it is necessary to be careful to not over-engage them, it is important to

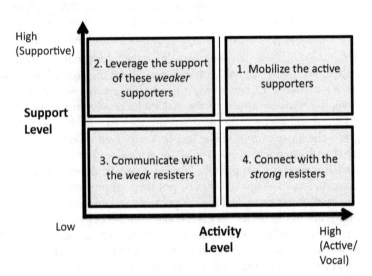

Ideally, the goal would be to turn every stakeholder into an enthusiastic supporter, but that is not realistic—*pick our battles.*

**Figure 4.3**   Stakeholder support grid

understand where they come from and what exactly is the nature of their resistance. When it comes to understanding these stakeholders' needs, it is often surprising to learn that the nature of their resistance may not be due to direct conflict of interest with what is being done. Many times, their resistance is due to confusion and other considerations about priorities and alignment. Engaging those strongly resisting stakeholders is about organizational politics and reaching out. Instinctively, when stakeholders resist the current initiative, there is a tendency for sponsors and PMs to get emotional and not want to engage them.

However, this is where you must show emotional resilience and reach out despite the differences in an attempt to find common ground and collaborate. Typically, the PM will not have the bandwidth or the desire to make such a connection, and the sponsor will need to drive it. To many people's surprise, engaging these strongly resisting stakeholders often yields a collaboration, opens doors to future interactions, and reveals that the differences are not about the merits, but rather about potential misalignment. Further, even if the differences are about substance, the line of communication that is established often leads to concessions and reciprocal action. Later in this chapter, the area of resistance (to projects and change) will be covered, along with how to deal with it.

3. *The stakeholder engagement roadmap*—the third tool to help with analyzing and articulating the findings about stakeholders is illustrated in Figure 4.4. The key stakeholder is listed, and for each one, the letter C (for current) and D (for desired) is located in the relevant column. The columns represent their states of mind or their stance about our engagement. The range of available attitudes includes the letters R (for resistant), U (for unaware), N (for neutral), S (for supporting), and L (for leading). For each stakeholder, the point where they currently are is marked C (for current) and their desired location is marked D (for desired). This tool is essentially a summary of the stakeholder analysis and it results in a roadmap for action. As can be seen in the hand-written diagram in Figure 4.4, there could be multiple combinations, but there are a few to pay particular attention to:

   a. When the C and the D are not in the same column, it is necessary to figure out a way to move the stakeholder from the current to the desired state.

   b. When the C and the D are in the same column, it will be crucial to find a way that will ensure that this stakeholder does not *drift* to the left; for example, moving from a support position to resistance. It is imperative to not take a stakeholder's disposition for granted. Since there are limited resources, there is a tendency to neglect to engage those who are supportive, but this risks losing support down the line. This problem is sometimes seen with service providers (e.g., telecoms) who fail to realize that it is much easier (and cheaper) to maintain an existing customer (supporter) than to obtain a new customer (converting a resister). The sponsor needs to ensure that sufficient engagement activities take place in order to ensure that important support is not lost (especially not for the wrong reasons or because of mishandling the engagement).

c. Note that it is not a necessity that all stakeholders support or lead. In many cases, a neutral position is acceptable, depending on the stakeholder and the situation. It would be a waste of resources (which are already limited) to try to shift all stakeholders into supporting positions. This illustrates the importance of *picking our battles* and considering where the stakeholders need to be and at what price.

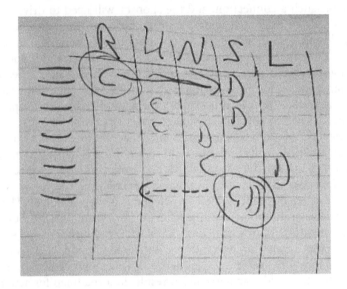

Legend:
1. On the left, the key stakeholders should be listed
2. On the top, the letters represent the stakeholders' attitudes or stance toward the engagement:
   R = Resistant
   U = Unaware
   N = Neutral
   S = Supporting
   L = Leading
3. For each stakeholder, identify two states inside the columns:
   C = Current state
   D = Desired state (for the future)

**Figure 4.4**    Stakeholder engagement roadmap

Many teams tend to overstate their relationships with stakeholders by being overly optimistic about stakeholders' support. In addition, teams often overstate stakeholders' support by brining hope into the mix of considerations and by confusing our desired state with the current state. Keeping this analysis realistic is key because it is imperative that the wrong approach is not applied or that misreading the stakeholders' map does not lead to neglecting to engage with a stakeholder.

Once the table is in place, the roadmap will be achieved by considering for each stakeholder the following list of factors:

1. *Is there access to this stakeholder?* If not, look for someone with a channel of communication to the stakeholder.

2. *Is there a rapport with this stakeholder and a position to engage them?* Once the channel is identified, it will be necessary to check whether or not a rapport with the stakeholder exists. This refers to a relationship, link, connection, affiliation, or a common level of understanding.

3. *Is there enough currency, or what it takes to move this stakeholder to where he/she needs to be (from current to desired state)?* Just asking someone to support what is being done does not guarantee that immediate support can be expected. Therefore, it will be necessary to think about whether the possibility exists to get this stakeholder to move to the right, toward where they are needed; and this means that a value must be provided for the cost, price, driver, or motivation that is necessary to do so. Even if the *currency* is available, it is important to double-check that there is enough of it, and that the stakeholder is worth the price. While *not having the currency* and *choosing not to pay the price* may lead to the same result (the stakeholder ending up not where he/she is needed), these are two different choices because choosing not to pay is a strategic choice, a result of a cost-benefit analysis, and a political move that is selectively taken.

## Additional Considerations: Stakeholder Requirements and Requirements Prioritization

It is important to understand and articulate stakeholder requirements because it is almost a guarantee that there will be some misunderstandings and conflicting needs. Between our initiative's objectives and the stakeholders' needs, we must determine which requirements are more important than others and in which order the requirements should be built, performed, or delivered. The prioritization and sequencing of the requirements are closely related. Prioritization is about determining which requirement is more important than others. It is not practical to prioritize all requirements against each other since many requirements do not *compete* with each other. Competing means competition for resources, bandwidth, time, money, or functionality. Many requirements will be viewed as high priority if they are *must haves*, and it will be the role of the sponsor to ultimately determine which requirement should be performed before the other. The criteria for determining requirements prioritization and sequencing is straightforward and must be communicated and articulated for consistency and transparency. This was touched on in Chapter 3 (see Table 3.8) and included the following considerations:

1. *Business value*—determined by the sponsor with consideration regarding functionalities, characteristics, and other stakeholders' needs. The sponsor is the final decision maker, but he/she must consider all points of view, political elements, appearances, impact on other initiatives, reputation, etc. The sponsor's decision-making criteria may not be consistent or transparent—and it may be different when it comes to different requirements. While each requirement's business value may appear clear, the sponsor may be under significant pressure to deliver on other considerations, including some that may not be visible, clear, or defined.

2. *Technical considerations*—these are needs that are related to the nature of the work and the product that is being created. SMEs, team members, and other stakeholders will provide input, but it is ultimately up to the sponsor as to whether or not to accept these considerations.

3. *Logical groupings*—here too, stakeholders and team members try to talk the sponsor into determining work sequence based on additional considerations, but it is eventually up to the sponsor. These considerations may include minimal feature set, efficiencies, economies of scale, or anything else that does not fall under the first two categories.

Requirements prioritization and sequencing may not just change the order by which the work is performed, but it may also (directly or indirectly) result in removing some requirements altogether. This is never an easy decision, especially since stakeholders get quite attached (sometimes emotionally) to *their* requirements. Moreover, cross-requirement dependencies and other considerations make the process much more complex than initially thought. One of the challenges with requirements prioritization is that there is often no easy or systematic way of checking which stakeholder is associated with which requirements—or to what extent they are *attached* to their requirements. In addition, it is often hard to even fully understand the dependencies, conflicts, or complexities among requirements, and as a result the process of prioritizing and sequencing of requirements may need to repeat itself multiple times throughout the project/initiative, regardless of the life-cycle type (agile or waterfall). It is important for the sponsor to gain and maintain relevant knowledge about the association of stakeholders to requirements (i.e., which stakeholder requested, paid for, or needed each requirement).

When it comes to requirements complexity, it goes beyond the technical considerations that are associated with the requirement since it is necessary to consider cross-requirement dependencies and the stakeholders' needs behind each requirement. In addition, there is the objective element that the sponsor has to look at for each requirement; what value and benefits it represents against the initiative's objectives and success criteria. Determining the relative importance of requirements should be done in such a way that it will not compromise the relationships with the stakeholders behind them and will not make stakeholders feel disrespected, unimportant, or that they are adversaries.

## Other Complexities Due to Stakeholders' Needs

Beyond the potential flare-ups between stakeholders, it is important to consider the specific needs that stakeholders may have. These may involve misaligned priorities, conflicting requirements, unrealistic expectations, or focusing on different objectives. In addition, there are the styles and personalities—where stakeholders may expect to be treated in certain ways or focus on certain areas that are not always in line with what and how things are done or how others view them. While it is fairly easy to identify product-related complexities, things get much more challenging when considering stakeholders' needs and views about the work, the product, and the benefits.

Figure 4.5 provides another visual tool that helps to determine the amount of value that each requirement represents versus the level of complexity (or risk) associated with the requirement. While it is not directly stating which stakeholder is associated with each requirement, it helps the sponsor in his/her decision-making process to determine which requirements are worth pursuing and at what price.

Note that if the values are all the same, it is best to pursue the completion of the high value, high complexity requirements first. This is to ensure that the high mountains are ascended early. By going with the low-hanging fruit first (high

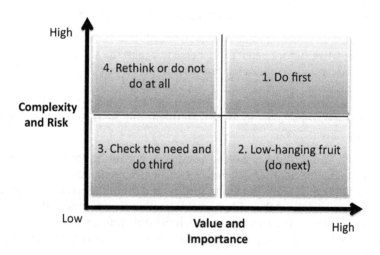

Grid map requirements for prioritization based on their importance (benefits and value creation) versus the complexity (or risk they introduce).

**Figure 4.5**   Requirement value and complexity grid

importance, low complexity), it is possible to complete them and then hit a wall with the high-complexity items. Therefore, the low-hanging fruit comes second. Third in priority will be low-low items, and last, it is necessary to reconsider—or not do at all—the high-risk/complexity, low-value items. The sponsor should lead the effort in challenging the need for items that present low value and introduce a high level of complexity and risk. Note that compliance or regulatory items are not low in value and importance and therefore, should not be in question.

## THE FOUR LAYERS

No stakeholder analysis should be complete without considering the four *layers* that will get us to better understand, engage, and ultimately work with our stakeholders. These layers also help make the stakeholder analysis more relevant and less removed since most practitioners view it as a chore. Further, most people do not see the benefits in investing the time and effort into stakeholder analysis because it usually produces just a list of stakeholders, along with some fairly obvious observations about them. Thus, the knowledge that is gained usually yields little value; especially in light of the time and resource constraints already being faced and also when considering the benefit-cost analysis. However, proceeding into the project/initiative with no understanding of stakeholder needs and without knowing about their drivers, motivators, agendas, and styles is like driving a car blindfolded—it is only a matter of time until you crash.

The layers are illustrated in Figure 4.6 and are explained here:

1. Position, role, and clear and visible needs that the stakeholder represents
2. Objective factors: reputation, behaviors, and the stakeholders' conduct
3. Observations: underlying factors and needs that impact the stakeholder's conduct
4. Subjective considerations: the sponsor's relationship with this stakeholder, the sponsor's ability to work with them, and the track record of their relationship thus far

Clearly, no two stakeholders are the same and, as a result, things will differ from one stakeholder to another—their level of involvement, interest, needs, stakes, impact, influence, decision-making capacity, and timing. Therefore, it will be necessary to map out the stakeholders and determine how to most efficiently utilize limited resources in order to gain as much valuable information as necessary. But clearly, there is no need to go through the same extent of stakeholder analysis for all stakeholders.

Before reviewing the four layers in greater detail, recall that the PM is typically in charge of the stakeholder analysis, but it is the role of the sponsor to enable the process and provide resources and insight in support of it—and, by the virtue of the stakeholder's position, some relationships and stakeholder engagement activities need to be led by the sponsor.

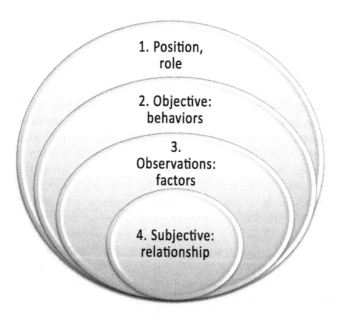

The model behind these layers makes the stakeholder analysis meaningful since it considers all that it is necessary to know about the stakeholders: from the (1) obvious (titles, positions), through the (2) objective conduct and behaviors, followed by (3) observations of underlying factors, to the (4) subjective view of the stakeholders and their relationships with the sponsor(s).

**Figure 4.6**    The four layers of stakeholder analysis

1. *Position, role, and clear and visible needs that the stakeholder represents—* this information is fairly easy to identify; it should include reporting lines, seniority, and involvement level in this (and in other) initiatives. It provides important information since each stakeholder represents the needs of their role and position. For example, when dealing with a person from the finance department, they obviously represent the needs of their department, including their processes, compliance factors, forms, and templates. It means that when the finance stakeholders are approached, they must be provided with information that resonates with them. When discussing things with them about the project, give them numbers, profit-loss information, and cost-benefit considerations. If the initiative is about improving productivity, they will want to see the financial justification for it. If new equipment is being purchased, they will want to see the financial justification for it. Stakeholders, the same as any other people, pursue their own needs and interests and often suffer from a double standard—which means that as long as something serves their own needs, they will not care much if it does not serve someone else's (or even the organization's) needs.

Everyone is under pressure to perform, and performance is measured by how the objectives are delivered. When it comes to conflicting priorities, people will promote their own priorities at the expense of others.

2. *Objective factors: reputation, behaviors, and the stakeholders' conduct*—the objective factors about stakeholders are still *above the surface*; they may not be as obvious as the positions and interests that the stakeholders represent, but they are visible. Watch stakeholders and learn how they conduct themselves, how they treat other people, the way they follow processes, and how they handle situations. Specifically, how do they respond to information that is less than favorable and conduct themselves in the face of uncertainty, change, and adversity? It is not easy to spot all of these things, especially early on, so there is a need to investigate, consult with others, and collect intelligence. Here again, the sponsor and the PM should work together and double up on their combined and collective knowledge, their access to information, and their ability to reach out to other people. Sometimes small pieces of information about stakeholders that may appear trivial at first can add significant value to understanding stakeholders, their needs, and their actions.

3. *Observations: underlying factors and needs that impact the stakeholder's conduct*—now a deeper layer is revealed that is under the surface: interests, underlying needs, agendas, drivers, motivators, influences, and currencies. These may be transparent, aligned with their behaviors, or different. Regardless, these factors and considerations drive people's behaviors, decisions, actions, and conduct. This is the most difficult layer of the stakeholder analysis to uncover and understand. It requires more time, rigor, and focus than any of the other layers (possibly combined). People do not walk around volunteering information about themselves, they do not always tell us what they care about, and they rarely reveal the underlying considerations and agendas that drive them. There is no one simple technique to discover all of the information being sought here, but there are elements that can support this process and make it more effective:

   - *Building an awareness of the need and importance of conducting stakeholder analysis*—this should be done early on and on an ongoing basis throughout the engagement, as needed.
   - *Allowing enough capacity for the process of understanding stakeholders and their needs*—capacity is not only about allowing time, but also about dedicating the right resources, skills, and techniques to collect and analyze the data of meaningful information that is actionable and will support the decisions being made.
   - *Utilizing the known*—information gathering, elicitation, and engagement techniques are the main ways to pursue this important information (including brainstorming, interviews, conversations, and document reviews)

- *Documenting and managing assumptions (also covered earlier in Chapter 2)*—making assumptions is an important part of planning, but once the assumptions are voiced, articulated, and documented, information can be pursued about them that will help to either validate the assumptions or, at the least, allow an informed decision to be made. It is not surprising to see that once an assumption is made, there is often someone who will immediately say that the assumption is wrong. This is ok; I would rather be wrong and know about it, than be wrong while thinking that I am right. It allows me to take the right action based on the situation. Changing people's views of assumptions is a step in the right direction.

- *An extension of the need for managing assumptions is communication*—opening the lines of communication can address many issues and solve many problems before they even occur (this is called *prevention*). It is necessary to eliminate the habit of not communicating to certain stakeholders or not calling stakeholders to the table (until it is too late), just to avoid the (short-term) need to engage in conflict. The earlier the expectations are set and the issues are addressed, the easier it will be to handle them, and the cheaper it will be to undo things if necessary.

- *Consider context*—it is beneficial to look into the context around stakeholders (could be demographic, geopolitical, economic, environmental, cultural, health, or safety and security). Consider both personal categories (i.e., information that is appropriate and relevant), as well as personal work circumstances (i.e., other initiatives or conflicting priorities). The context can provide valuable information about pressures and other personal considerations that may (and likely will) influence the stakeholder, their style, and their actions.

- *Impacts*—consider the specific impact the initiative does/will have on the stakeholder. Then extrapolate valuable information about that stakeholder and start identifying areas of concern, potential conflicts and flare-ups, or behaviors to expect.

Overall, look for the ability to articulate whether (and to what extent) the stakeholder is a supporter or a resister, and what type of actions should be expected. It is also helpful to find out about the stakeholder's potential emotional stance toward what is being changed (or toward the status quo), and in which times and areas he/she may impact or be impacted by what is being done. This entire layer is where most of the effort in stakeholder analysis will take place; it is most likely to produce the most valuable information for the project/initiative.

4. *Subjective considerations*—this is the sponsor's relationship with this stakeholder and his/her ability to work with the stakeholder. This is seemingly an easy layer. Try to understand and articulate the ability to work effectively with this stakeholder. It involves reviewing the history of the relationship in light of the context and the stakes, and determining whether it will be possible to work in partnership. Ideally, a genuine effort should be made to develop a productive relationship with every stakeholder, but this may not be realistic. Sometimes it is simply personalities and styles—rather than merits—that prevent people from being able to develop effective working relationships.

Once an understanding of this subjective layer is attained, it is necessary to come up with the available options for actions—those that are well-known and will work well together are what needs to be leveraged. However, it is likely that there will also be stakeholders with whom it is not possible to develop productive working relations, where one of three options should be pursued:

   a. *Work something out to improve and develop good working relations*—for this, it is necessary to utilize the knowledge that has been gained about these stakeholders and to understand where they come from, their drivers, and which currency can be utilized to make concessions. If this does not work, it is time to resort to the other available options.
   b. *Utilize other people to deal with them*—regardless of who is struggling to develop good relations with a given stakeholder, it is possible to resort to a colleague or to a higher authority for support and even to try to leverage their better relationship with the stakeholder.
   c. *Bypassing, if possible*—with the right level of escalation and permission, it may become necessary to resort to working with a different stakeholder instead of the one who has been labeled as *difficult*.

## Respect

Regardless of who the stakeholder is and his/her position, seniority, or needs, he/she needs to be treated with respect. Stakeholders do not need to be provided with the same information or level of detail, nor do they need to be engaged with the same level of rigor or effort. However, respect is about understanding their needs and working with them to find a way to address as many of their needs as possible (with minimal effort) in order to maximize the impact of engaging them and to keep them from resisting or harming the initiative. It is not about manipulating a stakeholder, but rather about serving the best interests of the initiative and attempting to ensure there is alignment between stakeholders' needs and the sponsor's needs.

Additional considerations about how to treat stakeholders include:

- Engaging stakeholders in a way that meets their expectations (within reason and within our capacity to do so).
- Keeping stakeholders involved in decision making.
- Managing rewards, recognitions, acknowledgments, and accountability through praise, celebrations, and acts of appreciation to help keep people involved and conformed to the process. It also helps to introduce, show, and maintain accountability.
- Keeping them involved: get stakeholders to the table early and work together to set expectations about needs and levels and timing of their involvement through the life cycle of the engagement. This also helps bring stakeholders closer, giving them a feeling that they matter and helping them plan effectively.

## One More Layer?

There is no fifth layer of consideration for stakeholder analysis, but there is a need to stop for a minute once this portion of the analysis is done in order to contemplate, one more time: Are there any other anecdotes or concerns about any given stakeholder, their agenda, style, needs, actions, interactions, or a combination of these? Is there anything else that is crucial to know? Is this possibly a situation where there is no one *alarming* area of concern about the stakeholder, yet overall, there is a combination of factors that add up to more than their individual components? People have a tendency to not like uncertainty or negative information, and as a result, they do not like talking about it or planning for it. But the unfortunate reality is that whether it is noticeable or not, whether it is spoken of or not—problems will surface either way. And if they are not noticed in advance, there will have been less preparation to handle them and the cost of addressing these problems will rise over time.

It is also important to keep in mind that having an agenda, even if it is misaligned with the project agenda, is not wrong. Everyone has agendas and everyone has things that motivate them—things that may not be clear or in line with the direction of the initiative. It becomes more challenging when these stakeholders' agendas outright conflict with that of the project, especially when driven by personal considerations. Table 4.2 discusses deeper and more specific or personal drivers that may dictate people's actions.

**Table 4.2**   The *additional* layer

| Additional Factors to Consider | What They Mean |
|---|---|
| Personal relationships | Friendships and social considerations within or outside of the organization. This includes any conflicts that stakeholders are involved in or are part of. |
| Fairness | A sense of fairness (to the stakeholder, by the stakeholder for themselves, or by the stakeholder toward others). |
| Ego and the need to save face/reputation/appearances and perceptions | Many people dig themselves into a rabbit hole only because they feel that they stand for something. Often, they will have a hard time giving up, moving away from their position, or taking a step back out of fear of loss of respect, disgrace, loss of reputation, or in an attempt to maintain a certain perception or appearance. |
| Sense of control | People's positions may be part of an attempt to maintain control (could be over processes, decisions, other people, or departments). |
| Handling change and uncertainty | In the face of changing conditions and uncertainty, people may react to situations in ways that may be perceived as irrational. This is a common source of misalignment. |
| Preserving | Many people take actions to preserve and maintain something (e.g., processes, realities, current state) in an attempt to prevent moving forward. |
| Setting a precedent | Some people try to make an impact and leave an impression, driving their actions to move forward fast, take a leap, rush something, or set a precedent. These actions may not be the best ones for the engagement. |
| Power | People have different sources of power and they tend to cling to them. Many actions will be driven by attempts to maintain existing sources of power, obtaining new ones, and potentially undermining other people's powers. |
| View of success | There may be gaps between how stakeholders view success or how the initiative's success criteria may impact stakeholders. |

These are additional considerations to take into account about stakeholders. While they may be explored as part of the third layer (underlying factors), these elements are more personal, specific, and removed from the actual nature of the work and project/initiative considerations. Note that these items, albeit potentially disrupting, are not about being unethical or disloyal, nor do they have a legal conflict of interest in any way.

# Engaging Stakeholders

First, it is important to start by using the right term: stakeholders are not *managed*, but rather they are *engaged*. If there is anything the sponsor manages about stakeholders, it is the engagement, the relationships, or possibly their expectations. The information that is obtained through stakeholder analysis will help to put together an effective stakeholder engagement plan and build a communication plan. Here too, the more granular it gets when it comes to addressing stakeholders' needs and communicating with them, the more it falls into the territory of the PM, but the sponsor still needs to oversee, know, guide, and enable the stakeholder engagement process.

The goal is to understand and address the stakeholders' needs and keep them informed at the expected and agreed-upon level so they add value to the initiative, get the benefits they expect, and remain satisfied with the progress, the process results, and their level of involvement. Stakeholder satisfaction is not only about the actual work completed or the benefits produced, it is also about their satisfaction and the way they feel about it all. In turn, stakeholder satisfaction ensures that they will not become adversaries or derail the project.

Utilize the information that is gained to set expectations up front and manage stakeholders' needs and expectations. Then, maintain those relationships by dealing in the drivers and currencies that stakeholders understand and care about. Following these guidelines also allows time to focus on what matters in the project/initiative, which is delivering value and benefits and reducing distractions.

Maintaining good relations with stakeholders makes it possible to respond faster, earlier, and more effectively to performance challenges. Happy stakeholders are likely to be more understanding when there are problems and more inclined to work with us even when things do not appear to go their way. But this takes place only as long as trust, accountability, transparency, and a sense of fairness are maintained. At times, the size of the problem may be beyond the PM's authority level and having the sponsor involved can appease stakeholders. When stakeholders are happy with the overall treatment they get, it creates more time, options, and leverage to fix performance issues.

The opposite also applies to initiatives with good overall performance that may get bogged down by strained relationships with stakeholders. Even if the team is on track to deliver according to plan, the distractions alone may lead to more performance challenges and issues downstream.

## Managing Attitudes

Attitudes are everywhere and can take projects and initiatives down, even those without performance-related issues. By learning about stakeholders' attitudes and monitoring them as part of the engagement process, it is easier to proactively manage stakeholders' attitudes and reduce the damage they may inflict if things should change for the worse. Certain attitudes—such as negativity, envy, cynicism, and greed—are contagious. If they are not dealt with quickly and effectively, they can spread like a brush fire through the project and it can destroy the team's dynamic and performance. These attitudes have the ability to eat through the fabric of relationships, destroying trust and triggering unconstructive conflict. The insights and information that are gathered through stakeholder analysis and the engagement process create a capacity to look for attitude problems in order to help provide the confidence, emotional resilience, and feeling of control to take a timely and sober look at the situation and apply the best and most appropriate approach available to solve the problem.

Earlier in this book, it was mentioned that managing change is a lot about managing attitudes. But even a project does not introduce an organizational change, it is still important to manage attitudes. Managing attitudes is similar to managing expectations, just more proactive. It is often a surprise when stakeholders change their priorities, views, support, or attitudes, but it is quite common and often happens with little to no advanced notice. Engaging stakeholders on a regular basis and understanding their drivers makes it easier to identify when their attitudes change concerning the project—and even better, it may reveal a sense of when they started to see things differently.

Whatever the nature of the changing attitude is, failing to address and contain it will most likely end up taking over and resetting the tone and direction of the initiative. Waiting until the backlash is more apparent will result in it being too late to effectively address and solve the issue.

## How to Engage

For effective stakeholder engagement, there is a need to determine the initial purpose and goals of the engagement—this includes who needs to be engaged and how to do it—taking into consideration all of the associated risks. Figure 4.7 provides a list of considerations for engagement planning and setup. These concepts serve as a set of guidelines for how to plan the process of managing stakeholders' expectations and from there, specifying the details of the engagement and communication plans.

Conducting stakeholder engagement can be broken down into three elements:

1. *Inform*—keep stakeholders informed by providing them with objective, consistent, accurate, and appropriate information. The word *appropriate* refers to making sure that each stakeholder gets the information that they *need*—no less, and especially not more. Giving stakeholders more information than what they need may lead to distractions and misunderstandings that in turn become escalations, consume time, and trigger requests for change.

2. *Work with them*—work together; provide information, communicate, gather needs, engage, and ensure the communication lines are open and that the feedback loop is in place and working.

3. *Collaborate and energize*—create working partnerships with stakeholders for decision making, inquiries, escalations, and process improvements. Make sure that stakeholders feel informed and included and that there is an awareness of their states of mind. This includes providing advice to each other, considering each other's points of view, and proactively seeking win-win solutions.

1. What is the nature of the engagement and the messages to communicate?

2. Who is responsible for the engagement?

3. What resources will be needed?

4. What is the nature of the relationship within the engagement (also based on the roles of both sides and their overall power)?

5. What are the technical aspects, such as timing, context, and methods to engage?

5. Outputs: what are the desired results from the engagement process?

6. Outcomes: what are the actual (measurable) intended effects?

These questions can help determine the nature of engagement, rigor, and focus that must be applied when dealing with stakeholders. Although this is well within the PM's territory, the sponsor often needs to step in for support, knowledge, and context.

**Figure 4.7**  Considerations for engagement planning and setup

To make the relationship with the stakeholder successful, the aforementioned elements need to be reciprocal, objective, responsive, open, and trusting.

There is no *silver bullet* approach that works for all circumstances. The specific needs of the initiative, stakeholders, and the situation are going to determine the full nature of the engagement process; but with the guidelines that were previously mentioned and by asking *what, who,* and *how* questions, it will be easier to organize thoughts around how to engage the stakeholders effectively, how much rigor it is necessary to put into the process, and on what information it will be necessary to focus on in order to understand stakeholders, their needs, their potential impact areas, and ways to manage their expectations.

# EVALUATING THE PROCESS

Throughout the engagement, the sponsor and the PM need to perform periodic checks to evaluate the stakeholder engagement process. Although they should not consume an extensive amount of time and effort, these reviews must be planned and the right capacity to perform them allocated. The goal is to look at the objectives of the stakeholder engagement process and check whether the process delivers its intended goals. If stakeholders feel unengaged or unhappy with how things are progressing, it will most likely be noticeable, and if there are regularly occurring touchpoints with the stakeholders, it will be possible to pick up on changes to their attitudes and demeanor as they occur. However, even if things seem to be going the right way, it is important to focus the stakeholder engagement review on a few questions in an attempt to gauge success.

An ineffective stakeholder management process may result in strained relationships, performance issues, or in extreme cases—outright failure. However, even though the deliverables may be finished as planned, there may still be underlying issues with the stakeholders that need to be addressed. Checking the effectiveness of the stakeholder management process may help to uncover hidden issues and may also serve as an indicator as to what extent things are (or are not) as they should be. Figure 4.8 lists questions to consider for the stakeholder engagement review. These questions may be introduced by the sponsor and at times need to be answered by the sponsor.

## Stakeholder Engagement Thoughts

*Handling* stakeholder thoughts (through analysis, engagement, and expectations management) serve as a crucial, underlying factor of project and initiative success. It shapes our ability to know what is really going on with the project/initiative and with those involved. There are many tools, techniques, templates, and ideas that can help us identify, analyze, engage, and manage stakeholders. It is not about quantity, but rather quality—perform the process efficiently and effectively so it yields the desired results without an excessive burden on our resources.

# ORGANIZATIONAL POLITICS

When it comes to communication and stakeholder engagement, keep in mind that whenever and wherever the sponsor and the PM surrender control of the process, someone will enter into this space to fill the void. Engaging stakeholders and having a regularly occurring and maintained line of communication and feedback are not only to keep stakeholders informed, but also to know what is going on with them and to address their needs. It is also about maintaining our presence and continuously engaging them so they do not feel left out or get a sense that they are not sufficiently engaged. When stakeholders feel that their communication and engagement needs are not being fulfilled, they will immediately default to any

1. Are the issues at stake understood?

2. Is communication taking place as planned?

3. Are the relationships with the stakeholders developing to be open, candid, and trusting?

4. Are assumptions and risks managed proactively and effectively?

5. Is there a sense of common purpose?

6. Is there an atmosphere of collaboration?

7. Is the decision-making process aligned with the objectives and stakeholders' needs?

8. Are there working mechanisms for early detection of roadblocks, problems, and escalations?

9. Do stakeholders feel properly involved, informed, and engaged?

10. Is feedback produced and collected on a timely basis?

A few focused questions are necessary that can help to determine whether or not the stakeholder engagement process is working. This list is for engagement challenges that go beyond performance issues or problems that surface through direct communication and engagement activities.

**Figure 4.8** Stakeholder engagement process review

other source of engagement and information that is available and accessible. When the sponsor and the PM (or the team) do not give stakeholders the attention they feel that they need, it is not only that the affected stakeholders will look for that attention elsewhere, but other stakeholders may take advantage of this situation to fill that void. Moreover, it may not be an actual void, but rather only a feeling or a perception—but it may be enough for stakeholders to disengage.

The stakeholders who step up into the engagement and communication void may not be there by chance. It may be part of a carefully orchestrated move. Those who attempt to take over the communication and engagement process may be driven by a specific agenda that they want to promote—one that is most likely misaligned with the sponsor's. These actions are part of the broader context of organizational politics and the sponsor not only needs to be aware of the politics in and around the organization, but also to be actively involved. An important part of the sponsor's role is to handle the political aspects of the engagement and shield the PM and the team.

## No One Likes Politics

Although no one likes organizational politics, they are everywhere and are essentially about considerations, drivers, and factors that are both visible (above the surface), as well as invisible (below the surface). Earlier in this chapter, the underlying factors were discussed as part of the third layer, but it goes beyond that. Politics help shape behaviors and attitudes based upon a specific combination of conditions and circumstances.

It is possible to learn how to cope with organizational politics. We are all political creatures in a way, so it is more—once again—about awareness and preparation. It is necessary to accept that organizational politics are part of reality and to exhibit the (physical and mental) capacity to learn about them. Many of these political forces are visible and clear, but others are not articulated, and this is where the sponsor needs to engage other stakeholders continuously to ensure that the initiative is the right thing for the organization and that it is championed accordingly. Conflicting priorities compete for decisions, capacity, money, and resources—and without a consistent push by the sponsor, some priorities will get the right of way at the expense of others. Organizational politics are viewed negatively when decisions and actions take place that are misaligned. The main challenge with organizational politics is that the *political rules* are not written anywhere, and often they are not transparent or even evident.

An attempt to change organizational culture or politics—in order to fight them, challenge them, or undo them—will most likely end in frustration, disappointment, and waste. Further, culture and politics are different from one organization to another, within the same organization, and sometimes even within the same department. It is hard to detect politics, yet it is something that has a significant and (at times) severe impact on essentially everything that goes on in the organization.

When it comes to understanding organizational politics, the results of the stakeholder analysis can give us significant insights into better understanding them, and subsequently how to deal with stakeholders based on who they are, when and how they are approached, and the surrounding situation. Some stakeholders are *straight shooters*—transparent, up-front, candid, or politically correct—while others are hard to read. Yet everything that people do, say, and react to, the way they do it, and sometimes even things that are not said or done, become part of the organizational culture of politics. An important thing to keep in mind when trying to get a better handle on politics is Simon Sinek's *Golden Circle* (which was reviewed in Chapter 2); for every stakeholder, explore the *why*, the *what*, and the *how* about what they say and do. Failing to figure out the political landscape is equivalent to trying to drive through a bumpy landscape in the dark.

Here are some examples of things that may be seen in organizations that can be attributed to organizational politics:

- People who behave nicely and professionally when certain senior stakeholders are present, but then act inappropriately when there is no authority around
- Team members who only do things to gain attention and appreciation from other stakeholders
- Stakeholders who make decisions based on what will make them look better
- Stakeholders who attempt to appease other people with their decisions or actions
- Stakeholders whose decisions are disconnected from the merits and the substance of what is being done
- People who act irrationally only to obtain advantages over others
- When there is a failure to address stakeholders' needs because they were not approached properly or their agendas were not understood
- When resources are diverted elsewhere despite the clarity of our needs, urgency, and priority
- When it feels like virtually every action or decision has been delayed, manipulated, and tainted by some sort of an ulterior motive

We can go on and on, but the message is clear: when people say or do things that are not aligned with what appears to be the right thing to do, that is politics. To better understand the underlying reasons for people's *political* behaviors, try to utilize stakeholder analysis to better understand their sources of power.

## Values

Organizational values are where politics and culture meet. Values are not necessarily documented anywhere, but it is quite easy to see them in action. No two organizations are the same, and even within the same organization there will be differences in values from one department to another. The sponsor can leave an important mark on his/her areas(s) of responsibility by sending the right message and establishing the right culture. The initiative's culture cannot be isolated from that of the organization, but when it comes to positive cultural change, this is the most effective way to start one. With that said, politics is partially about understanding the organizational culture and the values that the organization stands for. It is also about how closely people share the same values with the organization and their ability to fit in.

## Influence

One of the common reasons for engaging in organizational politics is an attempt to gain influence. Influence is an attribute associated with leadership and it is an important skill to have in today's world. At its origin, the need to influence comes to play when one has no authority over someone else. If someone has the seniority and authority, they do not need to influence others, but rather they simply tell them what to do. That can be seen in any hierarchical system, such as the military, where leadership is by command and control, based on rank and seniority. However, in the corporate world, even for people who have rank and seniority, their source of power will be much more effective and they will be much more impactful if they manage to exert influence, rather than just command.

According to Dictionary.com,[3] *influence* can be defined as: "the capacity or power of persons or things to be a compelling force on or produce effects on the actions, behavior, opinions, etc., of others." There are a few things to aim for when trying to build political power in an organization, ranging from building and understanding our personal power base, to staying focused and building respect and trust. The following list outlines the specific activities to do (including what not to do) to achieve political power:

1. *Build and understand your power base*—you should first become aware of the values that prevail in your organization and understand their meaning and your existing and desired interaction with them. You should then ensure that you understand the area, industry, and business in which the organization operates in order to develop or focus on your set of expertise.

2. *Think like a leader*—there is a story about Robespierre, the famous agitator of the French Revolution, that tells of how he leapt up from his chair as soon as he noticed a mob assembling outside and is reputed to have said: "I must see which way the crowd is headed, for I am their leader." Thinking like a leader is (among other things) about putting yourself in other people's shoes and trying to understand where they are coming from. It is also about being the *bigger person* by trying to form a win-win resolution regarding issues in a way that addresses both sides of a conflict and the organizational needs as a whole. If you no longer represent the organizational values and those of the team that you are trying to lead, you will lose the ability to influence them and your personal power will decline.

3. *Build trust*—it is a well-known fact that trust is difficult to build, hard to maintain, and even harder to regain once it is lost. It is the foundation of virtually any progress and achievement, and people must conduct themselves in a calculated and focused manner that delivers consistent insight, expertise, treatment of others, and responses to situations. More specifically, trust depends on a set of actions and behaviors as presented in Figure 4.9. It is common to see people engaging in behaviors that eat away at the trust they are trying to build. Other components of trust include maintaining behavioral standards and managing conflict in a transparent and effective manner.

4. *Stay focused*—the work of a leader never ends. Sponsors should constantly be on guard, check their actions, try to improve how they conduct themselves, lead by example, and do their work.

The sponsor must instill trust in the team and in
other stakeholders in order to lead effectively.

**Figure 4.9**   Trust ingredients

5. *Pick your battles*—this can be viewed as a subset of staying focused since it
   is about individuals channeling their efforts toward the things that matter
   for their causes. There is no need for anyone to prove they are right all the
   time; and when appropriate, it is important to be humble and admit mistakes. In addition, maintaining focus on the big picture will allow sponsors
   to step aside from lesser battles.

Overall, when trying to influence people, the focus needs to be on them, rather
than on making a point.

## It Is Also About What Is Not Said

Organizational politics, as well as influencing and leading, are not only about what
is done, what is said, and how it is said; but also about what is *not* said and done.
Sometimes the best response to a situation is to not respond (at least not immediately) and wait a little while until the dust settles.

Responses to situations must be calculated and the appearance, style, and tone
of the responses are likely to be even more impactful than the content. It is therefore important that leaders learn to control themselves and their responses. When
in a conversation and a negative comment or piece of information is received, the

most effective procedure is to count to 10 before reacting. If after the 10 seconds it is still relevant and applicable to say what had first come to mind, then go ahead. But in most situations, those 10 seconds will help to keep people from saying something that they shouldn't. The time will help you cool down, think straight, heal, or at the very least, figure out a way to respond while still showing respect to the other person and not escalating the issue. Of course, the counting to 10 is more figurative than anything else, but there are several techniques that can be utilized in a similar fashion:

- Ask for a recess
- If it is in an e-mail, do something else or physically get up and engage in a different activity before getting back to the other person
- Draft a reply outside of the e-mail application and then read it again later after doing something else (the 24-hour rule); this will allow cooler heads to prevail and prevent people from saying things that they should not
- Ask for clarification
- Paraphrase: this technique allows people to buy time, clarify their understanding, reiterate a point, or reframe what was just said to present a different point of view

## Emotional Resilience

It is hard to take the emotions out of projects. Emotions are usually the result of caring—and most people care about what they do. Moreover, emotions often dictate the course of action in conflict situations, especially if the stakes are high. People want to be successful; they invest time, money, and effort into doing something and they become emotionally involved. Yet, without removing the care, concern, and attention that come along with emotions, it is important to prevent those emotions from interfering with decision making, relationship building, or work. Showing resilience is about knowing what not to say, how to say things respectfully, and how to avoid hurting people, even though they open the door for it. Remember, it is about being the bigger person and the art of not speaking. People also refer to it as *Verbal Judo*,[4] which is a martial arts concept for managing communications, and in this context, it means: "if you are going to say something just for the purpose of making yourself feel better, do not say it."

## Win-Win

It is only possible to achieve a win-win resolution by separating the emotion from the situation and judging things by their merits; not by who said what or by attempting to make a point. It is not even about who is right or wrong, but more about the style and the way people feel about each other and the situation. To help the point come across as effectively and as distraction-free as possible, try to apply the following:

- Remain professional
- Focus on the problem
- Stay objective
- Maintain an image of trying to achieve a win-win resolution

The pursuit of a win-win resolution will bring the other side to a state of mind of potential agreement and will help you build a reputation as a composed individual who remains focused on the big picture—solving problems and ensuring that everyone gets what they need. It is not mandatory for people to genuinely like each other or be best friends in order to build productive and collaborative relations. In fact, many alliances have formed among people who had conflicting priorities, did not see things eye-to-eye, and who were not necessarily on friendly terms. Working together toward solving each other's problems can be achieved by taking emotions out of the equation, seeing past personal differences, identifying areas of mutual gain, and complementing each other's needs.

# TAKING IT UP A NOTCH: SPECIFIC STAKEHOLDER ENGAGEMENT DURING ORGANIZATIONAL CHANGE

In Chapter 1, the Kübler-Ross 5-Stage Model of change was discussed and an interpretation of this model was made that helped with understanding the different stages that people go through on the change U-Curve. As people journey through these states, there are different actions that should be taken in association with the challenges that were identified and addressed in Chapters 2 and 3. However, it must be remembered that even though people go through similar experiences based on the stage, people have different personalities and styles, and should therefore be treated accordingly, based on who they are. There are many personality assessment tools that *segment* people to different types; the discussion here is about one of the more straightforward ones—DiSC analysis, as it is illustrated in Figure 4.10. Although there are eight possible *types*, the interpretation provided here is simplified and refers to the four primary ones.

Table 4.3 provides more context on the characteristics of each *type*, how to identify them and what to expect, along with more information on how to understand them and how to make the dealings regarding each type more focused and effective. It is important for the sponsor to figure out his/her own type first, and then learn about the type of stakeholder who is about to be engaged. In the event that a stakeholder and the sponsor are *opposite types*, they should become aware of the other person's preferences and styles and adjust the engagement style accordingly. In the event that there is a struggle to provide the required engagement style, it is beneficial to work with other members of the team and leverage their styles if it improves the chances for a successful and a more effective engagement. Once the sponsor knows better about his/her own tendencies, along with an understanding of those whom he/she needs to deal with, it will be easier to prepare for the engagement and to set clear expectations.

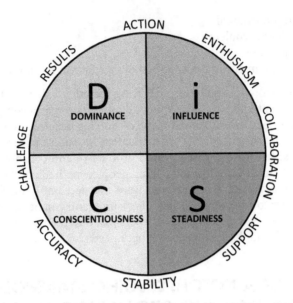

The four types (D,i,S,C) can be *coupled* with their neighbors into four additional sub-types (D-i, i-S, S-C, C-D)—for a total of eight. Conflict is likely to take place between opposing corners (for example, D-S and i-C).

**Figure 4.10**   DiSC overview

**Table 4.3**   DiSC interpretations and considerations

| DiSC *Type* | Interpretations for Main Focus | How to Focus and Work Effectively with Each Type |
|---|---|---|
| **D—Dominance** | Bottom line | Business and straight talk; get to the point quickly. Show them competence and realize they want to maintain control. |
| **i—Influence** | People | Be active and talk things through. Be personable, show interest in them, and provide options. Remember that they want acknowledgment and involvement. |
| **S—Steadiness** | Process | Be inclusive, give them time to talk and think, provide logical steps, maintain stability and harmony, and avoid sudden change. |
| **C—Conscientiousness** | Facts and data | Be low key; focus on data, facts, and details. Give them time to analyze and do not share personal opinions or feelings. Remember that they want structure and order. |

The *interpretation* outlined here makes it easier to focus efforts toward communicating with different stakeholder styles and types.

It is common for the sponsor to serve as an escalation point, where team members and PMs seek the sponsor's help in engaging stakeholders of *incompatible types*. It is also important for the sponsor to ensure that the change (or the project) team is well rounded and comprised of different types of people. This is critical not only for the ability to leverage the right *style* when communicating with stakeholders, but also for the team's performance. If everyone around the table is of the same type, that team is bound to dig itself into a specific rabbit hole, with everyone pretty much agreeing on everything, and most likely leading each other further in the same direction. Many sponsors and other senior members of organizations tend to surround themselves with like-minded colleagues and direct reports with the belief that it will improve communication and performance. While it may provide a sense of harmony, it usually does not end well because the harmony merely provides a consensus toward a specific, unexplored, and often *wrong* direction. In many places this is known as managers surrounding themselves by *yes* people, which has been proven to be ineffective.

# DEALING WITH STAKEHOLDERS THROUGH THE U-CURVE STAGES

## The Denial Stage

Different stakeholders will react to the denial stage in different ways (recall that different people may experience these stages at different times). With that said, it is time to review how to tailor your style for each of the *types* of stakeholders who are being encountered during the denial stage. Remember that these are not magic bullets and will not immediately *convert* stakeholders and bring them to where they need to be. However, the following guidelines may be the only chance to get these stakeholders to buy-in:

- *Denial: the bottom-line person*—these stakeholders, with their need to maintain control, will try to cling to the status quo. They are likely to step up their performance to show that there is no need for the change altogether; and it is important not to push back too hard and to recognize their accomplishments—both in ensuring the effectiveness of the status quo and in general. It is important to provide them with a full picture of the challenges and then turn those challenges into opportunities.
- *Denial: the people person*—we need to provide these stakeholders with the attention they feel that they deserve and it should include one-on-one meetings. Yes, one-on-ones are time consuming, but these will serve as opportunities to engage, reiterate our focus on people, and address stakeholders' concerns. Focus on showing progress, benefits, and accomplishments that are people-related. At this point these stakeholders have no interest in learning about the business benefits, so it is necessary to maintain the focus on people.

- *Denial: the process person*—here too, the way to reach out to these stakeholders is through one-on-one engagement, while keeping the focus on the team and how the change will impact them and their work. They should be provided with a genuine offer for support. Applying pressure on them to move forward will not yield the desired result since, at this stage, there is a need to give them time to process the information they see and get.
- *Denial: the data person*—these stakeholders need to know that their concerns are being listened to and that they have an opportunity to express them. They expect to be given facts and hard data—not promises, hopes, or feelings. An effort should be made to provide them the data in ways and formats that are meaningful to them, so they can review and analyze. In turn, the communication channel should be kept open to allow them to continue to express their concerns.

## The Resistance Stage

The stakes during the resistance stage are always higher. Progress is being made, more things are changing, but there is still a long way to go. In addition, the stakeholders during this stage are not happy. Chapter 6 provides an in-depth review of the types of resistance, their origins, and techniques to handle it. The following list is a review of the approaches that are used to deal with these *types* of stakeholders during the resistance stage:

- *Resistance: the bottom-line person*—this is not only about hearing what they have to say, but also about showing them that their frustration is being acknowledged. Justifying and making promises will not help much; rather, it is necessary to ask for their help, which will help them become, and actually realize that they have become, part of the road to the solution. Draw on their capabilities and their leadership competencies to help the initiative move forward.
- *Resistance: the people person*—just as it was in the denial stage, it is beneficial to listen to stakeholders' concerns. Similar to what is done with bottom-line stakeholders, it is necessary to acknowledge their frustration, but also to talk things through with them. As things get tough, the skills that stakeholders bring to the table should be leveraged and, in this case, it would help to appeal to their people skills.
- *Resistance: the process person*—remember that process people are not only concerned about processes, but also about people in general, just in a different way than how the *people person* feels. Here, the focus is more on the team. Therefore, keep the focus of the conversations with them on the team and the processes, and guide them to focus on the prospect of a calmer reality moving forward.
- *Resistance: the data person*—data stakeholders need facts and actual information. They must be given a chance and the appropriate amount of time

to analyze the data and, in turn, their input should be welcomed. They need to be shown appreciation for their analysis and there should be a detailed mutual discussion regarding their feedback. Some may feel that this is not a productive use of time since it can feel like a rehashing of the same information in different ways. It is, however, an important investment in obtaining this group's buy-in and in providing them with the reassurances they need in the way they expect it.

## The Acceptance Stage

Although this stage is called the acceptance stage, in reality it is still the neutral, or transition, zone. It still feels turbulent for people, but implementation is getting closer. As new processes are defined, there is also some experimentation. Here are some guidelines on how to approach stakeholders during this stage:

- *Acceptance: the bottom-line person*—the need to acknowledge accomplishments continues, but during this stage the acknowledgment should be more public in order for others to see. Momentum is building so an effort should be made to continue leveraging these stakeholders and keep them involved in moving forward.
- *Acceptance: the people person*—despite a chance that anyone can drift backward into self-doubt, at this stage and with these stakeholders, it is more likely. With their main goals to be involved and recognized, these stakeholders fear that they may appear incompetent. If this happens, they will slide back to self-doubt and, most likely, resistance. There is also the chance that they will simply check out or leave for that reason. It is therefore important to continue providing them with support and maintaining their involvement, while celebrating the success being achieved.
- *Acceptance: the process person*—here too, there is a need to celebrate whatever measures of success exist, but with more focus on the team. In addition, their struggles need to be acknowledged and they should be provided with support. This is a good time to leverage them to help increase the team's focus on moving forward.
- *Acceptance: the data person*—a show of appreciation is important here as well, but in this case it is in the form of keeping the facts and details in order. More effort needs to be put toward organizing all of that information for these stakeholders, while leveraging their need for standards and order to finalize the details moving forward.

## The Commitment Stage

We are now entering the refreezing of the new beginning and with it comes the process of embracing the new reality. It also marks the return of stability and productivity—until the next change. There is still a need to engage and to handle the different types of stakeholders according to their styles and expectations (even if unarticulated):

- *Commitment: the bottom-line person*—it is important to celebrate success and give them credit where deserved.
- *Commitment: the people person*—here the celebration should come with acknowledgment of their role in achieving success.
- *Commitment: the process person*—the celebration of success here has to be done more privately. This stage is where these stakeholders feel most comfortable with the newly reached stability, so it is a great opportunity to capitalize on their satisfaction with the comfort zone and get them to produce as per their roles. Unfortunately for those who thrive in stability, it will not be long before the next change is in progress.
- *Commitment: the data person*—the celebration here should be done in a low-key fashion by thanking these stakeholders privately. It might be a good idea to provide a written acknowledgment for the level of detail they demonstrated and for the accuracy of their work as it contributed to the success.

## SPECIFIC STAKEHOLDER ENGAGEMENT DURING THE PROJECT

The need to engage people differently based on their personality is important both when dealing with organizational change and with projects, especially since the two (change and projects) are often intertwined. There are, however, differences between what stakeholders go through during change stages and what they go through during the different project life-cycle phases, and with that comes the need to engage them the right way based on their *type* and the current project life-cycle phase.

There is a noticeable, strong alignment between the stakeholders' types mentioned in this book and the Project Management Institute's 2020 domain changes in the *Project Management Body of Knowledge (PMBOK® Guide)—Sixth Edition*, where the newly aligned domains are People, Business Environment, and Process.

### Pre-project

- ➢ *Bottom-line-focused*—if (and it is likely that this is the case) a decision maker is a bottom-line individual, a compelling and clear reason for the project needs to be articulated to them, along with a measurable set of benefits. A benefits management and realization approach will also help here. The stakeholders' needs must be satisfied in order for them to understand and support the *what* and *why*. The main focus of our conversation is on the potential benefits.

> *People-focused*—although the nature of the information that it is necessary to provide here is clear (people focus), the main challenge is to have enough clear and valid information to convey. The impact of the product (or the result) on people's routines, work, and benefits now enters into the change management *territory* since one of the primary focuses of managing change is managing attitudes and perceptions through communication, engagement, and development. It is therefore important to gain an idea of the direction being taken because these stakeholders need to know what the impact of the project and how it is being accomplished will have on them.

> *Process-focused*—the approach here is to provide stakeholders with information about the journey, processes, procedures, and policies, and how the project's product will impact the way people do things. It may be hard to obtain this type of information at this early stage, but it is necessary to work with these stakeholders and show them the approach (and process) to provide them with the information. There is also a need to focus the conversation on the risks, assumptions, and a comparison of the pros and cons of the proposed approach.

> *Data-focused*—Numbers, facts, and impacts are the center of attention here; mainly in the context of giving these stakeholders a clear picture of the current state, the desired state, and the gap, which must all be supported with facts.

## Planning

> *Bottom-line-focused*—they want to know what the plan means and how it's going to lead to the desired destination.

> *People-focused*—these stakeholders want to understand the details of the plan as it pertains to the teams, resources, and impact on other stakeholders. This group of stakeholders is likely to challenge the validity of the plan if the roadmap is not aligned with the capacity and capabilities.

> *Process-focused*—it is necessary to show them support as to how the plan will be executed and how it was developed. They may also ask about how the outputs, outcomes, and benefits that are being pursued will impact the organization as a whole.

> *Data-focused*—these stakeholders want to see the numbers behind the plan and traceability to information and data that are meaningful to them. They will also challenge estimates in search of supporting data.

## Implementation and Control/Reporting

> *Bottom-line-focused*—their main question: how are we progressing toward our goals and what stands between the present status and success? Since they are goal-oriented stakeholders, it is necessary to satisfy their need to see focus and determination. They want less conflict and expectations

management (unless these directly contribute to success) and more information about *what it means* and *what happens next*. The focus is on benefit-cost performance.

➤ *People-focused*—they want to see more of what is going on with the people (i.e., leadership, communication, conflict management, engagement, expectations management, and training), along with the alignment of these items to the product or the nature of the work. Some of their questions will be related to understanding not only the progress, but also to learn about the cost in doing it (when it comes to the impact on people).

➤ *Process-focused*—these stakeholders want to look behind the scenes, including how things are actually getting done and what kind of impact the progress is having and will be having on the processes and how they operate. If they haven't done so during the planning, they are now likely to raise questions about the impact on the organization the day after.

➤ *Data-focused*—their questions will seek the numbers behind the performance. They want to know the underlying data that leads to the reports, status updates, and interpretations. They want to validate that the performance numbers they see are aligned or are in support of the results being worked toward.

## Closing and Post-Project

➤ *Bottom line*—plan versus actual, benefits realization, why, and what's next.

➤ *People*—so what? What will the result be doing for the people (stakeholders and teams) moving forward? What can be done better in the future from a people perspective?

➤ *Process*—so what? What is the result doing for the organization and to the processes? What can be done better in the future from a process perspective?

➤ *Data*—numbers; cost, benefits, results, and why. These stakeholders are most likely to question the business case to see where it all started and to what extent success was delivered.

## PROVIDING GUIDANCE AND SUPPORT

When it comes to stakeholder identification, analysis, engagement, and expectations management, the sponsor's role is to guide and support the effort by the PM to set direction, engage certain stakeholders as necessary, and serve as an escalation point. It is important that the sponsor maintains involvement in the process of handling stakeholders, as well as to set the direction, provide the mandate, and send the right message about the importance of properly engaging stakeholders.

The sponsor's leadership style must match the needs of the team and the stakeholders in order to maximize their performance, contribution, and satisfaction. A leadership style that combines participative and contingent elements is important to lead effectively, set a direction, exert authority, and empower for growth. Leading effectively is about being there, being visible, and ensuring that the message is consistent and transparent, but also that it is meaningful, inspiring, and thoughtful in all aspects. The sponsor also needs to oversee team dynamics and development, as well as conflict. It does not mean that the sponsor handles conflict hands-on, nor that the sponsor needs to lead team development activities. However, here too, the sponsor acts as an enabler and facilitator to ensure that the sufficient amount of focus is maintained in these areas—primarily by the PM. When it comes to conflict, the sponsor needs to serve as an escalation point when there is a need so he/she can step in and address these matters as required. Further, the sponsor needs to establish, or at least oversee, the escalation procedures and proactively take part in ensuring that the culture enables constructive conflict and that the conflicts remain focused on the initiative's growth and objectives.

## Conflict

Even though the modern view says that conflict is a good thing (when it is focused on the substance and the merits of what is being done; not when it is about personal and petty differences)—it is necessary to be cautious as to how conflict is handled.

## Sources of Conflict

Many conflicts originate from underlying reasons that may be out of the PM's control. Therefore, the sponsor may need to handle them to contain these sources to minimize the impact of these conflicts on the engagement. The following list looks at a few typical sources that tend to lead to conflict if not handled effectively and in a timely manner:

- *Organizational and project priorities*—unclear or poorly communicated priorities lead to gaps in people's view of what needs to be done and their interpretations of the priorities are usually influenced by personal motives and agendas.
- *Unclear expectations*—one of the most important roles of the PM is to manage expectations with help from the sponsor.
- *Resource issues*—virtually every project has to contend with resource issues, whether it is a shortage of resources, timeliness, or duration of their allocation; *stealing* of resources in the middle of tasks; or a mismatch between the team's skill level and the task.
- *Values and interests*—people do not share the same set of values, interests, priorities, goals, definitions of success, and happiness. At some point, things may not turn out the way others feel they should, and from there it is a short road to conflict.

- *Work itself*—different views and approaches to the tasks at hand, work volume, task size, data interpretations, and processes are all possible sources of conflict.
- *Personalities*—personal styles and differences are likely to cause conflicts.

The PM's and the sponsor's ability to manage conflict effectively is a strong indicator of their leadership skills and credibility. It is a significant factor that impacts their personal power in the organization and, therefore, the individual's political clout. People constantly examine how effective the sponsors and PMs are at managing conflict and then establish an opinion about their ability to lead and deliver success.

## Norms and Ground Rules

Establishing norms and ground rules are, for the most part, under the responsibility of the PM; however, when it comes to certain situations and to some stakeholders, the sponsor may need to step in. Norms are a form of a team contract or agreement that it is necessary to establish as part of the effort to streamline communication, manage expectations, and ensure that the focus remains on the objectives. These agreements should include external stakeholders for the same reasons—maintaining owner communication, reducing the chance for misunderstandings, and ensuring that there is an understanding of the stakeholders' states of mind. It is easy to lose touch or to mismanage expectations—and once that grip is lost, it is hard to regain. It is also important to remember that once stakeholders do not feel informed or *in the loop*, they tend to seek information from other sources and can become influenced by them.

Some examples include:

- *Preferred forms of communication for different types of messages*—to make sure that people manage to convey and receive messages.
- *Best practices about e-mail use*—including expected reply and turnaround times, use of subject line, structure, length of a message, the use of CC (carbon copy), and when to reply to all.
- *Expectations for virtual teams*—due to distance, time differences, cultural gaps, and the lack of face-to-face communication, along with the potential of a lack of familiarity with team members and stakeholders, tighter controls in virtual environments need to be in place. These come on top of the controls that exist for a nonvirtual environment. Make sure to maintain ongoing engagement on a regular basis, touch base periodically, ensure that responses are sent and received, and establish clear escalation and troubleshooting processes so that simple misunderstandings do not quickly escalate to an out-of-control and unnecessary conflict.
- *Conduct around meetings*—meetings are likely the largest time consumer in most environments and, as such, tighter controls are necessary in order to ensure that less time is spent in meetings and that the time is used

more efficiently. While it would be nice to reduce the number of meetings altogether, it is likely going to be a tall order in most environments, so the norms and ground rules need to focus on reducing the duration of each meeting, reducing the number of participants in each meeting, and ensuring that the meeting is focused on the most important details (only the right people, preparation, participation, agendas, on-time start, time keeping throughout, focus, action items, and ownership).

# RECAP

There is no on-the-job training when it comes to how to approach stakeholder engagement, and since a lack of time and capacity prevails, the PM and/or the sponsor may drop the ball when it comes to dedicating the right (and focused) effort toward analyzing and engaging stakeholders. Early in the engagement, it is imperative to learn (and fairly quickly) where the speed bumps and the pillars are located—inside and outside of the organization. Speed bumps and pillars are the unmovable things that make up an organization's culture and politics, and their existence and positions must be recognized.

This chapter focused on the very important process of identifying, analyzing, understanding, and engaging stakeholders, along with managing their expectations. It focused on objectives and success criteria, but also on personalities, concerns, underlying currents, styles, conflicts, relationships, perceptions, appearances, and impressions. These are all *fluid* elements that are far from science and since they are volatile, they can change without notice, within a short period of time, and for no apparent reason. To cope with these conditions, some tools and approaches were introduced that can help to organize thoughts, articulate findings, and apply a more systemic and consistent approach to engaging stakeholders.

The sponsor does not need to perform most of the analysis or engagement activities, but he/she needs to establish context, set the tone, and guide the PM and the project team by maintaining a clear *big picture* and enabling the process through focus, time, and capacity. Without dedicating time and effort toward understanding stakeholders, there will be limited leverage and little knowledge on how to address their needs and manage their expectations.

Stakeholders have a significant influence on the engagement virtually at any stage—from the business case, through requirements, and all the way to final acceptance; and if their expectations are not managed properly, our engagement may be deemed as a failure even if it delivers what it was supposed to product-wise. Since the opposite is also true (we may fall short on product delivery, but keep stakeholders satisfied), it illustrates the importance of understanding and properly engaging stakeholders and addressing their needs.

Since stakeholder analysis can be viewed as the backbone of communication and expectations management, any piece of information and insight that can be gained from the analysis process may come in handy at some point in the project—for instance, how likely the stakeholder is to perform and deliver on their commitments, how to deal with them effectively, what damage they may inflict on what is being done, what is known about them, how predictable and rational they are, and how to access and engage them.

Regardless of who manages the project or the engagement, it is in the sponsor's best interest to ensure that there is sufficient knowledge, insight, and context around what goes on with the stakeholders.

## NOTES

1. Project Management Institute (PMI). *Project Management Body of Knowledge (PMBOK® Guide)—Sixth Edition.* PMI, 2017.
2. Schibi, Ori. *Managing Stakeholder Expectations for Project Success.* J. Ross Publishing, 2013.
3. Based on http://dictionary.reference.com/browse/leadership?s=t.
4. Inspired by the book *Verbal Judo: The Gentle Art of Persuasion.* George J. Thompson and Jerry B. Jenkins, HarperCollins Publishers, 2004.

# 5

---

# CHANGE SPONSORSHIP

---

## ABOUT ORGANIZATIONAL CHANGE

People say that they love change. In fact, politicians promise us change pretty much every election. However, these promises usually lead to disappointment for the electorate because the politicians only focused on the positive, never told us about the transition, and no one discussed with us that there was going to be pain to get there. Further, most people do not actually like change, especially when it is forced upon them—and this is when resistance begins.

A similar process takes place in organizations. A need or an opportunity introduces itself and there is a move toward it—promises are made but there is little understanding of or discussion about the transition, the full range of the impact, or the pain associated with the change. In addition, the change will not mean the same thing to everyone; some people will just not want to change and others will not benefit from it. Next, resistance ensues, people get disillusioned with the change, and other stakeholders with conflicting agendas take over the conversation. In most organizations, there is another compounding layer—the tendency to not wait until the change actually delivers on its promise before more changes are introduced, causing them to get intertwined. People then become change fatigued, while the organization becomes change saturated. But it is not all bad. The way for organizations to grow, improve, and develop is through change. Change leaders and sponsors just need to take the right approach to change, pursue the right change initiatives, and realize the organizational capacity to handle change.

John Kotter[1] articulated in 1995 that close to 80% of change initiatives fail, and today this number may be even higher. To put it into context, it is important to realize that not all initiatives under that 80% number fail outright—many of them just fall short of delivering on their intended benefits. Further, the failures are not because these are all necessarily bad ideas, but also because they are not implemented properly, not done in the right context, their timing may be off, or their tactical elements (specifically, project management aspects) fall short. Kotter pointed out eight common errors that lead to the staggering 80% failure rate, and this was the foundation for his 8-Step Change Model,[2] as presented in Figure 5.1.

Although quite prescriptive, this model is based on Kotter's analysis that identified eight common errors when going through organizational change. *Source:* https://frontlinemanagementexperts.wordpress.com/2016/02/08/john-kotters-8-step-organisational-change-model-pt1/

**Figure 5.1**   The Kotter 8-Step Change Model

Kotter identified these common errors:

1. *Not establishing a great enough sense of urgency*—people have different priorities and opinions as to the necessity and the type of change needed, and with a misaligned sense of urgency, it will not be possible to get the necessary buy-in.
2. *Not creating a powerful enough guiding coalition*—also related to buy-in, there is a tendency to move forward too soon and too fast without building the needed foundation of support; that is, support for the initiative and support along the way. The guiding coalition helps navigate the change process and picks the right people to lead and work with.
3. *Lacking a vision*—the vision is both something that is aimed for, as well as a driving force that will get people to enroll and join the team. A lack of vision and clarity will result in a failure to get people to join. A vision has to be inspiring, clear, and measurable, but still *high level.*
4. *Under-communicating the vision by a factor of ten*—even with a solid vision, if it is not communicated, it is as if there is no vision at all. The communication is not just about sending a message, convening a town hall, or sending an e-mail describing the idea and how great it is; different people need different messages and a different way to see the vision.

5. *Not removing obstacles to the new vision*—even a good vision does not mean that the road is clear toward achieving it. Those who articulate the vision might know that it is a great vision for a great cause, but not everyone will feel the same. It should not be assumed that everyone is aligned and that there are no problems with the way people see the vision.

6. *Not systematically planning for and creating short-term wins*—once the current status quo is unfrozen, there must be a plan for the transition, which is that long *chasm* where people will feel out of their comfort zone and where things will happen (good and bad) as part of moving toward the new reality. Part of the planning is slicing this complex space into smaller chunks (shorter, with smaller scope) and ensuring that milestones are in place to show progress, reinforce the direction, and keep people involved and informed. Failing to plan for these small wins will lead to a failure to show progress, and even if progress is made, it will not have the traction or recognition.

7. *Declaring victory too soon*—small wins are not the final victory, and in desperation to show delivery on the promise or because of a need to rush to the next change initiative, victory may be declared too soon. Besides the misleading message, people may not buy this "fake" news and what will be left is no victory and no credibility.

8. *Not anchoring changes in the corporation's culture*—this is related to the previous item of declaring victory too soon. Similar to jumping from one ledge to another, landing at our destination does not mean that everything is stable; there is still a possibility of falling back. Embedding and ingraining the new reality and refreezing it into the organizational culture is critical. When the change is perceived to be complete, this is when focus may be lost and people may default back to old behaviors since the *new* way of doing things is no longer enforced or reiterated.

## Connecting the Change to Project Management

Another reason for the high number of failed change initiatives stems from failing to connect the change to project management. Strategic changes need to be delivered through tactical elements—or projects. Everything that is accomplished about the change will be performed through these projects, but many organizations fail to realize that. The connection to project management is done through ensuring that there is a realistic plan with short wins that take the project through the transition. In many environments, the change initiative is revealed (usually through a big announcement) but gains little traction because there is no plan on how to move forward. Also, there is little to no consideration on ensuring that the right project manager (PM) is in place, and that the mandate is clearly articulated and is transferred to the project in the right context. Failing to install the right PM may drive the initiative in the wrong direction and a failure to properly convey the change message on the project level will lead to insufficient movement or meaningless progress.

This is where the sponsor or the change leader has to step up and ensure that the *why* of the initiative connects properly to the *what* and to the *how*. Without a seamless connection, the project team may move forward, but it may not be in the right direction or at the right speed.

## Portfolio Management

Connecting the change initiative to project management is done through a series of basic steps that are part of project management best practices, along with concepts related to portfolio management:

- *Strategic alignment*—the change leaders and the sponsor must ensure and show alignment between the change initiative (along with the projects that drive it) and the organizational strategy. This will help with prioritization, resource allocation, and decision making in general.
- *Capacity management*—there is a need to define and articulate the organization's capacity to take on the change initiative and to lead the project(s) associated with it. Capacity starts by understanding what is at stake and what organizational resources (people and other) are available. Most organizations fail at capacity planning because they tend to take on more than they can chew.
- *Prioritization*—within our limited capacity, it is important to prioritize what is more important and then plan the sequence of work. The sponsor should drive the process of prioritization, both across projects and initiatives (to determine what is more important and urgent) and within each project (to be able to articulate the project's objectives).
- *Defining success*—project success and acceptance criteria should reflect the prioritization scheme and strategic direction and are part of the trade-off between constraints and competing demands (scope, time, cost, and quality). Without an understanding of the project success criteria, the sponsor will scramble to make informed decisions and the project will struggle with its progress.
- *Resource management*—based on the priorities (within and across projects) and the success criteria, resource allocation will take place and decisions will be made about which project will get the right of way over others. When there are resource conflicts and disputes, the sponsor (or sponsors who are associated with the competing initiatives) needs to make informed decisions as to where resources will go. Resources are possibly the biggest *wildcard* constraint that plagues projects and can limit the progress toward achieving the organizations' strategic goals. More discussion about resource constraints takes place in Chapter 6.
- *Risk management*—while most risk management activities are led by the PM, the sponsor needs to make sure that there are big-picture considerations that go beyond the project and that risks are also considered at the operational level, the business level, and the post-project level. It is

important that actions that attempt to address specific project risks do not end up backfiring at the organizational level.

- *Assumptions*—make sure that assumptions are documented and managed, which in turn, will allow the sponsor to align expectations with other stakeholders and ensure that everyone is on the same page.
- *Project charter*—also discussed in Chapter 6, the charter is perhaps the most important project document and provides the mandate and link to strategy and the business case. It lists key pieces of information, sets expectations, and serves as the birth certificate of the project.

## Drivers of Change

To help better understand change, its origin, priorities, and drivers need to be determined. The drivers of change are essential triggers for the scope and the scale of the change initiative, and clarifying which drivers are triggering the change can help determine what must change in the organization and why.[3]

Table 5.1 serves as a tool to assess any of the applicable drivers and how it affects the change.

The following list expounds on each of the categories:

- *Environmental forces*—the dynamics of the larger context within which the organization and people operate; these forces include: social, business, political, governmental, technological, demographic, legal, natural, and economic.
- *Marketplace requirements for success*—includes the collective set of customer requirements that determine what is necessary to succeed in the marketplace and are usually the result of changes in the environmental forces. These forces include: product and service needs, speed of delivery, customization capability, level of quality, need for innovation, and level of customer services.

**Table 5.1** Determining the drivers of change[4]

| Factors | How Each Factor Drives Change (if Applicable) |
|---|---|
| Environmental forces | |
| Marketplace requirements for success | |
| Business imperatives | |
| Organizational imperatives | |
| Cultural imperatives | |
| Leader and employee behavior | |
| Leader and employee mindset | |

The left column provides a list of factors to consider that serve as drivers of change. The right column is where sponsors need to provide an assessment of how the driver is affecting the change (if the driver is applicable).

- *Business imperatives*—outline what the company must do strategically to be successful given the changing requirements that are identified during strategic planning sessions. This may require rethinking and changing: strategy, goals, products and services, pricing, branding, and e-commerce.
- *Organizational imperatives*—specify what must change in the organization's structure, systems, processes, technology, resources, skill base, or staffing in order to achieve strategic business imperatives. Examples of changes include reengineering, job redesign, and restructuring.
- *Cultural imperatives*—denote how the norms and the ways of relating and working together in the company must change in order to support and drive the organization's new design, strategy, and operations.
- *Leader and employee behavior*—collective behavior expresses an organization's culture. Behavior includes not only overt actions, but also style, tone, and the character that permeates what people do. This also includes how people must change in order to create the new culture. Leaders and employees much choose to behave differently in order to transform the organization's culture.
- *Leader and employee mindset*—mindset encompasses people's world view, assumptions, beliefs, and mental models. A person's mindset causes him/her to behave in the ways he/she does and underlies those behaviors. Becoming aware of one's mindset and its effect on his/her own feelings, decisions, actions, and results is often the first step in building the individual and organizational capacity to change. Mindset change is often required to catalyze and sustain new behaviors and for employees to understand the rationale for the changes being pursued. A shift of mindset is usually needed for organizational leaders to recognize changes in the environmental forces and marketplace requirements, thereby opening the possibility of new strategic alternatives and directions.

Determining the drivers of change is important not only for articulating the change and its scope, but also for determining the need for the change and the change urgency.

## VISIONING

A successful change starts with a vision. Figure 5.2 provides a short definition of what a vision is. The change leader or the sponsor needs to make sure that the vision is in place, clear, and understood. The sponsor may not be the one producing the vision, but the person leading this change needs to be part of coming up with and articulating it.

The vision is the internal compass of the organization and it directs the team toward the desired state that the change initiative is trying to achieve. It is not easy to put together a good vision so here are some characteristics it needs to have:

**Vision**
(vĭzh'ən) *n.*
1. An imagined idea
or a goal toward
which one aspires.

The vision captures the dreams, aspirations, and future we want to create.

**Figure 5.2**   Vision[5]

1. *Clear*—the vision has to be clear regarding what the goal is and what can be achieved.
2. *Inspiring and compelling*—it needs to have a message that appeals to and resonates with the subjects of the change and the stakeholders. The message has to appeal to a variety of stakeholders—often with different priorities.
3. *Realistic*—while the vision needs to be appealing and ambitious, it also needs to be realistic.
4. *Measurable*—not to a scientific level, but there needs to be a way to determine whether and to what extent the vision's goals and objectives are being achieved. There also has to be a time frame for when vision benefits will be realized.
5. *High level, but specific enough*—this is where it gets problematic. The vision must be high level, but not too high. It needs to point at a specific target, but not in too much detail. In fact, many people confuse high level with vagueness; but it must not be vague.
6. *It is not about the journey*—the vision is not about how to get there. Gap analysis, planning, and expectations management will focus on how to get there; the vision is about the *why* and the *what* and serves as a guide. It is important to set the right expectations that the journey toward achieving the vision will not be a straight line, but more like sailing—there will be tides, currents, winds, and shifts in how to get there, but the motion will be in the right direction.

Figure 5.3 provides an example of perhaps one of the best and more effective visions of our time: JFK had all six elements that were included in the previous list in that vision.

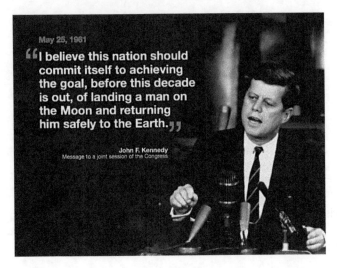

This vision by JFK had everything we should look for in a good vision: it was clear, compelling, realistic, measurable (including time-bound), and at the right level of detail. It was not about the journey, but rather about the aspiration for the future we want to create.

**Figure 5.3**   A good vision

## How to Build a Good Vision

One of the most common ways to perform a visioning exercise is a brainstorming session. Brainstorming events primarily are more attractive for extroverts who get energy from being around people and working together. Introverts go inside to mull things over, so they do not benefit much from the traditional brainstorming session. Depending on your introvert/extrovert mix, it might be a good idea to enhance the traditional brainstorming session either to a process that starts by collecting the round-robin input individually or by converting it into game-storming. Game-storming is essentially a facilitated session that fosters and encourages innovation by combining a series of methods to stimulate ideas through structuring large diagrams, introducing concepts, fusing words and pictures into visual language, and encouraging improvising. A common tool would be mind mapping or vision mapping. The process helps to solve complex problems and to look for questions by combining experiential learning and a little bit of simulation.

### Values and Vision Mapping

An articulation of the vision should be driven by values, which are the things that are believed to be important in everyday life and work. Values determine priorities and can be used as the measures that are used to tell if life and work are turning out the way they were intended. Vision mapping is a way of visually representing the ideas that people have about the future, based on their values. The process of creating a vision map is done through identifying association, extending them into new directions, and giving visual cues. It helps to activate the whole brain, and by listing all of the associations, the process helps to clear the mind and focus on what is at stake. Overall, the map exhibits the big picture and transforms ideas from short-term to long-term memory.

To simplify, the mind map (or vision map) connects the *why* with the *what*; the *why* comes from the question: what should the organization look like after the change (e.g., six months) and why? With the focus on the *why*, it will help to get the *what* out of it. A sample vision map is illustrated in Figure 5.4, which includes the following elements:

- A center concept
- Names
- Branches (brainstorming comes in through the off-shoots of ideas coming from the branches)
- Relatively few words—mostly in branches and connections
- The lines show associations but there is no need for any artistic talent

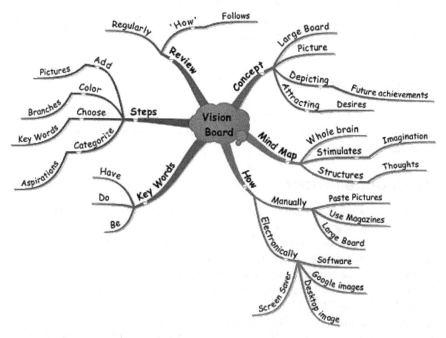

A vision map helps stimulate multiple parts of the brain. It can include drawings or images and it should be in color to make associations easy.

**Figure 5.4**   Vision map sample[6]

Branches can include (but are not limited to) items such as:

- Business environment—internal and external
- Products and services
- Customers and clients
- Key success factors

The steps to build the map:

1. Spend a few moments engaging and telling the story of your vision map.
2. Listen to your partner's story. What words and ideas stand out for you? What images resonate? What questions do you have?

At a minimum, make sure that your branches consider what you want to see and how you want to see it, and remember that the goal of the vision mapping exercise is to create an orientation and not the destination; so worry less about whether the branches are fully logical, reasonable, or rational—this will come later. The map will help create and articulate a compelling vision for change and from that, it will be possible to develop a transition path from the current to the future desired reality.

The vision helps set expectations, achieve stakeholder alignment, communicate ideas, clarify direction, articulate gaps, form plans, identify alternatives, define success criteria, and build a sense of urgency. To paraphrase an old saying: when you do not know where you are going, any road will do.

## MOVING FORWARD

With the vision in place, it is now possible to move forward with planning for the change. Start with scoping it, understand what is at stake, and realize what challenges may lie ahead.

### The Change Leader

The change leader (most likely, the sponsor) is the person who wants the change to happen and is in a position to work with the group to make it happen. His/her role is to provide a process that will facilitate a specific change easily and effectively with minimum disruption and with maximum support from group members. The change leader is the organizational leader of the change—even the champion—while the change agent is the person who is spearheading the process (might be the PM). There might be more than one sponsor for the change: an initiating sponsor—who is the originator or the person who starts it and a sustaining sponsor—who drives the change from that point. The sustaining sponsor may then utilize other stakeholders to support the change in order to provide the following:

- Develop and sustain *synergistic* working relationships with and among stakeholders
- Continually assess the level of commitment from both targets and other stakeholders
- Identify and manage resistance
- Select and utilize alternative styles of interpersonal communication to effectively announce the change and respond to questions
- Identify, relate to, and respect the diverse frames of reference of stakeholders

Change leadership revolves around the ability to obtain willing compliance to change. The more you can facilitate a person's willingness to accept and implement change without resenting either the change, the process, or you for requiring it, the more effective you are as a leader in that situation. In addition, keeping in mind that the status quo is not static; everything—the situation, the people, and the conditions—is evolving. As a result, leading the change is about the ability to stay flexible so that it is possible to respond to what is going on. Although the tendency is to focus on the future and the desired state once the change is completed, the more the change can be introduced in terms of what is presently happening, rather than in what *should be* happening or what might happen next, the easier it will be to work with the people who are facilitating change. Table 5.2 shows four primary change leadership styles, their meaning, and their application. Although it should go without saying, it is important to note that in order to apply the right type of leadership style to situations, the sponsor needs to have an understanding of the situation at hand, as well as a strong realization of his/her own leadership style and the ability to apply this style in the right context.

The change agent works within the parameters set by the sponsor and promotes and supports the change. The sponsor needs to learn about the source of power that the change agent brings (e.g., knowledge, position, and expertise), what the agent needs to do to help ready the organization, and whose support the change agent will need. In addition to the change leader/sponsor and the agent, identify and understand the needs of a few other key stakeholders: the change target, the customer, and the influencer/advocate:

- *Change target*—we need to define who will be impacted by the change and how they will be impacted. In some cases, the change target may also be responsible for leading elements of the change. A few questions to ask about each of the individual change targets involve whether any of them actually have had to change and how, assess the level of commitment that is required of them, and check if this person stands to win or lose from this change. This will give an indication about their type and level of resistance and what it will take to manage their resistance.
- *Customer*—there might be more than one customer, and for each one the following considerations need to be in place: identify which customers will be affected by this change and in what way; clarify the impact of the change

**Table 5.2**   Leadership styles for the change sponsor or leader

| Leadership Type | When Best to Use | Application |
|---|---|---|
| Autocratic | When demand is simple, with limited interest on the part of the group or when the need is imposed (externally) and is nonnegotiable | The leader makes the demand and the group is expected to respond.<br>Applicable when the change is not particularly important or when there is a need to save time. If used properly, it can reduce resistance because people will not fight for stuff that is not important to them. |
| Participative | When group input is needed to maximize outcome, when strong resistance is anticipated, or when ownership of the change is needed | This is the most used style since it maximizes individual input and ownership in the final implementation. When the success of the change depends on successful implementation by the group, it is necessary for the group to be part of determining the change process.<br>Important to clearly distinguish areas that are negotiable versus nonnegotiable early on. Also effective when there is a large amount of resistance by facilitating and maintaining control of the group process. |
| Supportive | When the group is competent to create and implement a change but needs support or when the group requires outside assistance or support to make change happen | Assist the group in developing a process to deal with the change.<br>Applicable when the group's working relationship and trust are low, when the group is newly formed, and when members do not know each other well enough to communicate effectively.<br>Focus needs to be on the process and making sure that everyone has an opportunity to speak up and participate.<br>Also applicable with a highly skilled and low-experience group or for a new application or design. The leader's role would be to identify resources and make them available to the group. |
| Laissez-faire | When the group is highly competent and experienced at working together on similar tasks or when there is little/no resistance | In this hands-off approach, the leader describes the change or the need for change, answers questions, sets boundaries, and then lets the group function on its own.<br>Suitable for a self-managing or well-functioning team that has successfully managed change before.<br>This approach is most effective when the group is highly experienced at working together and resolving process issues. |

In determining the leadership style, the sponsor must consider which style is most applicable to the situation at hand and, alternately, consider whether his/her prevailing style is the most suitable for a given situation.

on each of the customers; check whether, why, and to what extent any customer may resist the change; and determine what the organization will need to do to manage this resistance.

- *Influencer/advocate*—there is also a need to scan the organization's environment in search of any person or organization who might have influence on the change initiative. Such a scan often identifies stakeholders (i.e., influencers) in the organization who might support the change initiative but may not be in a position to sanction it. If this is the case, there is a need to check what type of influence they offer and what has to be done to manage their role.

## Force Field Analysis

For change to be sustainable, there must be alignment among the various forces that shape organizational execution. Start by identifying the forces that are driving and resisting the change initiative that help to determine what further changes are required in order to support the initiative. Figure 5.5 helps organize the driving

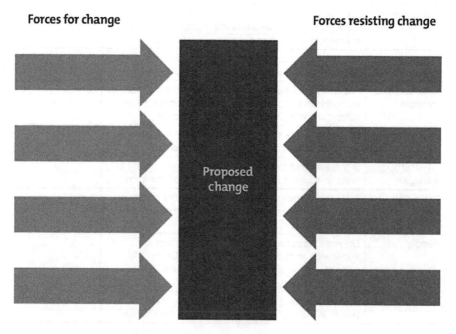

This template helps identify driving and resisting forces and the relative weight of the force.

**Figure 5.5**  Force field analysis template

and resisting forces toward the change. Based on the force field analysis, the following forces should be considered:

- Strategy
- Stakeholders
- Tasks, processes, and work methods
- Organizational structure
- Work teams
- Physical settings
- Technology and tools
- People
- Culture

Table 5.3 helps add context to the elements identified in the force field analysis.

**Table 5.3**   Force field alignment sheet

| Force | Questions to Ask | Required Actions |
|---|---|---|
| Strategy | Has the change revealed new opportunities and/or threats that require revisions to organizational strategy? | |
| Stakeholders | Are key stakeholders aligned with the change initiative? Are they aware of the change and what it necessitates? Have sponsors been identified? | |
| Tasks and work methods | Are employees/tasks/organizational processes appropriate and efficient in light of the change? | |
| Organizational structure | Are new positions required? Is there a need to transfer authority and accountability among positions? Are current reporting relationships appropriate? | |
| Work teams | Do current work teams have the correct composition and involvement of expertise and representation? | |
| Physical settings | Is there a need to revise the physical environment in order to support more effective work collaboration? | |
| Technology and tools | Does the current technology (tools, work processes, and automation) support the work environment and tasks during and after the change? | |
| People | Do employees have the skills, aptitude, and knowledge to succeed in the change? Do people understand the change and the anticipated impact it will have on them? | |
| Culture | Are the prevailing cultural norms, values, attitudes, and beliefs in the organization supportive of the change? | |

This table helps organize our thoughts around the forces that impact our change initiative by listing a few common questions to ask about each force and, based on the answers, come up with specific actions that are required. It subsequently helps with understanding the gap to be dealt with and planning for the transition stage of the change.

## Developing Shared Perspective

As part of the need for alignment and to manage expectations, there is a need to develop a shared perspective. As G. K. Chesterton said, "It isn't that they can't see the solution. It's that they can't see the problem." It is best to start with building a model. For an example, see Figure 5.6 depicting the parable of the blind men and the elephant. To begin the process of finding out what people are *seeing* as the problem, it is helpful to ask, "how does this system/problem/situation work," and if needed, ask people to draw it. As a result, there will likely be several different models or paradigms, and by ensuring that everyone is sharing assumptions, the model for the team/group/department/organization can be built. Keep in mind that the models that are generated will not represent the actual problem/situation, but rather they are a representation of an understanding of what people have in their minds. These models are therefore a starting point from which to work.

Once the model of the situation has been finished, the next step is to develop a shared sense of the current state. Ideally, the change initiative should be started before the current state ends or collapses, or even before the current state begins to peak. Peter Drucker called this *planned abandonment*, and it's the idea that the demise should be factored in from the beginning. In change theory, it is believed that the ideal time to institute a change is at the peak of current earnings/performance: sooner than that and the organization has not maximized its potential or earnings, and after that, the organization has started to subsidize the project/product. With that said, the tricky part to this is agreeing as to the current location on the curve, and without a shared perspective of where that is, it is next to impossible to agree on how urgent the need for change is. The result is an inability to agree on what should be done.

The current state is the starting point for any change; it is where understanding is gained as to why the change is needed, what may influence proposed changes,

It is not just the blind men who see different parts of the animal. We all see different parts of any situation/problem/organization/system depending on where we sit or stand, what position we hold, what our interests are, and what our intentions are.

**Figure 5.6**   The blind men and the elephant[7]

and in turn, what would the impact be of the proposed changes. Next, it is necessary to start identifying ways to measure and ensure that the change is impacting goals as desired.

To get everyone on the same page and on the same timeline, go through the following process:

1. Draw an S-curve and have each person mark where they think the system/problem is on it. This is not the *traditional* project management cost profile S-curve, but rather it is a different S-curve, as shown in Figure 5.7.
2. Note the differences and ask outliers to share their rationale with the group.
3. Keep discussing until everyone has a shared perspective on where the issue sits on the curve.

This is not the *traditional* S-curve from project management that shows the general spending profile of a project. This is about checking the team's current status on the product's earning peak so that it is possible to determine when the change should be proactively introduced before it's too late.

**Figure 5.7**  The other S-curve

## WHAT TYPE OF CHANGE IS BEING FACED?

The tools and techniques mentioned in this chapter can help the sponsor and the change leaders set up the change, understand it better, and build context around it. The context helps articulate the *type* of change being faced and with that, start the process of setting expectations or *bracing for impact*. Earlier in the chapter, the drivers for change were reviewed; that process will now be complemented by defining the *type* of change being faced, and this can be broken primarily into four types:

1. *Strategic or sustainable change*—think organizational (rather than local) and deep impact.

2. *Developmental change*—an improvement to what is currently being done with a focus on strengthening or correcting, rather than on going outside the box.

3. *Transitional change*—to replace what exists with something entirely different (a move to a new *state*). It requires dismantling and letting go of the old order. Once the vision and parameters are created, *projects* can be initiated to transition the organization.

4. *Transformational change*—this is a radical shift of behavior, culture, and mindset. The new order will emerge from the change initiative, as opposed to us transitioning into it.

The first type of change mentioned here—strategic change—can be combined with any of the others that are listed. Table 5.4 looks at the other three types of change (developmental, transitional, and transformational) and provides parameters to frame them and set expectations.

**Table 5.4** Framing the change[8]

| Type of Change | Expected Pain | Driver | Clarity of Outcome | How the Change Occurs | Orientation and Focus |
|---|---|---|---|---|---|
| Developmental | 1 | Improvement | 4–5 | Training, self development, communication, and process improvement | Improvement of knowledge, skills, or performance in a certain area |
| Transitional | 2–3 | Fixing a problem | 3–4 | Controlled process, support structures, timeline | Redesign of strategy, structure, systems, processes, technology, or work practices (not culture) |
| Transformational | 4–5 | Survival | 1 | Conscious process design and facilitation, high involvement, emergent process | Overhaul of strategy, structure, systems, processes, technology, and work. Requires shift in culture, behavior, and mindset |

Scale: 1 = Low; 5 = High.

The framing of the change helps realize the drivers behind it, the depth of the impact, and the pain expected. Then, you can set up the right level of approach, involvement, and activities to accommodate the change.

There are some questions to think about when going through any of the change types (developmental, transitional, and transformational).

## Developmental Change Questions

1. Does the change effort primarily require an improvement of the existing way of operating, rather than a radical change?
2. Will skill/knowledge training, performance improvement strategies, and communications be sufficient to carry out this change? Otherwise, what additional actions should be considered?
3. Does the mindset support the needs of this change?

## Transitional Change Questions

1. Does the change effort require you to dismantle your existing way of operating and replace it with something known, but different?
2. At the beginning of the change effort, were you able to design a definitive (and agreed-upon) picture of the new state?
3. Can the change occur over a predetermined time frame?

## Transformational Change Questions

1. Is there a need that pushes toward starting the change process before the destination is fully known and defined?
2. Is the scope of the change and its magnitude so significant that the organization's culture and people's behaviors/mindsets need to shift fundamentally in order to successfully implement and achieve the new desired state?
3. Does the change require the organization's structure, operations, processes, products, services, or technology to change radically in order to meet the desired state's requirements?

## Defining the Scope, Scale, and Initial Impact Assessment

Another step of framing the change, beyond its type, is framing the scope of the change. Table 5.4 helps determine the type of change and the respective characteristics of each type. Along with an initial impact assessment, it is possible to determine which aspects of the organization are likely to be impacted the most by the change initiative (see Table 5.5). The insight it provides can help better understand the change, its magnitude, scale and scope, as well as the process of considering which strategies to employ in an effort to absorb, handle, or minimize the negative impact of the change. The assessment also helps realize insights, obstacles, and related opportunities.

**Table 5.5**   Initial impact assessment

| D/I | Business/Strategic Impact | D/I | Organizational/ Operational Impact | D/I | Personal/Cultural Impact |
|-----|---------------------------|-----|------------------------------------|-----|--------------------------|
|     | Purpose/Vision            |     | Organizational structure           |     | Resistance and anxiety   |
|     | Business strategy         |     | Systems and processes              |     | Norms                    |
|     | Market position           |     | Technology and tools               |     | Relationships            |
|     | Mergers/Ownership         |     | Job definitions/team structures    |     | Leadership style         |
|     | Direction and reputation  |     | Policies and procedures            |     | Motivation, rewards, and recognition |
|     | Downsizing                |     | Resource needs and availability    |     | Workload                 |
|     | Growth/Expansion          |     | Union considerations               |     | Perception of fairness   |
|     | Succession                |     | Compliance and regulations         |     | Values                   |
|     |                           |     | Customer service                   |     | Attitudes                |
|     |                           |     | Governance                         |     | Team effectiveness       |
|     |                           |     |                                    |     | Culture sensitivity      |

An initial impact assessment helps measure how the organization will be affected. For each item, mark a *D* for a direct impact or an *I* for an indirect impact. Note that the initial impact assessment tries to assess the change impact for when it is fully implemented.

Changes can range from fine-tuning (e.g., refining policy at the department level); through incremental adjustments (e.g., improving technologies or organizational adjustments); to modular transformation (e.g., restructuring); and corporate transformation (e.g., major organizational redesign or a radical shift in business activity).

## Change Conditions and Strategies

Another thing to consider when assessing the change and trying to frame it is measuring the change conditions and strategies. In this assessment, the change is broken down into two dimensions: internal versus external and negotiable versus nonnegotiable. Figure 5.8 shows the breakdown into the two elements.

The following list further explains the change conditions shown in Figure 5.8:

1. The zone marked as number 1, external and negotiable change, is the most common change condition and it occurs when a source outside of the organization imposes a change or condition. In this situation, the organization is given latitude in implementing the change. Examples of this type of situation are broad policy shifts and organizational value statements or goals. The action to take involves describing the change in detail,

|  | Externally imposed | Internally imposed |
|---|---|---|
| Negotiable | 1 | 2 |
| Nonnegotiable | 3 | 4 |

Breaking the change into a two-dimensional set of considerations (internal/external and negotiable/nonnegotiable) helps provide context and frame the change.

1. An external-negotiable change is presented in terms of conditions/results, but the group needs to implement the actions.
2. An internal-negotiable change is where the group is initiating and implementing the change.
3. With an external-nonnegotiable change, the implementation must comply with the change as it is put forth to avoid a result of noncompliance.
4. An internal-nonnegotiable change is where the organization faces an immediate threat to itself or its members and a strong response is required.

**Figure 5.8**  Change conditions

explaining the benefits, articulating what will change and what will not, pointing out cost, and getting the stakeholders involved. There is also a need to listen to resistance and get agreement on specific actions and on roles and responsibilities.

2.  Internal and negotiable change occurs when the change creators and implementers are the same. This change generates the least resistance because it is initiated by the implementing group and it emerges from a perceived need to make something better. Examples include changes in work design, responsibilities, or groups. The action to take when facing this type of change involves gaining agreement on the conditions that require change and addressing the actual need for change. It is also important to gain a consensus regarding the causes that led to the current state, while keeping in mind that there are two primary causes to resistance: failing to acknowledge and work with the resistance, and moving forward toward implementing the change too quickly. There is therefore a need to involve the group in developing the change plan, identifying obstacles and resources, and installing a feedback process to monitor the implementation.

3. External and nonnegotiable change is demanding both regarding the implementation process, as well as the outcome. There is little room for variance, and it generates the most difficult resistance to overcome; but it is an easier type of change to implement. Examples include new regulations and legal statutes. Since employees have no input on why this change will be implemented, it is important to remind them of this reality. There is a need to explain why it is being implemented, define roles and responsibilities, and remove complexity as much as possible. Encourage people to ask questions; it is possible to reduce the impact from resistance by honoring the resistance and encouraging open expression of all the feelings about the change.

4. Internal and nonnegotiable change is less common to find. It is typically initiated through quick and unanimous consent, and in response to a clear, unanticipated, and unacceptable condition. Examples include a response to a safety risk or to illegal or unacceptable behavior. It is important to describe the existing condition or occurrence and ask for responses, while making sure that everyone in the group is aware of what has happened and what the impact is. There is a strong need to encourage an open discussion to allow airing a wide range of opinions. This should be followed by obtaining a consensus on the group's perception and on the remedy. Finally, ensure that everyone who would be affected is informed of the change.

## Gap Analysis

Gap analysis is designed to assess the distance between the current state that is being changed (or in need of change) and the future, desired state—that to be achieved. It may sound trivial to many, but to perform a gap analysis it is necessary to have the preconditions of understanding the current state and the future state firmly in place. The gap then essentially forms into the work (and sometimes project) that is to be performed in order to bridge the difference. It is important to have a realistic and sober read of the current state, as well as a meaningful and feasible future state. Failure to properly understand the current situation and what the pain points are, or aiming in the wrong direction for the future, will yield an incorrect or unrealistic gap.

Gap analysis can be performed formally, by identifying the difference between current state and future state capabilities, or informally, by thinking about the space between the current situation and the future goal.

Performing gap analysis is also about analyzing the organization's ability to initiate and manage the change effectively along a series of dimensions:

a. Understanding and articulating the change purpose
b. Successfully engaging the change and the power to go through it
c. The organization's and people's ability to learn new behaviors
d. Identifying and realizing a set of meaningful shared values and purpose

    e.  The capacity to engage in and effectively manage conflict

    f.  Being able to build a meaningful social contract to go through the change

Start the process of devising a strategy to bridge the gap. Then, review the gap against the needs, objectives, and constraints to establish a realistic roadmap to define, handle, and go through the change initiative.

## Readiness

With a better understanding of what lies ahead, it is time to perform a quick team readiness assessment for the change. Many people tend to confuse the need, urgency, or desires with *readiness*. The fact that there is a strong feeling about the need to go through a change does not mean that the resources are available to move forward—referring specifically to the team and the stakeholders. The exercise to go through involves asking a series of questions that can help assess the team's readiness for change. In the event that the team is not ready, they can: 1) not go through the change, 2) adjust it, or 3) break it into smaller and phased initiatives. The following sections contain lists of categories and questions to explore.

### Shared Sense of Purpose

- All team members understand the need for change
- There is a common understanding of the purpose and vision
- There is an understanding of the objectives and the change trying to be achieved
- There is a clear timeline for the objectives to be achieved

### Clear Roles and Responsibilities

- Team members and stakeholders have a clear understanding of their roles and responsibilities
- People understand their value and contribution toward achieving the goals
- Performance measures are in place
- People understand a realistic impact of risks, challenges, and issues on the initiative
- Critical success factors for the change are in place

### Team Processes

- Key milestones and decisions to be made are identified
- There are clear indicators of success
- Methods are in place to measure progress and meet goals
- Decision-making and escalation practices are in place
- Decision-making criteria, practices, and authority are defined
- There is a process to manage issues, assumptions, and risks
- There is a clear understanding of and a process for accountability

### Relationships

- Processes are in place for idea generation, feedback, issue management, and conflict
- There is commitment to the change effort
- Norms and behaviors are in place for working together to build and support trust, open communication, and participation
- Clear progress measures and integration points are in place
- Interlocking with other initiatives is established
- Responsibilities for integration and benefit realization are in place

## Post Initiative Review

Early in the initiative is the time to build a plan on how to capture meaningful lessons from the initiative, once it is complete. This is not about *traditional* lessons learned (to be performed throughout the initiative), and it is not about performing a post-implementation review (PIR)—which are both important and necessary. This is a look at the business case and the justification in an attempt to check whether it was the right thing to do and whether the right approach was taken. After the transition, and after the project is complete and the change is implemented, there is a need to look at what worked, what didn't work, why the organization is at this point, and whether this was the intended destination—in order to learn what can be done differently next time. What makes this different from a traditional lessons learned process is the need to maintain a more strategic and high-level (or organizational) view, as opposed to the tactical nature of most lessons learned exercises.

It is necessary to check whether the organization can label the initiative as a success from the organization's perspective. It is primarily the sponsor's role to check whether or not it was the right thing to do, whether the right approach was taken, and whether a similar approach should be pursued the next time. The main question to focus on is: with the current knowledge, should the same thing have to be done again, would it be done the same way? Even for initiatives that end up delivering their intended value, it is important to perform this exercise.

The PIR was first used by the military. It is a structured approach for reflecting on the work of a group and identifying strengths, weaknesses, and areas of improvement in an attempt to maximize their effectiveness in their working process. It can be a formal process (facilitated) or an informal discussion (group leading itself). The main questions to consider include:

- Why was the organization here?
- What was expected to happen?
- What actually happened?
- What was the approach taken? Were the goals achieved?
- What approach could have been better?
- What was done that was effective? What made it effective?

- What was done that was ineffective? What made it ineffective?
- What can be done differently the next time in work groups/teams to improve group/team performance?

Note that the questions may seem somewhat pedantic, but it is critical to address each one thoroughly.

## Working *On* or *In* the Business

This is less of an assessment and more about helping sponsors check to what extent they add value in their role. In a recent initiative, a senior stakeholder who was acting as a sponsor received a performance appraisal that had many *opportunities*, which was the HR department's way of implying that there was room for improvement in one's performance. The opportunities were in the area of leading and driving change in the organization. As it turned out, this individual used to have a strategic role in the organization and she performed it very well. She drove change and created tremendous value for the organization until she was assigned a series of several tactical portfolios that ended up consuming the majority of her time. Although she performed her work as described and delivered above the expectations on her tactical objectives, the strategic ones got pushed aside, and the optics around her value creation turned negative. This was a textbook example of how work volume and capacity issues end up consuming many people's time and casting shadows about their ability to add meaningful value for their organizations. In short, the individual mentioned before still delivered value for her organization, but she was working *in* the business, rather than *on* the business. She was working on tactical and more mundane elements, as opposed to the visible, strategic, and *driving* items.

Leaders, and specifically sponsors, need to make a distinction between working *on* and *in* a business, and set blocks of time to allow themselves to add the more strategic value creation associated with working *on* the business. It is easy to drown under the high volume of work created by working *in* the business, and to be consumed and overwhelmed by it. Further, many people end up using working *in* the business as an excuse for not working *on* the business.

### Working On the Business

This includes setting strategic direction, transforming systems, identifying new opportunities, causing creative tension, defining a direction, addressing creative problem solving, defining a desired state, changing and transforming, and setting a vision. It is ambiguous and it may reach into unchartered territory.

### Working In the Business

Working *in* the business includes operating the business *as is*, implementing strategy, servicing current lines of business and customers, and keeping things running smoothly. It is more mechanical and time-consuming and necessary for efficiency.

# THE NEXT CHANGE AND WHY ORGANIZATIONS KEEP FAILING TO MEET THEIR OBJECTIVES

Kotter's finding that 80% of change initiatives fail to deliver on their objectives was staggering at the time when it was first identified (in the 1990s), and it is even more surprising to find that number is higher today. With all of the knowledge, techniques, tools, and concepts that have been developed in both change and project management, one would think that an improving trend would show in the rate of successful initiatives. It therefore begs the question of why impactful gains are not being made—and there are several potential causes.

## The Way We Measure

Things are measured differently; the objectives and challenges today are more aggressive than ever before.

## More Initiatives

There are many more initiatives, projects, challenges, and opportunities today than ever before due to the faster pace of change and the growing list of needs. It can therefore look as if things are improving in the way they are done, but the improved tools and techniques do not equate with improved overall results.

## Playing Catch Up

The processes and techniques lag behind the needs and they often play catch up by addressing yesterday's needs for tomorrow's challenges. Necessity continues to be the source of most innovation. When it comes to products and services, there is an effort to constantly try to innovate, but by nature, when it comes to processes and methodologies, there is never a specific time to do the right thing. Therefore, businesses are reactive and often introduce new ways of doing things only when forced to and when the old ways simply will not stand anymore.

## Methodologies in Silos

The methodologies that come to support our needs are developed and applied in silos and in almost complete isolation from each other. Project management, change management, agile, business analysis, and other approaches and methodologies keep picking up on leadership concepts and evolving, but they mostly evolve within themselves. For example, project management and business analysis are supposed to work in full collaboration with each other, but they do not. In my book, *Effective PM-BA Role Collaboration* (J. Ross Publishing, 2015), I addressed the matter and introduced a series of concepts on how to improve the working relationship between the PM and the business analyst (BA) and how to promote both disciplines in collaboration.

Unfortunately, most organizations fail to provide the setup and the message to enable such collaboration; the result often suppresses the BA's effort and leads to product-related challenges downstream. In my third and most recent book *Agile Business Analysis* (J. Ross Publishing, 2017), I expressed a connection between agile and business analysis—two disciplines that have grown around the same time frame but have almost systematically failed to integrate. In fact, in most environments, when I mention the need to incorporate business analysis skills (more specifically, a role for the BA), I face resistance because the majority of agile methods (specifically Scrum) tend to ignore the role and the work the BA would perform. We need to introduce more cross-discipline collaboration in organizations to realize the benefits these methodologies and approaches offer.

## Back to Project and Change

Project management is the (tactical) means to achieve the strategic goals that the change identifies and mandates. It is therefore imperative that project and change management are integrated together. If project management is done properly, it essentially addresses the change side (e.g., through communications, stakeholder engagement, and visioning). It is also clear that most projects fail to address various key aspects, which in most cases include the key success factors to manage change. Communication and stakeholder engagement are two of these elements that are critical for change success, and yet they are also easily dropped. Since there are fewer tangible deliverables associated with these two elements, it is easy to ignore them and clear the way for more *urgent* and tangible deliverables—such as requirements, schedules, and budgets. However, without sufficient and effective communication and stakeholder engagement, any progress being made may lack the foundation for success in the form of stakeholder buy-in. If performed properly, project integration management (the Knowledge Area per PMI[9]) is where PMs need to focus on change management.

## The Big Picture

The message that most organizational leadership gives is to focus primarily on short-term wins, which in turn prevents PMs, change practitioners, and even sponsors from focusing on the big picture, long-term benefits, and overall organizational benefits. The result is that solutions are not properly integrated into the operations of the organization or they lack context for the long term. The result may help individual projects deliver and get recognized, but as evident in Kotter's 80% failure findings—it does not really serve the organization as intended.

### *Re-freezing* Change for the Next Change

Another root-cause issue of change initiatives starts with failing to position the change and its benefits in a way that can be integrated with the ongoing strategy and the operation of the organization. This is then exacerbated by a failure to deliver the change in such a way that positions the organization to benefit long term and then to *refreeze* the new state in such a way that can easily enable the start of the next change.

A few actions are required to make sure change benefits are realized and that the change is done in such a way that enables the next change to take off (see Table 5.6). As expected, if the current change is managed properly, it is likely to provide

**Table 5.6** Actions to enable the next change

| Actions to Help Enable the Next Change | Details |
|---|---|
| Business case | Ensure clear justification and feasibility for the current change (emotional, rational, and tangible). This will help in going through the change and to evaluate the extent of success once it is completed. |
| Expectations | Set clear and transparent expectations. Make sure stakeholders realize that it will not be quick, simple, and cheap to implement. Through the change, with effective leadership and a clear plan, achieve buy-in and handle resistance. |
| Leadership | The change leaders need to first and foremost serve as role models. Clear and strong sponsorship, along with role definition, are critical. |
| Manage the transition | Perform communication and reinforcement activities in context of the change's pace, stakeholder needs, and the events around you. Prioritize opportunities against each other and make adjustments based on the interlocking events across initiatives and on the sense of urgency within each opportunity (i.e., deadlines, impact, and visibility). Consider cross-initiative impact, coordination, and resource management; provide clear ownership on the change pieces; manage risks and account for them; establish awareness and processes toward continuous improvement. |
| Finish properly | Many sponsors declare a victory prematurely. Embed the change in the fabric of the organization and avoid diverting focus and commitment away too early. Integrate the change properly into operations and in alignment with strategy. Ensure proper handoff of the change. |
| Make it stick | Acknowledge lessons learned through a post-action review and a proper lessons learned process that goes back to the business case and views the strategic impact of the change results versus the intent. Question the reasoning for deciding on the change and the approach taken. |
| Continuous improvement | Investigate how to engage and involve employees throughout and over the long term and how to institutionalize best practices to capture the full benefit of the change and any future changes. |
| Follow-up | Reinforce, realize, and measure benefits to make the change stick. Check that there is a full realization of the current stage in the new status quo so it is possible to consider the upcoming needs realistically. |

These are a series of actions to ensure organizational alignment and readiness for the next change. Most of them originate from the start of the current change and have a lot to do with the process of going through the current change. It is critical to complete the current change in such a way that enables the next one.

the context and the setup for the next change. Achieving the goals for the current change is not enough, though; it is also important to fully realize exactly where the initiative is in comparison to where it was intended to be, and also against where the sponsor *thinks* it is (these three may not be the same place). It is common that change initiatives fall short of their original intent, and it is more common that the extent of success and benefits that were actually realized are less than what was initially believed. These may result in a misconception as to the new position and capabilities of the organization and, accordingly, it may be tempting to think that things are ready, aligned, or in place for the next initiative. If we are starting further back than we thought, there is already going to be a gap between expectations and reality for the next change.

# KEY PERFORMANCE INDICATORS (KPIs) AND ANALYSIS TOOLS

One of the main challenges when trying to go through organizational change is that many initiatives are not about producing tangible products. Whether it is the nature of the change or the nature of the business, when it comes to producing results that are nontangible, it is hard to measure success. This problem also takes place in organizations in which their core business is service oriented. Even when the product is more tangible (i.e., process improvement), it is often hard to articulate the benefits even if the intended product was produced. For that, there is a need to access business analysis skills that will support the effort of identifying service performance levels and measurements that are meaningful, along with providing a clear indication on whether success is delivered and to what extent.

## The Change Process

In order to introduce any type of improvement, start by identifying, analyzing, and articulating the current state. The findings of such a study will provide an understanding of how things are currently done; the strengths, weaknesses, challenges, and areas where there may be an opportunity to improve; or other areas that pose threats. The next step would be to define the future state, identify the areas of improvement, and determine how things should be performed after the change is complete. The vision exercise from earlier in this chapter is an important step in this process. Once a current and a future state are established, the gap is identified and analyzed and the change strategy forms. The following is a review of a series of tools that can help in the process:

- *Business needs, goals, and objectives*—the business need is the problem or opportunity of strategic importance that the organization faces; it serves as a high-level strategic requirement that comes to state a business objective and the intended impact of the solution. The business need may originate from various sources, including from the top down—where there is a need to achieve a strategic goal; from middle management—where there might be an emerging need for additional information to make informed decisions or to perform additional functions to meet business objectives; from the bottom up—through a problem or opportunity with the current state of a process, a function, or a system; or from external drivers, including customer demand, market conditions, or competition.

- *SWOT analysis*—this exercise needs to go beyond merely identifying strengths, weaknesses (internal), and opportunities and threats (external). It needs to help us formulate strategies that help leverage the *intersections* between strengths and opportunities/threats and, in turn, weaknesses and opportunities/threats. SWOT analysis also helps distinguish between symptoms and problems. It is imperative to realize what the problem actually is, so that scarce resources are not wasted in an effort to fix symptoms rather than the actual problem.

- *Generic problem analysis*—this is a technique to brainstorm a list of answers to the question: *what is the problem*? It then helps define who is impacted, who might resist the solution, and what the magnitude of the impact will be. Next, there is a need to separate the real problems from the symptoms and the proposed solutions. The goal is to ensure that a real problem is identified that has potential multiple solutions and that at least one of the solutions will actually eradicate the related symptoms. This helps facilitate the brainstorming process for solution options and yields a list of several potential solutions.

- *Fishbone diagram*—this old tool (articulated around 1945 by Dr. Kaoru Ishikawa and subsequently forgotten until getting "rediscovered" in the mid-1990s) helps with finding the root causes of a problem. This tool intends to lead to a solution where the *disease* is eliminated. It seeks to discover and treat the conditions that led to the symptom in the first place, as opposed to troubleshooting where the effort is only on trying to alleviate the symptoms of a problem. Keep in mind that the root cause of a problem is often hidden under the surface and is hard to find; hence, the need for this tool and thinking process.

- *Causal factor flow chart*—this is essentially a flow chart where a chain of events is examined in order to look for the points in the process where decisions were made or where there were opportunities to change the course of action to prevent the problem.

- *Benchmarking*—compares organizational practices of best-in-class firms; assesses how these organizations achieve results; focuses on strategies, processes, and operations; and leads the process to learn and adapt based on the findings.

- *Problem/opportunity statement*—once the problem has been analyzed, it is necessary to try to document exactly what the problem is. Usually the problem statement is included in subsequent documents such as the business case, the scope definition document, or the as-is business processes, and it includes the impact on company goals. The statement needs to be concise and specific.

- *Constraints*—limitations that must be identified so we know what choices may be restricted on our way to the future state. Constraints can include but are not limited to: time, funding, personnel, facilities, bandwidth, capacities, and management limitations. The various available solutions to accomplish the objectives are analyzed to determine the best, most technically sound, and most viable solution.
- *Decision criteria*—decision criteria can be quantitative (objective and expressed as a number or quantity) or qualitative (subjective, where the characteristics can be described but might not be able to be numerically measured). Decision criteria may come from previous business cases or projects, goals, and objectives identified for the current initiative, business strategy documents, or the sponsor and other important stakeholders.
- *Acceptance and evaluation criteria*—typically used when only one possible solution is being evaluated and are generally expressed as a pass or fail. These are minimum requirements that must be met and, if not, the solution option will not be considered. Evaluation criteria are used to compare multiple solutions or solution components that allow for a range of possible scores. These are requirements that will be used to rate multiple solutions and once they are rated, recommendations are made.
- *Generating alternative solutions*—these alternatives can provide a wide range of options, one of which can be to do nothing. To make the process easier, a decision matrix can be utilized where the criteria are prioritized, the measurements for each criteria are determined, data are obtained, and the matrix can be analyzed to recommend the best solution.

## Back to KPIs and Solution Evaluation

When solutions do not have built-in performance measures, stakeholders need to work with BAs to determine and collect the measures that will best reflect the performance of a solution. The performance of a future-state solution (and by saying solution, the reference is not only to a tool or technology but to any type of process, service, or result to be produced) can be measured in multiple ways, including objectives, processes, or KPIs.

Once the best method to measure the success of an initiative or a solution is identified, it will be necessary to look at the data and analyze whether or not the solution is achieving/delivering the intended value. Analyze the data by trying to answer the following questions:

a. Is the solution meeting the (strategic) goals and objectives of the organization?
b. Is the solution meeting the targets identified in the metrics and KPIs (project goals and process goals)?

    c.  How risky is the solution? Is it working within the constraints? Are there risks that it will go outside of those boundaries?

    d.  Are there other targets that have been identified that the solution is intended to address (portfolio targets, regulation targets, etc.)?

KPIs intend to measure the performance of solutions, solution components, and other matters of interest to stakeholders. A good indicator has six characteristics:

1. *Clear*—precise and unambiguous
2. *Relevant*—appropriate to the concern/issue
3. *Economical*—available at reasonable cost
4. *Adequate*—provides a sufficient basis on which to assess performance
5. *Quantifiable*—can be independently validated
6. *Trustworthy and credible*—based on evidence and research

Not all factors can be measured directly and proxies can be used when data for direct indicators are not available or when it is not feasible to collect it at regular intervals. For example, in the absence of a survey of client satisfaction, an organization might use the proportion of all contracts renewed as an indicator.

Once the KPIs are in place, it will be necessary to assess the solution limitations that may be directly linked to the product, service, or result that was implemented. Then perform the following steps:

- Identify internal dependencies and any interrelated components of the solution that may be limiting the solution performance
- Investigate and identify solution problems by examining instances where the outputs from the solution are below an acceptable expected level
- Finally, perform an impact assessment using the information from the previous two steps, review any identified problems, and assess the effect they may be having on the organization

The next move is to identify enterprise limitations by looking at factors that may impact the solution—with a focus on the following:

- *Cultural assessment*—check whether stakeholders want the project to be successful by assessing stakeholders' beliefs, values, and norms, keeping in mind that this is a subjective assessment
- *Operational assessment*—check if stakeholders and the organization are ready to make use of the solution, including whether stakeholders are trained, whether policies and procedures have been updated, and whether the resources have been put into place to support the solution

Make sure to look for ways to define, measure, and articulate every aspect of the performance. Even if the indicators are loosely defined or hard to measure, it is critical to develop the ability to measure them so that they can be tracked and managed. Any type of improvement must start with the ability to articulate and understand how things are currently done; it is followed by what things should be like in the desired future state; and only then will the gap be revealed so that a plan for it can be made.

## *"PLUS ÇA CHANGE, PLUS C'EST LA MÊME CHOSE"*

French novelist Jean-Baptiste Alphonse Karr once wrote, "Plus ça change, plus c'est la même chose," which translates to *what goes around comes around*. This could have referred to change management, as well. Changing an organization is difficult and painful and doing so effectively while minimizing pain means having leaders who communicate the vision and walk the talk—leaders who realize the importance and the magnitude of changing organizational culture and people's attitudes.

There is another analogy that stands out for me when it comes to organizational change. Earlier in my career, when I mentioned to a colleague that I was involved in an organizational change, she told me that change management was like a marshmallow: you poke it with your finger and it moves; you poke more and it makes a dent; then you start seeing how easy it is to alter the marshmallow, so you poke your finger into it all the way and the marshmallow wraps around it and all of the sudden you are surrounded by marshmallow and you cannot move or get out. This analogy serves as a reminder that no change is fast or easy and if things appear to be too good to be true, they probably are.

Gareth Morgan, a world-renowned author, researcher, and Professor Emeritus at the Schulich School of Business, York University, articulated another interesting thought about organizational change—the 85:15 concept. He imagined it as an iceberg, but his focus was on the amount of effort being spent under the waterline where the bulk of the iceberg lies. According to him, most of the time and effort (85%) was spent working on the 15% of the iceberg visible above the waterline. This is in opposite proportion to what should be done. This disproportionate effort, as illustrated in Figure 5.9, serves as a major challenge in many environments.

## FRAMING THE CHANGE

There is a need to properly frame the change, beyond the scoping discussion that was mentioned earlier in this chapter. Framing is about identifying whether the change being undertaken is a shallow change that is more structural by nature (e.g., adding new technologies) or a deep change that is more transformational by nature, and hence, more difficult to manage. Few shallow changes are truly shallow since most changes involve transformation. With that said, few managers of shallow change attempt to address the deeper aspects of the change, and this is another significant contributor to the reality of why so many change initiatives fail. The need to frame the change and manage it accordingly takes us to the

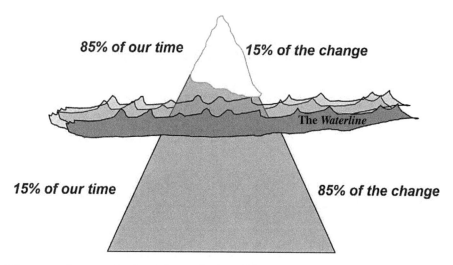

It is easy to focus on the level above the waterline since it is visible and accessible. However, there is a tendency to spend too much time and effort on that level instead of looking below the waterline where most of the action is needed. The result of the disproportionate amount of time and effort allocation leads to an 80% failure rate in change initiatives. Because most of the needed change is below the water level, it may not be seen and it is possible that no one even knows that it is there.

**Figure 5.9**   Morgan's 85:15 ratio

importance of visioning and to the need to focus on managing the transition—that time and space from when the change is announced, until the new, future state is achieved.

An important part of moving from the vision to an actual change initiative is the change charter. There will be a more detailed discussion of the charter in the context of project change (in Chapter 6), but the idea is to take the level of understanding of the change initiative and organize it into a short and concise document that mandates the initiative and helps convey that understanding to the various stakeholders. The charter captures the reason to change (the why) and provides context on the degree of choice about whether to change. This will help to articulate and assess the present in terms of the future, while leading to a better understanding of the work to be done and how to manage the transition state.

## Four Frames

To understand stakeholders, culture, and resistance, there is yet another iceberg metaphor that is helpful. Figure 5.10 helps demonstrate the different layers or frames of change. It is necessary to be able to define what frame of change is being

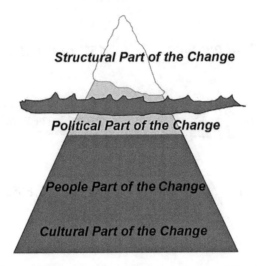

The four frames of change help us better understand the depth that the change initiative will reach.

**Figure 5.10**    The frames iceberg

faced, so the change can be managed accordingly, based on its type. The sponsor needs to drive the process of spending time analyzing who the stakeholders of the change are. The analysis naturally gravitates to who is important in the organization or who thinks they should have a say about the change initiative; but the main focus of the stakeholder analysis should be toward those who have direct connection to the common goal of the change initiative. It will help to identify hot spots of where resistance is going to come from so it is possible to better understand the lay of the political landscape.

### *The Structural Frame*

Above the water is the structural aspect of the change where there are many elements and moving parts, but most of them are tangible and can be broken down into smaller, more manageable components. Most of these items can be captured through charts, graphs, reports, meetings, and budgets and they have a lot to do with rules, efficiencies, money, timelines, goals, policies, and procedures. The items in this frame address how to achieve common goals and how to conduct ourselves in a rational and objective manner. This frame is also about identifying accountability, responsibility, and resource acquisition and allocation. In this frame, an understanding of the interests is gained through stakeholder analysis, rules are established, and the details of the goals and plans are communicated.

## The Political Frame

At the waterline is the political frame, which is about *interests*. One of the challenges with this frame is that it may fluctuate and move both above and below that level. It is important to try to bring most of this frame above the waterline so things in it become more visible. In this frame, it is necessary to know the stakeholders and what their interests are, which stakeholders have power (and what type) and how they (can) exercise their power, how the allocation of scarce resources and the diverse interests create conflict, and how stakeholders can influence the decision-making process. The reality in virtually every organization is that there will be competition over resources (not to mention having a shortage of key resources) and each stakeholder will act based on their own interests and needs. This leads to the realization that the most important decisions in an organization are around the allocation of resources—based on prioritization, portfolio and strategy considerations, and senior management guidance.

Since the political frame sits right at the water level, some of the interests can be seen that are related to the organization's resources and positions. Managing these interests is complicated because of the negotiations, power bases, relationships, coalitions, and alliances. The reference to the word "complicated" was also made in the structural frame section earlier where the distinction was made between *complicated* (multiple moving parts that can be broken down into smaller, easier-to-manage items) and *complex* (something that cannot be broken down and that has to be dealt with as a whole). The below-the-water portion of the political frame is invisible, where the interests cannot be seen. This part of the frame has to do with people's complex needs, desires, values, beliefs, and dreams. Managing these interests is complex; people's motives are complex, diverse, and many times contradictory. The needs for the initiative are often unclear and difficult to articulate—even to the sponsors themselves—and their beliefs may be incorrect. Overall, the sponsors are not clear statements of the interests, but rather a complex and often confused manifestation of them. As a result, it is necessary to sort out what is actually known, what is believed to be known, and what cannot be known for certain, so that the complicated and complex can be managed effectively. It is also necessary to gain some understanding of what *we do not know that we do not know*.

## The People Frame

Moving further under the water level takes us to the people frame and this is where it is possible to begin to examine the origins of resistance. As we get further below the water level, things tend to get progressively complex. Deeper under the water level, the necessary skills for sponsors are more related to being part sociologist, part anthropologist, and part psychic. People typically have a need to know and it is easy to get frustrated by the lack of certainty, the lack of analytical proof, the lack of clear and linear reasoning, and very little scientific theorem.

The people frame helps us learn about whom to be careful of and what drives their adversarial view of the change or of the method being used to carry it out. It is during the transition (the neutral zone) that people generally get disoriented, disillusioned, and dispirited and go through a defensive retreat where they hold on to the current way of doing things, while feeling angry.

## The Cultural/Symbolic Frame

A deep dive under the water is where the cultural frame can be found. It can also be referred to as the symbolic frame; and this is where the change becomes the real deal—a transformational change. In the symbolic frame, what is most important is not what actually happens but rather the meaning given to it. Culture is the glue that holds the organization together; and people create symbols, stories, and rituals to increase predictability, reduce confusion, and find a source of direction. The symbolic frame is completely in the territory of the subjective and perceptual because it is all about the meaning that individuals give to an event or object. It is therefore imperative that senior management spend sufficient time managing the meaning and not just the tactics.

When going through a change that touches on the cultural aspect of an organization, it is necessary to check the symbols that are important to the people of that organization and the stories that people tell. Then explore the meaning of these stories, what they tell about the organization, and what is revealed as being important to the people. The symbolic frame is also about what the symbols or artifacts of success and failure are in the organization—and what symbolic *land mines* are likely to be encountered. From here, there will be a clearer change path that can be followed as implementation begins.

The breakdown of the change initiative into frames can also help us identify the critical factors for the success of the initiative, including what new skills, processes, techniques, and tools the people will need to learn. With this knowledge, it is possible to learn how different these skills and tools are from what is currently possessed and what types of concerns and anxieties the newness may introduce. In turn, it will help to determine what needs to be designed into the change process in order to ensure that the right thing will be done the right way, the first time.

A correlation can be seen between the degree of change and the impact on the culture. Figure 5.11 helps show this correlation, and with that information, it is possible to anticipate the amount of expected resistance and the chances of delivering success. Remember, it is important for people to give things meaning, beyond what is actually said or done. This frame helps focus on what is done to manage the meaning of the change.

The frames should also be looked at, and they will appear in a different context depending on the current status of the change process (i.e., beginning, middle, or end). The main questions to ask for each stage are whether there is a consensus about the position and what people are seeing about the change, its progress, and its direction. The answers will serve as a guide toward what is needed in order to build commitment.

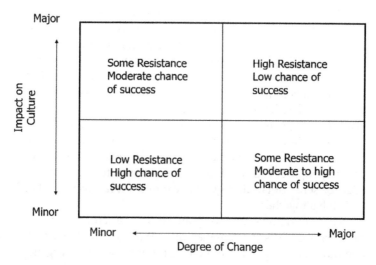

There is a clear and direct correlation between the degree of change and the impact of the change on the culture. From these two factors, it is possible to realize the degree of resistance and the chance of success that should be expected.

**Figure 5.11**    The degree of change and its impact on culture[10]

# RESISTANCE

There is an old Chinese proverb that says: "When the winds of change blow, some people build walls, and others build windmills." Resistance is likely in virtually every change initiative, yet it is one of the most difficult items to plan for and one of the most challenging to manage. The result—resistance may take down our change initiative. In order to achieve an equilibrium, it is important to understand where the resistance comes from and what the forces are around the initiative—both the driving forces (mainly complicated, above the waterline) and the resisting forces (the complex ones below the water). While going through the very volatile and vulnerable period of the transition, resistance serves as one of the most potent dangers. Even with confidence in the potential benefits of what is being done and even if a clear plan and direction exists, people's resistance (depending on who resists, why, and how) may spell the difference between success and failure. Without resistance, a fairly smooth ride can be expected, but it is resistance (like risk) and how it is handled that will make the difference.

To understand resistance, it is necessary to first realize where it comes from. Kotter identified seven reasons for resisting change, and they are often seen in most change attempts:

1. *Fear of the unknown*—in many organizations there is not much information revealed about the change beyond the initial announcement. A

significant source of resistance is a lack of knowledge. If people do not know what exactly is going to change, they are more likely to resist.

2. *A lack of good information*—people often do not know what awaits them on the other side of the change. Sometimes there is a lack of clear information, but on many occasions, management fails to communicate to people what to expect, or to provide them with the information about what it takes to deal with the future state.

3. *Fear of loss*—people love their comfort zone. They know how things are, they know how to do their work, and they feel comfortable with it. A change, even if it provides a great promise, may also bring with it a fear of loss: people are afraid of losing their status, stature, recognition, knowledge, or sense of familiarity. The fear of loss may also be related to losing their job altogether.

4. *No sense of urgency*—not everyone knows the same about the change and not everyone feels the same about it. With different levels of knowledge and buy-in among different people, different senses of urgency should be expected. This misalignment may cause confusion and frustration and it may unravel any effort toward progress.

5. *A lack of resources*—resources (human, financial, and others) end up being a major factor in virtually every change initiative or project. It is not uncommon to chronically fail to manage resources effectively when it comes to planning, utilization, allocation, and sharing. A lack of capacity management, conflicting priorities, and double dipping (where resources are allocated toward an initiative in addition to their full-capacity *day job*) all contribute to the siloed mentality in resource management—making this area the biggest wildcard in the planning process. Time and money constraints are known, but often the extent of our other resource constraints are not.

6. *Bad timing*—this sounds more like an excuse than a true reason for resisting change, but it is still a common one. Bad timing may simply be on a personal level, where people are engaged in something else that consumes their attention; but it may also be on the organizational level—when two initiatives interlock with each other, leading to competition over resources, priorities, or other bandwidth elements. With the lack of cross-project and cross-initiative planning, and (on a higher level) a lack of proper enterprise planning, there is little visibility as to competing priorities and limited consideration as to how to stagger initiatives so they do not compete with each other. Bad timing is also the result of change saturation or change fatigue—people are tired of all the changes that are intertwined with each other and any new initiative is simply viewed as bad timing.

7. *Habit*—this may be a combination of any of the previous reasons or a reason on its own, but habit is a common cause for resistance. People do not want their familiar environments, processes, and routines to change, even if there is a promise that things will get better afterward.

## Grouping the Causes of Resistance

Most people who resist the change will not announce their resistance. They may actually express support toward the initiative, but their actions will show differently. When it comes to handling resistance, it is not only important to focus on what happened and what is about to happen, but also about the meaning that is given to it; and here too, management (and particularly the sponsor) needs to manage the meaning. Everyone should not be allowed to interpret things through their own frames, but rather the symbolic elements should be managed in order to create a collective sense of meaning. People give meanings to things from the time they are babies (e.g., the teddy bear or any other favorite toy or stuffed animal) and all throughout their lives (e.g., the corner office and other status symbols).

It is safe to say that in most work situations, people do not feel safe to begin with—let alone when change is introduced. For example, a few years ago I witnessed an incident at the Toronto airport, and not too long afterward it was described almost play-by-play by Simon Sinek on a TED Talk—as if we had witnessed the same thing. As a flight was boarding, the call was made for zone 1 passengers only. An individual tried to board, even though he was in zone 4. The airline employee who was boarding the passengers raised her voice at that person and shamed him in front of everyone. As a result, someone asked her why she was treating people almost like cattle, and her response was very surprising. She said, "Because if I do not follow the rules, I could get fired." It got me to thinking that many times when service providers mistreat customers, it is not for any other reason but for the employee fearing for their own job if they do not follow the rules.

This story about employees feeling unsafe in their own positions goes back to the discussion about leadership. Leadership should not be about headcount, but more about *heart count*; quoting Simon Sinek, "If you had hard times in your family, would you ever consider laying off one of your children?" Leadership is about choices and not only about exerting authority, but about looking at the people involved, setting an example, inspiring them, and leading them; and when the followers see the conduct and sacrifices made by their leaders, they will reciprocate.

### Signs of Resistance

No matter the reason for someone's resistance, it is important to detect it—and that starts by looking for the signs of resistance and understanding its origin. The following list includes *common signs of resistance*, which may include one or more of the following behaviors:

- *Criticism*—people may criticize the situation, how things are being done, or criticize others. Criticism is a common sign of resistance and it can be spotted when the criticism is almost just for the sake of criticism; those who offer blind criticism do not look for a resolution and often they do not even look for answers. Even if their criticism is addressed, it will not satisfy them and they will find something else to focus their criticism on.

- *Blaming and finding fault*—these items are related to criticism and can be spotted when people look for someone or something to blame. Here too, there is no search for answers, reasoning, or resolutions, but rather it is an attempt to shift the focus, stall, or shirk responsibility in a way that will create a distraction or provide an excuse for why not or why not now.
- *Loading on and appealing to others' fears*—there is such a thing as constructive criticism that is made to help, support, or alleviate concerns, but then there is criticism that is the exact opposite. And many times, people look for partners to rant about the change with, and this often becomes a contest about who can come up with a more pessimistic outlook or who can instill more fear in others. There is nothing constructive about it and it just lures people into this turbulence with no resolution or positive outlook.
- *Distortion, exaggeration, or selective use of facts*—it is easy to take things out of context and overemphasize certain numbers, information, or facts. This often leads to concern, fear, and even panic. This is not about lying or about making up false information, but rather it is about focusing on specific elements from the big picture, overstating them, isolating them, or implying that the most extreme scenario is going to take place.
- *Ridiculing and intimidation*—whether it is ridiculing the situation, the way things are being done, or certain people, this is all part of a similar *technique* to change course and slow down, derail, or stop the change process. It creates a distraction and takes the wind out of any momentum that might be in the making.
- *Sabotage and blocking*—here people take things up a notch when they actively try to disrupt and damage the initiative. It may be under the disguise of misunderstanding, confusion, or surprise, but the intent is to stop what is being done at almost any cost. It is hard to blame these people outright for attempting to sabotage things and it is probably not going to help with mitigating their resistance, but it is important to work with them on the reasons for their actions.
- *Manipulation, undermining, and starting rumors*—these are behaviors that are a little more subtle than outright sabotage, but they can be just as damaging, if not more. Many times, it is hard to detect these behaviors or their impact and by the time they are realized, it may be too late.

The following list includes *passive signs of resistance*:

- *Agreeing, but with no follow through*—this is a common sign. It is hard to detect and difficult to handle since the resisting individual does not express any resistance. He/she actually agrees with the decisions and actions and is even agreeable during conversations—except that they do not follow through on the decisions or on their commitments. It is difficult to realize that these people are actually resisting the change initiative since they seem positive and agreeable; and by that, the sponsor's guard is lowered because they tend to look for more obvious signs of resistance. When this behavior is demonstrated, it is necessary to resort to other techniques to find those individuals before it's too late.

- *Avoiding*—this can also be thought of, essentially, as stalling. They may do things slower than they should, procrastinate, or simply not do their part. They will not rock the boat with questions and doubts, but they will leverage their position to stop the change initiative.
- *Pulling back*—some people will have knowledge or information or they may be in a position of power, but they will simply take a step back, not interfere or help, maybe even withhold information, and allow the initiative to go sideways. If asked about it, they will usually hide behind their inaction or blame it on not knowing, not seeing, or not realizing what was going on.

## Positive and Negative Resistance

When looking for signs to help recognize resistance, another distinction that can be made is between the signs of positive and negative resistance. Positive resistance is when people challenge the change, and although it is still resistance, it is good when these signs can be detected. It means that people are not settled with the change and that they are exploring their options by challenging it to see if they get the answers that they are looking for. Some common signs of positive resistance include the following:

1. *Open-minded questioning*—when people inquire about the change with a genuine intent to learn about it rather than asking questions that are aimed at judging it.
2. *Disagreeing with the solution*—this is when people do not agree with what is being done or how it is being accomplished. They do not express resistance to the notion of the change, but they do not like where it ends up pointing. They try to challenge and explore what the change will look like.
3. *Lobbying for alternative solutions*—this is similar to number two on this list; it is not an indication that people feel negatively about the change, but they want to see what other options there are that they may like better.
4. *Questioning the need or challenging the vision*—this type of resistance is still positive since people may want to take another look at why the change is necessary or its general direction.

Positive resistance can give people a good feeling about the change, answers they are looking for, or just the sense that they are included and that their needs are considered. Many times, these types of signs are invitations for us to engage with them and provide assurances.

Negative resistance is when people resist almost just for the sake of resistance. They do not like what the change represents or where it goes and they are not interested in learning more about the change. Many of these people can be viewed as lost causes when it comes to converting them into supporters; yet it is still necessary to look for ways to reduce the resistance—or at least reduce their behaviors or their impact. Some common signs of negative resistance include the following:

1. *Being too busy*—people will find ways to make themselves look and even feel busy so they cannot attend to anything related to the change. This includes being too busy to attend meetings or to handle their assigned duties.

2. *Starting another initiative*—creating a distraction is another common type of negative resistance. People will start another initiative that will consume their time and attention so they do not or cannot deal with the current change initiative. It can be hard to argue with people who are engaged in some other important activity and ask them to drop it. Another way to create a distraction is the introduction of a phantom initiative, where people do not actually have another initiative that consumes their time, but they make up a story about how busy they are with this or that. Often, being "busy" is a distraction for people from attending to things they prefer not to.

3. *Questioning the plan*—Monday morning quarterbacks appear in all sorts of forms, and one of them is when people question aspects of the change plan, including the budget, timelines, or resource plans, without offering a way to make them better.

4. *Ignoring the change initiative or encouraging others not to attend to the initiative or comply with commitments*—these people do not even go through the effort of making an excuse for their lack of time or focus; they simply ignore and, in some cases, try to get other people to also ignore the initiative, or at least slow it down.

## How Much Resistance Should Be Expected?

The amount of resistance will change based on multiple factors, including the organizational context, the circumstances, and the nature of the change. Additional factors include the stakeholders' style (as covered earlier with the DiSC discussion) and the amount and type of information provided. In most change situations, people's sentiments toward the change initiative can be broken down into three primary groups:

1. *Strong supporters and early adapters*—there will be some stakeholders who will strongly support the initiative. They may be part of it, they may be

the primary beneficiaries of it, or they may simply believe in it. This is not a large group of people, but they are ahead of the curve and already feeling the *warm and fuzzy* vision of the future, desired state. It is safe to say that they are on the other side of the change U-Curve. It is important to make sure that they continue to be content with what and how things are being done. It is also necessary to ensure that they do not drift toward a weaker level of support (or even toward becoming resisters); although, there should not be a disproportionate amount of time spent on satisfying their needs.

2. *The busy center*—most people will be on the fence. In most situations, this group consists of people who are *neutral* about the initiative, and even if not exactly neutral, they can be split into two groups, somewhat equal in size: the *lukewarm supporters* and the *lukewarm resisters*. The bulk of the effort should be spent on working with these large groups by communicating, supporting, clarifying, and informing them as required. The goal is to turn some of these people into strong supporters, reinforce the support of those who are already supportive, and gain more supporters from those who currently demonstrate weak resistance.

3. *Strong resisters*—there will be some people who will strongly resist (what is being done, how it is being done, or who the sponsors are and what they represent). Before even going through the reasons that fuel their resistance, it is necessary to remember that this is a small group. While it is natural to gravitate toward focusing on them more, it is beneficial to refrain from spending too much effort (and time) on trying to buy their support or to weaken their resistance. It is important to further analyze the source and cause of their resistance and engage them accordingly, depending on who they are and what source of power they have. If there is any hope of weakening their resistance, it is important to do so. In fact, just by engaging and working with them it is possible to develop a rapport that encourages working together and moving forward, now and in the future. However, with that in mind, it is crucial to not spend a disproportionate amount of time with them because it may send the wrong message. When other stakeholders (who may be supporters or weak resisters) realize that the bulk of your time is being spent on the strong resisters, they may realize it will be worth their time to resist too.

Figure 5.12 helps provide a generic demonstration of the expected ratio of supporters versus resisters.

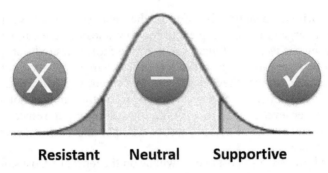

**Resistant    Neutral    Supportive**

Although there is no such thing as a *typical* situation, the number of supporters versus resisters should be expected to follow a normal distribution on a bell curve, where most people are in the center (weak supporters or weak resisters take up the middle two-thirds with one third on each side of the neutrality line). Approximately 16% could be considered early adapters who strongly support the initiative with the other approximately 16% strongly resisting. It is necessary to be cautious about spending a disproportionate amount of effort on the strong resisters so that the others do not get the wrong message that they should also resist.

**Figure 5.12**   Breakdown of change support and resistance rates

## Grouping the Reasons for Resistance

People will resist for various reasons and it is imperative to spot the symptoms, identify the resistance, figure out its source and reason, and deal with it. When it comes to strong resisters, there may not be any way to sway them from their resistance; thus, trying to reduce their resistance may be a lost cause. Therefore, it may be better to simply learn to live with their resistance. This could be through accepting their resistance, making concessions, bypassing them by dealing with other stakeholders, or by finding *messengers* that will help to further engage these stakeholders, if required.

The drivers or reasons for resistance (with the various symptoms, signs, and behaviors) stem mainly from three sources:

1. *A lack of awareness*—when people do not know what goes on or what will happen as a result of the change, they are more likely to resist.
2. *A lack of knowledge/ability*—when people do not know what it will take to deal with the new, future state or how they are going to deal with the new reality, they are likely to resist. They want to know how they will do their work afterward.
3. *A lack of desire*—this category is all about resistance because people may simply refuse to accept the new state.

Figure 5.13 shows the breakdown of the resistance drivers by group. The largest group will contain those who lack awareness about the change, followed by those

Similar to the fact that Tylenol is not the remedy for all pains, all resistance cannot be dealt with by using an off-the-shelf consistent approach. Learning about the causes of and the reasons behind resistance will help to apply the right technique to deal with it. The reason for the triangular shape is that most resistance takes place due to lack of awareness, followed by concerns about not having the ability or knowledge to deal with the future state of the change initiative. Lack of desire, or refusal, accounts for the smallest portion of resistance.

**Figure 5.13**   Causes of resistance

who lack knowledge as to how to perform their work post change, and then those who simply refuse to accept the changing reality.

## Dealing with and Mitigating Resistance

Generally, doing the *right things* will help minimize resistance. What are the *right things*? These include proper change sponsorship, leadership, communication, engagement, a plan for the transition, and guidance. Although there are many different stakeholders with different styles, expectations, and personalities, and who are in different places on the change U-Curve, we need to make sure the following elements are addressed:

  a. *Explain the need for change*—this may need to be done in different ways for different stakeholders, but literally everyone must know about the need.
  b. *Provide information*—the information is about the status of the current state, the sense of urgency, the journey through the transition state, expectations about the future, and information about the future state.
  c. *Consult and negotiate*—people love to feel included and involved; they want to be in the loop, to be heard, and to be part of the decision-making process. While it is not always possible to keep everyone equally involved and included, it is still necessary to make an effort to consult and present

people with the options so they can express their concerns and negotiate the trade-offs.

d. *Offer support and provide training*—people are being taken out of their comfort zone and are expected to follow along into something that they may not be fully aware of yet or that they may not know how to handle with their current knowledge and skills. Thus, they need to be provided with assurances and the relevant knowledge to cope with the coming new reality.

e. *Involve people in the process*—make sure that people are not only informed, but that they also feel included as part of the considerations and decision-making process. People need to know that their needs, views, and opinions are heard and considered.

f. *Assess the team's readiness for change and anticipate employee reactions*—desire and need should not be confused with readiness. Check to make sure that the team is ready for the coming change and if they are not, take it into consideration and make the necessary adjustments (a team readiness tool and a set of questions were reviewed earlier in this chapter).

g. *Build trust and a sense of security through an investment into building commitment to the change*—trust is the first ingredient of every success story and it can be established only through the process of building commitment, participation, and engagement.

## More Specific Actions

We can take the three categories of *reasons for resistance* that was just listed in this chapter and identify a series of actions, per category, that should be considered when trying to deal with and mitigate change (see Table 5.7).

Overall, since people are looking for guidance, it is important to give it to them. There are three areas[11] to focus on, regardless of the type or origin of the initiative:

1. *Prepare*—provide an explanation as to why this is being done, reduce the uncertainty, and increase the sense of urgency by increasing the dissatisfaction of the current state of affairs.

2. *Lead*—come up with and communicate an inspiring vision, set meaningful milestones, energize, engage, and communicate.

3. *Involve*—empower people and leaders, make them part of the solution, reward those who adopt, and celebrate progress and victories.

Table 5.8 provides a list of additional approaches for dealing with change, along with situations where they can be applied and the pros and cons of each of these approaches.

**Table 5.7**   Specific action to handle resistance by category

| Resistance Category Type | Potential Actions and Remedies |
|---|---|
| Lack of awareness | Communication<br>Engagement |
| Lack of information, ability, or knowledge | Training<br>Support<br>Growth |
| Lack of desire; refusal | Involvement<br>Buy-in<br>Rewards and recognitions<br>Negotiation<br>Demonstration |

Realizing the origin of the resistance can help to determine which approach to take to reduce, mitigate, and address resistance. While actions can be useful across different categories, they have the most potent impact as per the category in which they are listed in this table.

**Table 5.8**   Methods for dealing with resistance to change[12]

| Approach | Commonly Used in Situations | Advantages | Drawbacks |
|---|---|---|---|
| Education + communication | Where there is a lack of information or inaccurate information and analysis | Once persuaded, people will often help with the implementation of the change. | Can be very time-consuming if lots of people are involved. |
| Participation + involvement | Where the initiators do not have all the information they need to design the change, and where others have considerable power to resist | People who participate will be committed to implementing change, and any relevant information they have will be integrated into the change plan. | Can be very time-consuming if participators design an inappropriate change. |
| Facilitation + support | Where people are resisting because of adjustment problems | No other approach works as well with adjustment problems. | Can be time-consuming, expensive, and still fail. |
| Negotiation + agreement | Where someone or some group will clearly lose out in a change, and where that group has considerable power to resist | Sometimes, it is a relatively easy way to avoid major resistance. | Can be too expensive in many cases if it alerts others to negotiate for compliance. |

*continued*

**Table 5.8**  *continued*

| Approach | Commonly Used in Situations | Advantages | Drawbacks |
|----------|----------------------------|------------|-----------|
| Manipulation + co-optation | Where other tactics will not work or are too expensive | It can be a relatively quick and inexpensive solution to resistance problems. | Can lead to future problems if people feel manipulated. |
| Explicit + implicit coercion | Where speed is essential and the change initiators possess considerable power | It is speedy and can overcome any kind of resistance. | Can be risky if it leaves people mad at the initiators. |

Each of the approaches listed here is associated with common situations to apply it, along with pluses and minuses. Note that even the most effective approaches will have some negatives and it is important to recognize the nature of those issues. Realizing the pluses and the minuses of each approach can reveal context and a better understanding of how to apply it and, even more important, in which situations it should or should not be applied.

# THE CHANGE SPONSOR/LEADER

The role of the change leader or sponsor is to ensure clarity about the purpose of the change, assess individual and team readiness, communicate the change management plan, and build and inspire trust. In addition, he/she needs to set realistic expectations and subsequently manage the *pace* of the change effort, build momentum in the form of tangible and meaningful progress along with milestones, and anticipate stakeholders' needs and reactions to the changing situations along the way. The change leader also needs to establish and use the change processes, set up and provide support, and remove obstacles along the way. In addition, the sponsor needs to facilitate people's change acceptance and adoption, set an example as a visible leader, provide direction and authority, and influence stakeholders to buy in and act in line with the change. The change sponsor also needs to be the backbone behind the process of building and leading the teams and of communicating effectively.

## Overseeing the Formation of Effective Teams

The sponsor is not going to be directly involved with the change team on a daily basis, but it is the sponsor's role to provide the context, support, environment, and drive that enables and supports the formation of effective teams that become high performing. The measure of the team's performance will be by directly assessing collective work products. The following list consolidates a few characteristics that make great teams:

1. A clear, meaningful purpose that the team has helped shape
2. Mutual accountability and commitment to get things done

3. Defined roles with a mix of complementary skills
4. Specific performance goals that flow from the common purpose, align with the roles and responsibilities, and are supported by accountability
5. Open and clear communication, conflict management, and effective decision making
6. Balanced participation
7. Participative leadership

The change leader needs to facilitate the process of building and developing the team and ensure effective and streamlined communication (as discussed in Chapter 4, which covered stakeholder engagement and communication management). Keep in mind the importance of active listening, asking the right questions (question structure), establishing effective communication lines across organizational boundaries, and understanding other people's needs so they can be engaged. Also keep in mind that influencing is an art that is an extension of effective communication and it requires remembering and considering the following:

a. Be prepared to know who it would be beneficial to influence, what needs to be achieved, and how to do it
b. Make and validate assumptions about the people whom it will be necessary to influence and what their needs are
c. Consider all possible options and plan accordingly
d. Do not try too hard, provide too much information at once, talk too much, or ignore the other side's needs and interests
e. Do not assume an unrealistic ability to influence people or assume that the other side will buy in just because they have been asked to—or because it is the right thing to do

## So, What Really Changes?

Managing change is tough all around, but a big part of the problem is that there is little agreement on what factors most influence transformation initiatives or what parts of the organization really change. Every stakeholder focuses on a different part that changes based on their point of view, and the different views introduce different priorities and approaches. With a lack of clear guidance from the top, too many attempts will be applied simultaneously to tackle multiple differing priorities, thereby forcing organizations to spread their resources and skills too thin. In addition, different approaches will be applied differently in various parts of the organization, exacerbating the turmoil that is already in place due to the change. A clear vision, a strong direction, and a consistent, calculated, and patient approach from the sponsor is therefore key to success.

Many change leaders and sponsors realized in recent years that change is not only about the tangible or *hard* things that actually change (i.e., symbolic frame). They started shifting their focus toward the important *soft* aspects of the change (i.e., culture, leadership, and influence). However, in many organizations that shift was too hard because leading change only through these soft aspects is not enough for transformational changes. Things such as vision and communication are critical success factors for any change, but they are not sufficient on their own.

*Soft* aspects are hard to measure and influence. In the past, there was not enough focus on them, but now many organizations seem to overfocus on them without even realizing it—wasting organizational resources and yet failing to meet the change objectives. A balanced approach is needed to ensure there is enough of the soft aspects in place to support the change, while leading the way with the hard, tangible, and symbolic elements that are easier to measure and influence. Keep in mind that the hard elements are not only the symbolic ones, but they are also about the approach that is being taken.

## At the End of the Change Initiative

At the end of the change, it will be necessary to be able to not only declare that it is complete and to measure the benefits, but also to check the true impact of the change on the organization:

a. *How much of the intent of the change has been realized*—there has to be a sober review of what happened, which of the benefits were realized and to what extent, which benefits have not been realized (at all or partially), and whether new benefits were introduced that had not been considered prior to the change.

b. *To what extent the organization is benefiting from the change*—the intended benefits for the change were identified early on in the process and at the end it is necessary to check whether and to what extent the organization is benefiting from the change. This is not about specific change benefits, but rather whether the organization is benefiting from it overall. There might be (or even is likely to be) misalignment between some of the change benefits and the overall value they produce for the organization. Maximize alignment between the two and realize the hits and misses will make the organization more equipped to cope with the next change.

c. *What other impact the new reality has on the organization*—this starts with checking if there are any *side effects*; that is, anything that the change initiative has introduced that veered off from the intended results. Some of the side effects may be positive, but often they are not. Most changes are likely to produce some side effects and it is not only important to realize them, but also to check what impact they really have on the organization. Further, understanding the full impact and results of the change will help to realize the new reality (the refrozen, future state and new status quo), learn about our true new capabilities, and position ourselves better for future challenges.

d. *Real lessons*—this is the time to perform a meaningful lessons learned process to check the change results, the process of going through the change, and the business case. The results review is about the PIR of the change impact and the benefits; the process review is about what happened through the change, the transition, and the journey, and what can be done better; and the business case review is perhaps the most important from a strategic perspective: if the team had to do it all over again, would they do it and what would they do differently? It is the final attempt to look back and consider the entire approach and the mandate for the initiative. There might be various misalignments; for example, between the benefits and the mandate. That is, the team may have realized most of the benefits, but in hindsight, the mandate should have been different. As part of the lessons learned, the team should also create a measurement that allows for not only assessing individual changes, but also to compare changes to each other and check at what rate the organization realized benefits from the change initiatives and what these initiative do to the organization as a whole—from all three perspectives: the mandate, the benefits, and the process.

e. *Readiness for the next change*—the success of the previous change should also be measured by how well the completed change has positioned us to cope with the current reality and the upcoming challenges. It is possible that a successful change still hasn't managed to position us with the right capabilities to deal with what's next. For example, the benefits that were realized are not applicable or are outdated, or the new challenges are different—of a kind that no one saw coming before. Since organizations do not properly do lessons learned for their change initiatives, they often overstate (over-believe-in) their new capabilities.

Peter Drucker pointed out that organizations spend 80% of their time trying to solve unsolvable problems, and much of this problem is a result of not being properly positioned to deal with the future. Further, not realizing your post-change capabilities is also a significant contributor to this problem. Ensuring alignment and understanding the capabilities and state of readiness to deal with the next change is therefore a significant step in the right direction toward focusing on Gareth Morgan's 15% of what is within the team's control.

Another consideration at this stage is to check whether there have been any impacts as a result of interlocking considerations, dependencies, and touchpoints across change initiatives. These often have impacts that are difficult to measure, but it is important to articulate them at the end of the initiative.

A final thought about the lessons learned process: at the very least, encourage people to think about one thing they would do differently with the knowledge they now have. This can be about any aspect of the change—ranging from the mandate, approach, process, timing, or result.

## The Proxy

When the sponsor is either too senior and/or too busy to attend to the initiative's needs as required, he/she should consider appointing a *proxy*. The sponsor proxy (for a change or for a project) may need to be introduced where there is a need for someone, on behalf of the sponsor, to be involved to a greater extent than the sponsor can provide. The proxy works within the mandate and guidance of the sponsor, but he/she needs to have a sufficient level of seniority to be able to provide answers and direction, enough context to make informed decisions, and the right level of organizational and domain understanding so that he/she can properly escalate and engage the *real* sponsor. It is therefore important to have the right person as a proxy in place, considering the following: availability, seniority, context, communication skills, relationships with both the sponsor and the PM/change manager, and decision-making capacity.

Having a proxy sponsor can bridge the gap between the sponsor's availability or involvement and the needs of the initiative—especially when the initiative's velocity and events require more involvement than what the sponsor can provide. It is important to plan the engagement needs and check whether the sponsor can provide the level of involvement and support required. But even though planning is important, keep in mind that in most situations, the sponsor's involvement will end up being greater than anticipated and the initiative will likely be more demanding than originally planned. The planning for the sponsor's involvement should take place with the PM or the change managers, and it needs to involve clear role definitions and a breakdown of responsibilities so that everyone knows what is expected of them and it is clear what is expected of the sponsor.

Determining the need and level of involvement of the proxy depends on the stakes of the initiative because it is better to have a proxy on the ground than a missing-in-action sponsor. Agile projects (discussed in Chapter 6) are a common place to see proxy sponsors since the product owner may act as one, under the executive sponsor. Keep in mind that having a proxy sponsor can also backfire, for several reasons:

    a.  A lack of context or timely decision making
    b.  The wrong seniority level
    c.  Involvement is insufficient or there is too much meddling
    d.  Misalignment with sponsor and mixed messages
    e.  When there is a need for the actual sponsor to be involved

Also keep in mind that relying on certain team members or BAs to act as a sponsor is a common mistake since they lack seniority, context, and clout to make timely and informed decisions.

## For the Post-Corona World

The post-corona reality the world has been dealing with does not alter what change management means, but similar to other shocks throughout history, it leads to changes in the way we do things. It also happens to reinforce many of the concepts that are covered in this book and specifically in this chapter.

Moving forward, change leaders need to focus on two different fronts. First, they must reduce redundancies and waste and improve collaboration and efficiencies, since there is now an elevated sense of urgency around the need to do things the right way. There is also less money and no tolerance for chasing failures and lacking change readiness. Second, they must take a hard look at change initiatives that were taking place or those that were rushed through during the pandemic. These initiatives may have to be re-done, adjusted, or abandoned—this time with better planning to realize more benefits at less cost.

In addition, our new reality should further push our change leaders to focus more on building resilience through change, properly shifting organizations to distributed workplaces, developing virtual leadership capabilities, and making communication more pointed and concise.

## RECAP

The set of tools and concepts covered in this chapter is intended to help sponsors and change leaders review their change initiative from different perspectives. The chapter offered techniques to define the vision and articulate the scope, scale, and frames of the change. It also covered ways to perform gap analysis, check impact areas, measure team readiness, understand and deal with resistance, and realize the forces that are applied to the change. These tools should be part of a toolbox for the change sponsor to consider based on the context and circumstances at hand.

Change and project sponsorship are similar in nature. This chapter provided the change sponsor with a set of tools to ensure that he/she pursues the right initiative with the right approach that the team is ready for. Chapter 6 provides more specific information regarding project sponsorship.

## NOTES

1. https://hbr.org/1995/05/leading-change-why-transformation-efforts-fail-2.
2. https://www.kotterinc.com/8-steps-process-for-leading-change/.
3. The source of some concepts in this chapter is SIGMA Strategic Solutions Inc. and these concepts are used, with permission, from Rhona Berengut.
4. Anderson and Anderson. *The Change Leader's Roadmap*. Jossey Bass Pfeiffer Publishing, 2001.
5. https://likeateam.com/how-to-define-a-clear-vision/.
6. http://www.usingmindmaps.com/mind-map-vision-boards.html.
7. https://williepietersen.com/the-lessons-of-the-blind-men-and-the-elephant-2/.
8. Adapted from Anderson and Anderson. *Beyond Change Management*. Jossey Bass Pfeiffer Publishing, 2001.

9. Project Management Institute (PMI). *Project Management Body of Knowledge (PMBOK® Guide)—Sixth Edition.* PMI, 2017.
10. Adapted from Harvey and Brown, *An Experiential Approach to Organization Development,* 7th ed. Pearson, 2006.
11. Based on: http://www.1000ventures.com/design_elements/selfmade/change_resistance_h2overcome_10tips.png.
12. https://workplacepsychology.files.wordpress.com/2016/11/methods-for-dealing-with-resistance-to-change-kotter-and-schlesinger.png.

# 6

---

# PROJECT SPONSORSHIP

---

We do not expect project managers (PMs) to understand everything there is to know about project management just because they are given the title of PM; yet for some reason, senior managers are expected to automatically understand what is involved in sponsoring projects. After a comprehensive review of the role of the change sponsor, this chapter takes a step back and looks at the foundations of project sponsorship. Keep in mind that despite the specific things that the sponsor needs to understand as part of the change initiative, there are no significant differences between the roles of the project sponsor and change sponsor; in fact, the way to drive a change is through projects, and therefore, the similarities and overlapping aspects of the roles.

Projects are the means by which organizations achieve goals and satisfy client needs. The means to drive organizational change and successful implementation of projects is critical to an organization's performance and overall profitability. Senior management must have an understanding of project management needs and the skills required to lead projects and build and integrate a sound project management culture. Project success is a team effort, and when the project sponsorship role is better understood, the entire team, as well as the organization as a whole, benefits. This chapter addresses some portfolio management concepts in support of its focus on streamlining the working relationship between the PM and the sponsor—so that both roles *speak* the same language.

## THE ROLE OF THE SPONSOR IN PROJECT SUCCESS

The project sponsor is an individual (often a manager or an executive) with overall accountability for the project. He/she is primarily concerned with ensuring that the project delivers the agreed-upon business benefits and acts as the representative of the organization by playing a vital leadership role through a series of areas:

- Provides business context and guidance; establishes a mandate and objectives
- Provides expertise or access to subject matter experts (SMEs), including the PM and the team

- Champions the project throughout the organization to ensure priority, capacity, funding, and resources for the project
- Acts as the ultimate decision maker for significant items—such as changes; not required for minor, non-project-altering items
- Acts as an escalation point for decisions and issues that are beyond the authority of the PM
- Serves as an additional or alternate line of communication and observation with team members, customers, and other stakeholders
- Serves as the link between the project, the business community, and strategic-level decision-making groups

These are well-known roles of the sponsor; however, there are different perceptions and levels of understanding on the styles of the sponsor's involvement, as well as on how to ensure that the sponsor is sufficiently involved. Unfortunately, many sponsors have the awareness of what needs to be done, but they do not have the capacity to be there for the project or knowledge of the techniques on how to perform their duties as sponsors.

## Sponsor's Responsibilities

In addition to the previously listed items, which are more general, there are also more strategic considerations that the sponsor has in relation to the project. The sponsor is typically responsible for initiating, establishing, and approving a series of key project aspects, which can be summed up under the categories of vision, governance, value creation, and benefits realization. These are not clear-cut categories since most items can appear under more than one (e.g., approving deliverables can be placed in multiple categories).

### Vision

- Ensure the validity of the business case and the ongoing alignment to business objectives
- Define project success criteria that align with the business objectives
- Interact informally with the project team and other key stakeholders to stay informed of events and underlying trends in and around the project
- Check (both formally and informally) that the project remains viable

### Governance

- Define project success criteria that align with the business objectives
- Prioritize the initiative and ensure that it is launched and initiated properly (e.g., priorities in relation to other initiatives, as well as priorities for the project's success)
- Serve as a voice for the project and ensure appropriate organizational support and priority are given to it throughout

- Identify roles and responsibilities, as well as reporting structure
- Serve as an escalation point for issues and obstacles that are beyond the control of the PM
- Provide financial resources for the project and approval on go/no-go decisions

### Value and Benefits

- Ensure risks and changes are managed properly and make associated decisions
- Check the impact of project events, risks, and progress on the organization and other initiatives
- Ensure reporting, control mechanisms, and reviews are in place
- Ensure the project delivers the intended value
- Evaluate progress and status
- Approve deliverables
- Make go/no-go decisions
- Be responsible for the overall quality, value, and benefits of the project from both the process and the end product

The sponsor is also responsible for recognizing, addressing (both proactively or reactively), and initiating appropriate action when issues arise. In the event that business conditions significantly change during the life cycle of the project, he/she is responsible for checking that the project remains viable and that the PM has what it takes to continue leading the project.

## Where Is the Sponsor?

In many environments the sponsor is nowhere to be found (sometimes right from the beginning, and at other times, just at some point in the project); whereas, in other situations, the PM does not even know who the sponsor is, how to access him/her, or what the project success criteria is. Organizations are often reluctant to delegate project sponsorship and may keep these responsibilities in the hands of a steering committee. This often leads to problems concerning the committee's involvement level, timeliness of decisions, or the nature, support, or quality of those decisions.

## Selecting a PM

The discussion should not only be about the sponsor's fit and his/her ability to act as the sponsor; there is also a need to look at the PM's fit and relevant skills. After all, it is the sponsor who, in most cases, appoints the PM. Often, PMs are appointed to their role with no view of business objectives, leaving the PMs to focus on the most visible and measurable items—time and money. It is the role of the sponsor to find a PM that is suitable for the job and who is up to the task. In most environments, the focus when looking for a PM is on the candidate's technical or product-related skills—which in the majority of cases ends up being the least important factor. It is important to have product-related expertise; however, the PM does not (with some exceptions) need to be an SME. It is also easier to focus on product and technical expertise since these are fairly tangible and measurable.

*Hard* PM skills, such as requirements and scope management, planning, scheduling, and budgeting, are fairly easy to detect, assess, and measure and most PMs can demonstrate these skills. Therefore, most of the focus should be on the less tangible, more difficult to detect, *soft*, or interpersonal skills that help determine the candidate's suitability for the role. These include the candidate's style and aptitude toward working in the project's environment (based on pace, amount of change, stability, reporting structure, and governance), influence, communication, relationship building, and resilience (how the candidate can handle the compounding effect of multiple project and organizational factors).

## Building an Effective Sponsor-PM Relationship

The working relationship and rapport between the sponsor and the PM often become critical success factors in projects. The sponsor and the PM depend on each other for the project's ability to deliver the intended benefits and business needs. The sponsor and the PM must trust in each other and meet regularly; define rules of engagement, roles, and responsibilities; and set clear and realistic expectations of each other early on. Unfortunately, despite the importance of project sponsorship, there are no associations, organizations, methodologies, and approaches that exist for project sponsorship. In the absence of a "Project Sponsorship Institute" to establish guidelines and encourage education and qualification of project sponsors, there is a growing need to address it from the point of view of project needs and the PM.

When it comes to sponsor-PM working relationships and boundaries, many PMs prefer that sponsors remain out of their way and not interfere in order to allow the PMs to do their thing, while other PMs find it beneficial when the sponsor acts as a senior PM for some project matters. The most common form of friction between the sponsor and PM is when a sponsor is too busy to attend to his/her project's details—treating the project as hands-off. In these cases, there is little definition or clarification of the objectives, no proper empowerment of the PM for the tasks at hand, and an overall attitude by the sponsor that "when the PM needs me, they will reach out." In most cases, when there is no clear role definition or involvement by the sponsor, things tend to go offtrack before the PM has the ability to reach out to the sponsor, and before the sponsor has a chance to notice the trend.

In order to foster and enhance the collaboration between the roles of the sponsor and the PM, and with it the quality and success of projects, it is necessary to first articulate in a greater level of detail the specific elements and actions that make up the role of the project sponsor. While this is started here, Chapter 7 provides a set of checklists and considerations for the sponsor to determine what he/

she needs to look for, measure, ask, and review in order to perform his/her role both effectively and efficiently.

## Sponsorship in Organizational Context

Project sponsors should understand the organization's business and corporate strategy very well, and be in a senior enough position to have good—or at least workable—relationships with other members of senior management, with the board, with other departments, as well as with the relevant external stakeholders. Sponsors should also have sound knowledge of the business case and an understanding of project management practices. However, with little attention and guidelines as to what good sponsorship entails, the area of sponsorship has become a growing pain in many organizations. With the introduction of multiple methodologies and approaches over the years—and the rapid growth of some of them (i.e., agile, business analysis, and change management)—it sometimes appears that organizations are looking for answers to project failures in the wrong places. This is not to suggest that these various disciplines are not effective or that they cannot introduce results, but the reliance on more complex concepts may have distracted people from looking in a more obvious, foundational, and impactful place—project sponsorship. This area has not received the right amount of attention and only in recent years has there been a noticeable growth in the number of organizations that realize the importance of improving their project sponsorship practices.

# WHO IS THE RIGHT SPONSOR?

Let's go back to the role of the sponsor as the owner, funder, and champion of the project—actually the project's customer. Earlier in this chapter there was a list of roles and responsibilities that are expected from the sponsor. Most sponsors know about these roles and responsibilities yet they either cannot find the time or capacity to perform them or they do not know how. This is a good time to review some items that if in place mean the difference between a good and mediocre sponsor (see Table 6.1).

One of the main causes of problems with the role of the project sponsor is that there is no clear definition of what a sponsor is. It is therefore hard for senior managers who get appointed to become sponsors to know what to aim for. To paraphrase a Lewis Carroll quote, "If you don't know where you're going, any road will take you there." So, if there is no clear understanding of how to be a sponsor, every case will look different. Those who become project sponsors are senior members of management; they are busy, experienced, and knowledgeable; and they have a reputation and some form of power. There is usually no question about their skills or stature, but rather about their fit for the specific task, and about their understanding of what it takes to be an effective sponsor.

As established earlier in this book, many of the problems faced today when it comes to project sponsorship can be attributed to a lack of time to attend to the

**Table 6.1**   What makes an effective project sponsor?

| Characteristics of a Good Sponsor | What It Means | How to Do It |
|---|---|---|
| Commitment to the role and the project | Allocate enough time to attend to the project, especially at critical junctions (e.g., decisions, sign-offs, phase gates) | • Block time on the calendar for scheduled items; otherwise allow flexibility to attend to as-needed items<br>• Set up role definitions and boundaries with the PM<br>• Delegate to a proxy if needed |
| Availability and access by PM and team | Must be within reach and on a timely basis as needed | • Become available when there is a need by the project<br>• Establish rules of engagement for the PM to escalate |
| Own the business case | It is not about writing the business case, but about owning and being accountable for each element of strategic impact | • Ensure traceability to strategic objectives; each item needs a purpose and an approach to achieve/measure<br>• Each item must deliver a piece of value |
| Stakeholder engagement | Engage stakeholders and ensure alignment and context; this is not *instead* of the PM engaging stakeholders, but as a complementing layer | • Address stakeholders and matters that are not within the authority or ability of the PM<br>• Deal with conflicting needs among stakeholders<br>• Appropriately address matters that require attention<br>• Ensure transparency and focus on project priorities and objectives |
| Drive the project | Sponsors must own the project and leave their mark on it | • Proactively participate on a regular basis (ask questions, inquire, and challenge)<br>• Do not over-delegate<br>• Know what goes on<br>• Make sure the PM leads based on the sponsor's parameters and mandate<br>• Articulate success criteria<br>• Ensure the PM is aligned and delivers intended value |
| Organizational considerations | Maintain alignment: consider organizational change impact areas the project may introduce | • Address misalignment between project objectives and stakeholders'/other initiatives' needs and priorities<br>• Manage capacity and prioritization against other organizational needs<br>• Serve as an escalation point for organizational matters that the PM cannot address (e.g., resources) |

*continued*

| Characteristics of a Good Sponsor | What It Means | How to Do It |
|---|---|---|
| Decisions | Make informed and timely decisions | • Consider all information available for decision support<br>• Be prepared to make decisions with ambiguous and limited amounts of information<br>• Make tough decisions that are in line with the project and organizational needs, even if unpopular<br>• Make timely decisions; time usually works against us<br>• Always consider the alternatives<br>• Remember that there is an option to do nothing |

The project sponsor needs to maintain a level of involvement in the project that not only complements the areas covered by the PM, but also ensures there is another set of eyes in place to see things independently of the PM's view. At times, PMs may not see the full picture or may get tangled in paradigms or in certain aspects of the work. The sponsor is then in place to challenge and address any concerns before it's too late.

project's needs and a lack of awareness of what it takes to become an effective sponsor. A lack of time is understandable since these individuals who become sponsors have day jobs, they are busy, and they are attending to their part of addressing organizational needs. With that said, one of the keys to success as a project sponsor is to make a conscious effort to ensure that there are blocks of time and available capacity toward attending to the project. This begins with raising awareness. Once people become aware of something, they will make the effort and obtain the tools to look after it.

To make sure the *right* sponsor is in place, the mandate of the role, along with the time allocation and awareness, needs to come from the highest levels of the organization—senior levels of management, the C-suite, or the CEO. Organizations need to look into clearly mandating the role of the project sponsor by introducing a role definition and ensuring that those who take on sponsorship roles know what it entails to be successful. Performing a proper lessons learned process that looks into the project benefits in comparison to the business case can also help highlight the importance of the role of the sponsor. Reviewing project results against the business case can also help better understand additional aspects of the sponsor's role, such as project selection, definition of success criteria, and selection of the PM.

Project sponsorship is not a numbers game. It is puzzling to learn that many organizations not only *double dip* into resources (where resources are over-allocated between their day jobs and projects), but organizations also double dip into the PM's time. For example, if a PM manages five projects, he/she can attend to each project an average of one day per week, but is that enough? The same goes with sponsors. Most sponsors not only maintain their day jobs as members of senior management, but they also take on more than one project and, at times, multiple projects. When the sponsor oversees several projects, none will get the level of attention it needs. It is therefore safe to say that no one person can effectively sponsor multiple projects at the same time. Organizations therefore need to make a choice and put some order around the role of the project sponsor by:

a. Identifying what the role of the sponsor entails and providing a role definition
b. Measuring the amount of capacity it requires from the person who takes on the sponsor's role
c. Checking whether the sponsor's experience, seniority, leadership style, and availability are aligned with the nature of the project
d. Ensuring that the sponsor has enough capacity to perform both his/her day job as well as sponsor responsibilities
e. Providing role definition, boundaries, and a relationship between the sponsor and the PM
f. Ensuring governance, escalations, sign-offs, and reporting are in place in support of the project and organizational needs

With a growing number of initiatives failing due to conflicting priorities in the organization or a lack of sufficient support, it is time to look into providing a clear role definition and expectations when it comes to project sponsorship.

## Types of Sponsors?

There may be more than one sponsor for a project upon inception. Sometimes there is an executive sponsor, who is a C-level executive, and beneath him/her there is a project sponsor who acts on his/her behalf—in a similar fashion to the proxy concept. There is, however, a need to make another distinction between different types of sponsors.

There are sponsors who, for lack of a better word, are *leader sponsors*. These are the *original* sponsors; it is their initiative, their idea, their drive, and the project will bear their fingerprints. These sponsors are typically involved, passionate, and proactive and the initiative is strongly associated with them. In the event that these sponsors leave the organization or move to a different position (depending on the nature of the initiative), there is a significant danger to the initiative's existence and direction. From the initiative's perspective, the leader sponsor is the backbone of the initiative and, as such, he/she is most likely to ensure funding, priorities, and resources to support the cause.

There are also the *agent sponsors*. These are sponsors who are appointed to lead initiatives or who just happen to be under the umbrella, mandate, or portfolio that this initiative *falls*. In these cases, there is rarely any special connection between the sponsor and the initiative (e.g., no emotional attachment). This loose connection leads to lower stakes and a lower level of involvement. Accordingly, the direction of the initiative is likely to get impacted by the more sporadic and even distracted nature of the sponsor. It is also likely that the agent is the sponsor of multiple other initiatives, meaning poor results may follow. In the event that the agent sponsor should leave his/her role, another will be installed and he/she may or may not continue the initiative in the same direction.

# BUSINESS CASE AND PROJECT SELECTION

It is not easy to determine which project or opportunity an organization should pursue. There are multiple considerations, competing priorities, agendas, and valid reasons for or against any initiative. From a project management point of view, the PM is announced, appointed, or installed to a project after the selection process is complete, and typically, upon chartering the project (the charter will be looked at later in this chapter). The selection of the PM should show a fit between the candidate's skills and style and the project type and needs. Since it is the sponsor's job to find a PM, it is also his/her job to lead the project selection process.

An idea, initiative, problem, or opportunity is selected to become a project through what should be a consistent and transparent organizational process. It is necessary to have criteria to determine which one(s) is worth pursuing and why, by comparing them apples to apples. While it is difficult to have a set of transparent and consistent criteria for project selection, there still has to be some system that allows organizations to pursue the things that make the most sense for their strategy and needs.

## Business Case

Before selecting a project, all under consideration go through a business case study and analysis. This involves looking at all the challenges, opportunities, and problems that are in the pipeline and comparing them to each other under a similar set of criteria in order to determine which item(s) should be selected and pursued. The process involves considering the justification of each of the items based on the criteria to help determine what would be the best course of action and which initiative gets your limited resources. The criteria are typically considered against strategic objectives and other portfolio considerations (i.e., comparing initiatives to each other based on the *lanes* they fall under). For example, organizations will consider two competing research and development (R&D) items against each other but not against an unrelated initiative, such as employee retention.

The business case analysis will look for justification of which is the best initiative to pursue. The justification process may involve financial considerations, benefit realization, timing, strategic alignment, potential savings—or any other consideration that is deemed important. Once an idea or initiative is deemed *worthy* of pursuit (or justified), another analysis needs to take place—feasibility. The feasibility analysis takes us one step further and checks whether the initiative that was just deemed justified is within reach, and whether the proper components are available to pursue it. The feasibility analysis ensures that needs or desires (addressed by the business case analysis) are not confused with ability, capacity, or readiness (that may be addressed by the feasibility study). At times, cash flow, timing, resource availability, interlocking with other projects, or any other organizational considerations may present themselves and stand in the way of success.

Since this is the pre-project stage, the person who will become the project sponsor may not have this title yet. With that said, the business case process is typically driven by the person who will, in due course, become the sponsor of the project once it is chartered. Although the sponsor title may not be in place yet, this person *owns* the analysis process and the need. The business case and feasibility study are not performed by that individual, but rather by someone who acts as a business analyst (BA). It is important to note that the business case and feasibility analysis provide the sponsor and the organization with accountability and rationale:

- *Accountability*—the nature of a business case means that the purpose, costs, and benefits need to be clearly articulated; and this means that the anticipated benefits will be baselined, tracked, and measured. As a result, the person who becomes the sponsor will be held accountable against the promise of the initiative and its expected value creation and benefits. In a way, the business case serves as a contract between the sponsor and the organization, and when benefits fall short or are late to be realized, the sponsor is held accountable and he/she needs to justify the variance.
- *Rationale*—the business case forces the rationale for the project to be clearly articulated and to be aligned to the strategy. It therefore introduces organizational scrutiny in order to ensure that the rationale is met. The need to articulate the rationale reduces the chance that the sponsor will proceed with a *pet project* that is misaligned with organizational needs or with an initiative that does not present a clear idea of what he/she wants or how the initiative will solve a problem or realize an opportunity.

Regardless of who actually performs the analysis and writes the report, the sponsor of the would-be project champions and drives this process.

## Project Selection

An extension of business case analysis is the project selection process. Here too, there has to be criteria as to which projects to pursue and the sponsor is once again the main driver of the process—and therefore, the accountable person. Table 6.2 provides a brief look at practical items to consider when performing the process of project selection. In addition to the items that appear in Table 6.2, it is important to look at the following:

- *Probability of success*—based on the circumstances, the current conditions, and with all things considered, there is a need to assess the real chance of success.

**Table 6.2**  Project selection considerations

| Project Selection Considerations | Meaning |
|---|---|
| Financials | Financial considerations make up some of the most significant weight considerations for projects since they are visible, measurable, and directly related to the organization's bottom line. Financials are typically performed by finance/accounting departments and include one or more of the following: NPV—net present value, IRR—internal rate of return, payback period, benefit-cost analysis, and ROI—return on investment. Note that financial considerations may still be subjective, and if taken out of context, easily manipulated. |
| Scoring models | Take into consideration multiple criteria and provide a relative weight for each item, then give each candidate option a score. The result is reached by multiplying the relative weight by the score, and the project/option that scores the highest is the one that should be selected. Considerations may be financials and/or others. Keep in mind the notion of *garbage in, garbage out*. If the criteria selected does not reflect the true needs, the scores will be out of touch with actual needs and we could select an option or a project that is not right for the organization. |
| Opportunity cost | This is also a financial consideration where one option is weighed against an alternative. It is necessary to make sure that the comparison method is apples to apples. |
| Strategic alignment | There has to be strategic alignment; that is, ensuring that the opportunity selected is in line with the direction of the organization or that it is part of or a step toward the big picture. |
| Urgency | Beyond the other considerations, there is a need to determine the level of urgency that is associated with an option or an opportunity (e.g., timing, impact, visibility, market consideration, or action by our competition). |
| Benefit definition/realization | It is imperative to consider the benefits that each course of action promises—especially the type of benefits, their timing, and areas of impact. Benefits are not only financial or tangible; you must also consider intangible benefits (e.g., customer loyalty, user experience, reputation, brand awareness, employee retention, employee morale, and customer satisfaction). Intangible benefits are typically associated with a longer time horizon. |
| Political considerations | These can be internal or external. They should not be the only item under consideration, but they definitely need to be taken into account. Under this category, also include changes to management and to organizational structure, consideration of competing priorities, and stakeholders' needs. |

The process of project selection is directly linked to the business case analysis. The project selection process is about ensuring that the project that makes the most sense for the organization in context and under the circumstances is the project chosen. None of the items discussed here should be considered on its own, but rather as a compilation of virtually all of these items together, where a specific item can serve as a tie-breaker or deciding factor.

- *Availability of information*—take a look at data, information, and knowledge and check their level of availability and accessibility, as well as at their quality and reliability. The wrong set of data may result in choosing the wrong project.
- *Savings/growth potential*—these are a combination of financials and other factors; albeit mostly tangible.
- *Potential for side effects*—perform an environmental scan to look at the potential for less-desired outcomes or impacts as a result of the initiative. This also includes the overall customer impact. Do not get blindsided by significant unexpected consequences.
- *Resource availability*—this is related to the capacity of the organization. Check to make sure that the resources to perform the necessary work are available.
- *Core competencies*—beyond resources, check the capabilities and whether (or to what extent) the goal being pursued impacts (or is impacted by) our core competencies. Organizations often confuse a good idea with those that impact their core competencies or their competitive advantage.
- *Risk assessment*—risk should be considered in several dimensions:
  - Project risk—asking what could go wrong
  - Business/operational risk—asking what may happen to the organization as a result of the project
  - Scenario analysis—asking *what if*, to consider all possible outcomes; or asking *what if not*, to check what might happen if this opportunity is not pursued or if it is aborted (going back to what the pre-project situation looked like)
- *Life-cycle approach capabilities*—some projects may require a different approach to their life cycle (e.g., agile). It is necessary to check whether the capabilities are present to support the necessary life-cycle approach.

## Benefits Realization

The process of benefits realization starts with business case analysis and the project selection criteria. This is when the initiative's first set of benefits is identified, even if on a high level. While going through the process of refining the benefits and articulating them in a measurable way, it is necessary to develop criteria on how to measure the benefits and how to realize them. The criteria need to be both consistent and, at the same time, stand the test of time because by the time the project is done and the bulk of the benefits are due to be realized, there may be a different view on how to measure the benefits, how to realize them, how they should impact the organization, or any other deviation from the original view when the benefits were first defined. It is also necessary to consider and define criteria to measure both the tangible and intangible benefits. Be mindful of the timing of the benefits—which benefit is expected when and in what form. Some benefits may be realized throughout the project (especially when projects are pursued with an empirical or agile life-cycle approach). Most benefits are expected to be realized at the end of the project, while others—especially the intangible ones—may be realized over time, well past the completion of the project.

# STRATEGIC ALIGNMENT AND PORTFOLIO MANAGEMENT

When selecting an initiative to pursue, it should go without saying that it needs to have strategic alignment. Whatever is decided must be linked to, be part of, or work toward the organizational big picture. It must address a need, opportunity, problem, challenge, or an idea that is aligned with the organization as a whole, what they are about, and what their objectives are. At the end of the day, if it does not add some sort of meaningful value, our scarce resources and time should not be spent on it.

# A QUICK REVIEW OF PORTFOLIO MANAGEMENT

Portfolio management is the alignment of projects with organizational strategy by selecting the right programs or projects, prioritizing the work, and providing needed resources. It is the *centralized management of one or more portfolios to achieve strategic objectives*.[1] Portfolio management is about prioritization and capacity management to ensure that resources are allocated based on organizational priorities and needs. It is essentially the thread that connects organizational strategy to the tactical elements of projects, programs, and operations. Therefore, portfolio management is a major driver that maintains the focus of the business case and project selection process. Through portfolio management, organizational governing bodies can make decisions that control or influence the direction of portfolio components as they work to achieve specific outcomes.

A more tangible way of looking at it is through realizing that portfolio management is about coordinating the projects within the organization and ensuring they are streamlined based on a set of strategic objectives and priorities. In a way, it is about treating the projects as investments that consume organizational resources and capacity with the intent to maximize the overall return from the investments in all projects. Like an investment portfolio, we are looking at a mix of things that take place in the organization and that represent the organization's values, strategy, and objectives. As such, it is a collection of projects, programs, and operations that are grouped together to facilitate effective management and alignment with the strategic objectives. Portfolios are often represented as strategic business units, geographical areas, lines of business, or any other breakdowns of organizations into buckets. The programs, projects, initiatives, and operations are placed into the buckets where they compete with like projects within each bucket.

When it comes to project sponsorship, it is important to have some context around what portfolio management is since the sponsor plays an important role in the process of pursuing opportunities, leading the business case analysis, and selecting projects. With the context provided by portfolio management, the sponsor can compare apples to apples, focus on strategic objectives, and learn about organizational capacity and its prioritization process. Figure 6.1 provides a look into the *hierarchy* or the layers in organizations. It is important to note that portfolio management is not necessarily an exclusive layer in the organization because it serves as a *thread* that connects the strategy and objectives to the tactical elements. However, this connection may also be viewed as a diagonal layer, as opposed to a horizontal layer, since it works as a connection from the top to the tactical, below. In addition to the breakdowns to portfolios listed before (e.g., strategic business units), an arm of portfolio management can also be in the form of the project management office (PMO), the activities associated with project selection and cross-project prioritization, and even some committees that engage in these activities.

The project sponsor in most cases is not the portfolio manager, but he/she participates in (and even leads some) portfolio management activities and has to work with the portfolio manager. The role of the portfolio manager involves monitoring, evaluating, and validating portfolio components against the following:

- Organizational strategy and alignment
- Overall performance and risk in relation to the portfolio's priorities

Portfolio management is "located" between organizational strategy (from above) and tactical elements (programs, projects, and operations) from below. By saying tactical, it does not imply unimportant, but rather on the ground.

**Figure 6.1**    Where is portfolio management located?

- Evaluating components against each other based on capacity
- Ensuring sufficient and relevant resources and that changes are addressed
- Providing guidance, reviewing for context, measuring, monitoring, and providing support

# Breaking Down Portfolio Management: Capacity Management and Prioritization

A significant part of portfolio management is alignment, which includes breaking things down into components, categorizing them, and evaluating them against objective and consistent criteria so that it is possible to select the right thing to do, authorize it, and communicate the mandate. Doing it the right way helps, in turn, to articulate success criteria and identify and respond to risks. As progress is made, it becomes possible to conduct effective reviews and reports on performance, monitor progress against strategic changes, and adjust for changing realities, performance, resources, and needs.

## *Capacity Management and Prioritization*

Capacity is the total ability or bandwidth of an individual or an organization. Essentially it is the measure of all the resources an organization has and how much throughput or productivity they can produce with the time they have. Capacity management is about ensuring the organization maximizes its potential production. Measuring capacity is about figuring out how many resources are available to work on something, how many hours they have available, and at what rate they produce value. Measuring how many resources (people and potentially other things that produce value) are on hand and their amount of work hours is fairly straightforward. The most difficult part is determining the resources' *velocity*—or the rate at which they produce work. For example, if there are two resources, working for eight hours per day (16 hours per day in total), producing at a rate of 50% (that is, four hours per person, per day), there is a total of eight hours of productive time per day between the two of them.

Most people, teams, and organizations do not have a clear understanding or awareness of their own capacity. The result is that they make commitments and take on work and activities that they subsequently do not have the ability to deliver on—with all the negative consequences and ramifications. Portfolio management helps break down the organization into buckets, where it is easier to measure capacity, and it helps to determine what the team can take on and which items are in competition for the same limited resources. Since every organization has a limited capacity—and virtually every organization has more work and needs than it can handle—there is a need to prioritize whatever items are under consideration and rank them in order of organizational capacity.

We all remember the days when there were no automatic payments for toll roads through a Transponder or an EZ-Pass. These toll-booth traffic jams are a perfect example of what happens when there is no clear prioritization process and everyone feels that they are most important. It leads to chaos and a reality where what advances is not necessarily the highest priority or most important.

**Figure 6.2**   When there are no clear priorities[2]

Prioritization is about deciding the relative importance (or urgency) of an item against other needs. Within a limited capacity, it is necessary to make sure that the order by which things will be done is understood, otherwise it will lead to chaos and most likely to failing to complete the more important items. Organizations need to have a clear prioritization scheme that helps compare apples to apples and makes the right decision about what is more important and why. Figure 6.2 helps illustrate a situation where there is no clear understanding of priorities and where no one and nothing is going.

Once the portfolio management process helps us gain an understanding of (limited) capacity, it also acts as a guide through the prioritization process—both across initiatives to determine which project gets the right of way, as well as within each initiative to determine project success criteria.

### Prioritization Across Initiatives

Start this process with the strategic objectives that act as a guide toward pursuing items that add value toward achieving these objectives. Each portfolio needs to have a mechanism to help determine what is more important and how to *direct traffic*. This could be done through a prioritization matrix that can help determine which tasks/projects are critical or urgent for the organization. The matrix graphically displays options and criteria and ranks the options based on the criteria that

## Prioritization Matrix

| Options / Issues | Criteria | | | | | | | Total |
|---|---|---|---|---|---|---|---|---|
| | A | B | C | D | E | F | G | |
| Option / Issue 1 | 2 | 3 | 4 | 5 | 5 | 2 | 4 | 25 |
| Option / Issue 2 | 1 | 3 | 4 | 2 | 3 | 1 | 1 | 15 |
| Option / Issue 3 | 2 | 4 | 5 | 3 | 4 | 3 | 1 | 22 |
| Option / Issue 4 | 4 | 1 | 2 | 3 | 4 | 1 | 3 | 18 |
| Option / Issue 5 | 5 | 2 | 4 | 4 | 2 | 2 | 4 | 23 |

A prioritization matrix helps rank items based on a set of agreed-upon criteria. We list all options, provide a set of criteria (can also be done with a relative weight for each item), and tally up the score each item gets. If we are truthful in our criteria and relative weight, the most suitable item will get the highest prioritization score.

**Figure 6.3**   Prioritization matrix example[3]

the organization determines to be important. The criteria are then weighed, based on their assessed importance, to help highlight the most suitable option to pursue. This process can also help narrow down options and compare the choices systematically. Figure 6.3 shows a generic prioritization matrix.

Cross-project prioritization helps determine which project is more important than others in delivering value toward strategic objectives. The priority of a project or initiative may change throughout its life cycle, but usually not significantly.

### Cross-Project Urgency

Although the priority of a project may not change much, the relative *urgency* of a project is likely going to change. The sponsor needs to establish mechanisms for allowing cross-project collaboration that will help address the changing sense of urgency among projects throughout their life cycles. The process of cross-project collaboration improves the way that teams compete for resources and involves the following steps:

a.  A RACI chart (responsible, accountable, consulted, and informed) is completed that assesses the timing of the resources needed by PMs over the next two weeks.

b.  A recurring meeting is convened where the PMs, resource managers, and corresponding sponsors sort out which project gets the right of way based on its urgency. It is likely that the respective sponsors will also disagree on the priorities or resource allocation, but these meetings provide a platform to discuss, escalate, and collaborate in ways that are more effective, more senior, and with the bigger picture in mind. This beats the alternative of a simple exchange between the competing PMs.

   c. Resources are allocated to best reflect organizational needs by promoting the projects with an elevated sense of urgency

Figure 6.4 helps identify which project gets the right of way. It is important to maintain focus on what matters for the organization and not turn this process into a shouting match where PMs focus on their own needs and are screaming, "me, me, me." The urgency will shift from one project to another every cycle and the urgency measure has little to do with the overall priority of the project. The rationale behind the two-week cycle is similar to work package sizes in a work breakdown structure where the recommended guideline is that they remain smaller than two weeks. It is also reasonable to expect that PMs will know the needs they have for the next two weeks, as well as for the resource managers to be able to provide resource commitments (to the extent they can) for a two-week period.

In order to determine urgency, it is necessary to look at a few criteria that can help articulate what *urgent* means. People tend to overuse the word, as well as its synonyms, and this dilutes its meaning. On a recent project, I received an e-mail from a colleague with a subject line that read: *Urgent*. I immediately opened it to realize that, indeed, there was an urgent matter with which to attend. A few weeks later, the same individual sent me another e-mail. This time the subject line read: *Urgent Urgent Urgent*. Again, I opened the e-mail expecting to read about a matter that was three times more urgent than the previous one, but it was hardly more urgent than the original item. Inevitably, there is a tendency to up the ante when using descriptive words and terms and, as a result, it dilutes the meaning of those words, and with that, makes people oblivious to true calls for help. In turn, there seems to be more usage of even more dramatic words—and once the vicious cycle has begun, the crying-wolf effect is exacerbated. Figure 6.5 shows a set of considerations based on actual urgency to focus the discussion on which project should get the right of way.

| | Project A | Project B | Project C | Project D |
|---|---|---|---|---|
| **Project A** | | ? | ? | ? |
| **Project B** | | | ? | ? |
| **Project C** | | | | ? |

Measuring the relative level of urgency for a project, as part of a two-week cycle of cross-project collaboration, has to be facilitated or at least overseen by the sponsor.

**Figure 6.4**   Cross-project urgency face-off

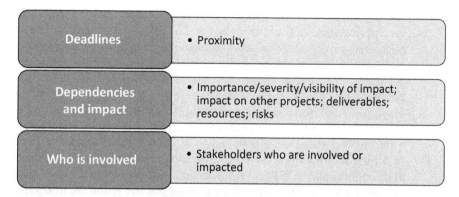

| Deadlines | • Proximity |
| --- | --- |
| Dependencies and impact | • Importance/severity/visibility of impact; impact on other projects; deliverables; resources; risks |
| Who is involved | • Stakeholders who are involved or impacted |

Establishing criteria for discussion makes determining urgency easier and more consistent. To determine which project is more urgent, it is necessary to determine time sensitivity, the nature of the impact, and who is involved. This criteria opens up a constructive discussion that is based on the merits and the situation on hand, as opposed to description drama by the respective PMs.

**Figure 6.5**   Criteria to determine urgency

## *Cross-Project Collaboration*

Throughout this book, multiple references have been made to the need for cross-project collaboration. This collaboration is about establishing a mechanism that allows PMs to work together, as well as with those who manage and own resources (i.e., team leads, functional managers, and department heads). This means collaboration regarding resource planning and allocation—so projects can maximize the utilization of resources and reduce waste. Resource waste includes a lower than necessary resource capacity, as well as over-allocation. These resource problems lead to delays, missed deadlines, and failure to meet objectives; which in turn, lead to budget overruns and project failure. The mechanism to enable cross-project collaboration is fairly simple to establish, but it needs to be facilitated by the project sponsors and maintained throughout. Establishing such a process involves the following:

a.  Ensure that PMs identify their resource needs. Ideally, the planning intervals should correspond with a period of about two weeks to ensure that the planning horizons are not too long. It is reasonable to expect that PMs should know their resource needs for the coming two weeks and that the organization (i.e., resource owners) can provide some level of understanding about the commitment to make these resources available.

b.  The resource planning process in the project should be performed through submitting a RACI chart (or a responsibility assignment matrix; RAM) and a schedule where resource needs are identified. It is then necessary to identify the projects that compete over shared resources and specify when each project needs any of the resources. The RACI chart is an effective way to connect project stakeholders and team members with the project scope and deliverables, and it can be useful at several levels: for the actual project work, for project management related activities, for division of work between the PM and the BAs or between the PM and the sponsor, and for sign-off and decision making among stakeholders. Keep these goals in mind: (1) ensure that each deliverable, activity, and task is going to have a resource or stakeholder assigned to it; (2) safeguard that there is skill matching and that the most suitable person is assigned to each activity and at the right capacity; (3) get resources and stakeholders to understand the nature and level of their involvement in each activity; and (4) find gaps— completing the RAM will show whether there is someone who can be assigned to each activity. In the event that there is no one assigned to an activity, it means that it is not going to get done. It sounds straightforward, but in reality projects often go ahead without having all tasks and activities mapped out. Many times, PMs mix hope with strategy and, thus, activities with no resources assigned to them on the RAM often get dismissed (we will figure it out later). Unfortunately, gaps are usually discovered the hard way—later, at which point it is even more pressing than it was previously and the team may not be able to perform certain activities on the project.

c.  Meetings should be convened regularly (once every two weeks) that include the PMs, the managers of those resources, and the projects' sponsors where the end goal is an understanding of each project and department needs, along with ranking of the projects based on organizational needs, constraints, and project urgencies. These include deadlines, dependencies, and the impact of the actions to be performed by the resources in question, including the stakeholders associated with these impact areas.

d.  The process, the makeup of the meeting, and the presence of the sponsors all combine to ensure that the discussion remains focused on the merits of the needs and that it is free of emotions, agendas, made-up urgencies, and drama.

e.  Once the rankings have been completed, resources will be allocated. The process also ensures that resource needs will be followed by commitments and in meeting those commitments by sending the right person, with the right skills, at the right time, and for the right amount of time. As a result, projects will be staggered based on the availability of the resources and the downtime (as well as over-allocation) of the shared resources will be minimized. Resource allocation will follow organizational needs and be driven by strategic objectives regarding which project requires more focus right now. Inevitably, this may harm certain projects, but this is the correct price to pay from a portfolio and overall prioritization perspective. It is also the right thing to do. A project that was deprived of resources in the current period will probably be a natural candidate for more focus for the next period, but this should not be the driving force.

f.  The ranking and the resource allocation in each period will serve as a starting point. Any game-changing events that may occur throughout the coming two weeks may require a change in the allocation of resources. But at the very least, there is now a starting point, a healthy discussion on merits, a focus on organizational needs, and the allocation of resources based on capacity without double-dipping or over-allocation. If a change occurs that requires a shift in the resource allocation, it will most likely create a chain reaction downstream that will favor the project(s) that has been deemed more urgent.

The concepts and rationale behind this process have been inspired by Eli Goldratt's Critical Chain.[4]

## *Prioritization Within the Project*

The sponsor also needs to facilitate the process of determining the priorities within the project—including the requirements prioritization and the project success criteria. While these activities will be led by the BA and the PM respectively, the sponsor provides the mandates and guidelines, and has the final word.

Prioritizing the requirements involves four sets of considerations that will determine the sequencing of the work to be performed: the business value of each requirement, technical dependencies, logical groupings, and product viability. Although the process is called *prioritization*, it is really about a sequencing of the requirements and scope items. The process must involve multiple team members and other stakeholders, as well as SMEs, but it is ultimately up to the sponsor to determine which requirement has more business value.

## *Project Success Criteria*

Next comes the need to determine the project success criteria. The sponsor provides guidelines, a mandate, and the business value to articulate the success criteria; yet there is an alarmingly high number of PMs who do not know what the project success criteria are or can articulate them. Generally, most PMs focus on delivering the project on time and on budget, yet the mix of success criteria varies from one project to another and there is a need to define it, communicate it, and ensure that it is consistently understood among all stakeholders. The factors that determine project success include scope, time, cost, and quality.

With scope, there are the priorities that were previously discussed that serve as a guide to sequencing the building of the project's product. However, even if the scope items are properly sequenced and prioritized, it is necessary to determine the relative priority of the other items that help articulate the project success criteria. Figure 6.6 can serve as a tool to help gain an understanding of the project success criteria based on ranking the main project constraints against each other.

| | Scope | Time | Cost | Quality |
|---|---|---|---|---|
| **Scope** | X | ? | ? | ? |
| **Time** | X | X | ? | ? |
| **Cost** | X | X | X | ? |

The success criteria face-off helps with understanding which of the four competing demands that help determine success are more important, and then to sequence them. The scope needs to have a separate ranking and sequencing, but regardless, it is imperative to gain an understanding of which item is more important relative to the others. Each intersection of two items provides an answer as to which item is more rigid (i.e., more important to prioritize).

**Figure 6.6**   Project success criteria face-off

When considering all of the potential intersections on the face-off matrix, it is imperative to get answers as to which aspect of the project is more important to meet. For example, if a project for moving into a new facility is considered, time is of the essence and one would assume that the PM would be better off delivering on time, rather than saving money. Although the constraints face-off is not an exact science, it provides a strong guideline as to which aspects of the project are more important. The sponsor is supposed to provide the answers to the PM about these guidelines. When looking at any of the intersections, the PM must not provide any of the following answers: (1) I don't know or (2) It depends. If the answer to any of the intersections in Figure 6.6 is either of these two, more information is needed from the sponsor.

Determining the project success criteria is not only critical to the ability to pursue and deliver value, but it is also a critical step in performing effective risk management. Risk is not just an event, but rather an event that has an impact on project success. Without understanding what constitutes project success, it will be impossible to perform a proper risk management process. It will be riddled with wasted effort in the form of managing events that are not risks and, in turn, missing valid and important risks. Effective risk management also helps determine which risks the project's actions and results introduce to the organization.

Project success criteria also helps articulate acceptance criteria and the definition of *done* (in agile). Acceptance criteria helps articulate technical performance and technical measures of success. This, in turn, serves as an important input to testing and the creation of test cases.

When it comes to defining project success, not all stakeholders view success in the same way and different stakeholders may have significantly different views of what success should look like. Some stakeholders focus on certain features, functionalities, or performance measures; others focus on timely delivery; and some on keeping within budget. Additional stakeholders' considerations also include focus on specific processes, impact on operations, and addressing specific stakeholders' needs. It is virtually impossible to satisfy all stakeholders so, overall, the success criteria originates and is defined by the sponsor. The PM should try to maximize the value creation toward the sponsor's mandate, while minimizing the negative impact on other stakeholders. Both the sponsor and the PM should try to align stakeholders' view of success as much as possible, but it is expected that some views will remain inconsistent with each other. Most important, it is necessary to ensure that the project success criteria align with the strategic objectives for which the project was undertaken.

It is not uncommon to see projects in which some of their success criteria vary significantly from the target; or projects that were initially perceived in one way, only to be viewed differently later on. The Sydney Opera House, as shown in Figure 6.7, is an example of a project that was significantly late and over budget, but years later, people no longer question the viability of the project's outcome since it turned out to be one of the most iconic and visited tourist attractions in the world with close to 11 million visitors per year.

The Sydney Opera House was hardly viewed as a success in its early days. Construction commenced in 1959 with the expectations that it would take 4 years, but it actually took 14. The original cost estimate was $7 million, but it finished at over $102 million with an almost 1,500% budget overrun.

**Figure 6.7**   The Sydney Opera House

### Project Approach

With an understanding of what success should look like, it is time to think about the project approach. This involves picking a life-cycle approach, such as water-fall or agile (sponsorship of agile projects will be discussed later in this chapter), as well as establishing a framework and high-level supporting guidelines for the PM to follow:

- *Resource management and allocation*—how the project will identify its re-source needs and obtain resources
- *Cross-project collaboration mechanism*—how to manage shared resources and coordinate their availability across projects to minimize waste and over-allocation
- *Governance and sign-off*—establish project governance including sign-off, decision-making processes, turnarounds, and criteria; assigning and defi-nition of authority levels, gates, and milestones
- *Escalations*—establish escalation procedures, along with thresholds and criteria
- *Roles and responsibilities*—in relation to project management, business analysis, sponsorship, and governance; make sure roles, responsibilities, and ownership areas are defined

It is not the role of the sponsor to build these items or to dive into their details, but rather to provide guidance, support, a mandate, and a framework for the PM to use.

## PROJECT CHARTER

The project charter serves many purposes, but it should mostly be viewed as the birth certificate of the project, its mandate, a summary of the knowledge regarding the project, the official hand off from the business case to the project, and a con-tract between the sponsor and the PM. It is common to come across projects with charters that are too long and vague, but there has been noticeable improvement in recent years as the number of projects that do not have a charter has gone down significantly. There is an increased awareness regarding the role and the impor-tance of the charter. Many organizations focus on producing charters for larger projects that require more rigor and scrutiny to ensure they are successful, while for smaller projects a charter is not needed. This is fine as long as the smaller proj-ects are not mismanaged.

The charter has to be short (generally up to three pages) and serve as an op-portunity to show the organization and the team how important the project is, the project's focus, and the potential value it brings to the organization. It takes on the role of a legal document (to authorize the project), a marketing tool (to show the value it brings), and a way to set expectations (a short and articulate review of what the project is about).

The view on who writes the project charter has shifted through the years. It used to be associated with the sponsor, then PMs began to handle it, but now the consensus is around having the sponsor *own* the charter but with either the sponsor or PM writing it. In the event that the PM writes the charter, the sponsor needs to provide support and guidance. It is quite easy to create a list of items to include in the charter, but populating the document with *quality* information is a challenge, especially when it has to be done in short form. The charter should include the following information:

a. Business objectives (why the team members are here)
b. Project objectives (what)
c. High-level project scope (and boundaries), along with key deliverables
d. Governance, approach, and life-cycle type
e. High-level expected cost
f. High-level timelines and milestones
g. Naming the PM, along with authority level
h. Key roles and responsibilities
i. High-level risks, assumptions, constraints, issues, and dependencies
j. Signatures of the sponsor, PM, and the customer

For the most part, the charter should not change throughout the life of the project. If it does, a change in the charter should be viewed as a new mandate and most likely a new project.

## SELECTING AND WORKING WITH THE PM

Finding the right PM is one of the most important things for the sponsor to do since it is critical for project success that the PM is suitable for the role and the challenges. It is also important to ensure that the sponsor and the PM develop a good rapport and are able to work effectively together. Unfortunately, in most environments, there is limited attention to this matter and virtually no formality or consistency. In many cases, PM selection is based on availability, and naturally it takes place under time pressure and budgetary constraints. One of the challenges when it comes to selecting a PM is that there is no consistent *off-the-shelf* set of criteria. There are some hard skills and typical soft (or interpersonal) skills to consider, but there are three other subjective factors to address:

1. *The specific needs of the project*—the project objectives, nature of the work, aggressiveness of the constraints, resource management, and authority of the PM
2. *Organizational context*—competing priorities, cross-project collaboration, support level (e.g., PMO, templates), change management, and political considerations
3. *The fit*—the working relationship and rapport between the sponsor and the PM

These three considerations are up to the sponsor's judgment, experience, and understanding of the context. Table 6.3 provides a review of important traits that the sponsor should look for when choosing a PM for his/her project. In addition to these traits, the sponsor should also look for capabilities related to the following:

- Be able to contribute to the creation of a shared vision and to relay the vision to team members and other stakeholders
- Demonstrate team building and development skills
- Be able to pick up and maintain context on organizational considerations, as well as familiarity with organizational change concepts and impact
- Demonstrate enthusiasm about the role and the challenge
- Be trustworthy—demonstrate and maintain integrity, credibility, and accountability
- Demonstrate effective prioritization and time management skills, including the ability to delegate
- Be able to measure and articulate needs, plan for and manage resources, and work within defined capacity
- Show appropriate level of support for the team; beyond the rapport with the sponsor, the PM needs to be a good fit with the team

**Table 6.3**  Key traits for the PM

| PM Traits | How to Identify |
|---|---|
| Adaptive and flexible | Easily and quickly adjusts to changing conditions; ready and able to change as needed, while remaining positive and focused. |
| Collaborative | Works well within the team and across with other stakeholders, PMs, and managers in a constructive manner. |
| Outstanding communication skills | Strong and effective communicator, relationship builder, and expectation manager. Includes nonverbal communication, being empathetic, being good at providing feedback, demonstrating active listening, engaging in discussions and a variety of question-asking techniques, minimizing redundancy, providing clarity, building trust, and *owning* communication. |
| Problem solving | Looks for root causes and win-win solutions systematically and timely. |
| Works effectively under pressure | If all of the previous items are in place, it is likely that the individual can handle pressure effectively. This includes maintaining professional conduct, staying focused on the objectives, refraining from allowing personal agendas to take over, minimizing emotional responses, showing resiliency, and maintaining composure in the face of turbulence. |

These traits should not be taken lightly or viewed as trivial. Not all PMs will possess all of these traits, or to the same extent, but it is important to check which of these traits are more applicable to any given situation and ensure that the PM is a good fit. Also, note the absence of technical skills from this list, as well as *hard* PM skills (e.g., schedule, cost, and risk management), which are easier to learn and acquire.

## Mistakes Related to Choosing a PM

Many sponsors end up with a PM who is not a good fit for the job, the challenge, or the organization due to a variety of reasons—ranging from a lack of experience to a failure to demonstrate the traits and capabilities listed in this section. When there becomes a need for a PM, time is usually a pressuring factor. It is common for the sponsor to rush through the hiring process (especially because in many organizations the hiring process is cumbersome and too slow for the needs) and, in some cases, upon the start of the project, there is no PM in place. In addition to the danger of ending up with the wrong PM once they are hired, having no PM at the start of the project will force the new PM, once hired, to *play catch up* from day one and to lack important context and information about the project and the charter.

Sponsors should also ensure that they do not confuse a candidate's desire or enthusiasm with ability or fit—or confuse someone's availability with being a suitable candidate. Another potential problem is when PMs impress the sponsor in the interview with war stories and abilities that are either irrelevant or non-transferable to the current context and challenge. In addition, it is increasingly common to see overlaps in roles and responsibilities that may lead to confusion and, subsequently, to problems—due to unclear role definitions between PMs, BAs, delivery managers, and change managers. In case additional roles are associated with the project, it is important for the sponsor to define the roles and responsibilities, boundaries, and touchpoints. This is also applicable for when there is more than one PM in place, or in many agile environments, where there are both Scrum Masters and PMs. Last but not least, the sponsor cannot just deposit the project in the hands of the PM, hoping that he/she will immediately take over and be fully responsible and accountable. The sponsor needs to work toward building rapport, articulating the PM role, and ensuring that the boundaries and touchpoints are in place.

## PROJECT VERSUS PRODUCT THINKING

Sponsors need to shift their thinking from project-based to a more holistic product-driven approach. In environments where it is not relevant to think *product*, sponsors need to shift into a more business or portfolio type of thinking. The need for the more holistic approach means taking on initiatives *not* on a project-by-project basis, but rather more systematically in a way that will serve the organization better. A focus on projects is not detrimental to delivering on the project objectives, but it may not best serve the organization. When focusing on the project level, there is little use of the planning processes that are listed in the following sections.

## Portfolio Management

Lack of portfolio thinking may lead to decisions that favor short-term project needs over long-term organizational goals. It may also encourage PMs to focus on project-specific or siloed goals, as opposed to long-run benefits. Additional challenges as a result of the lack of portfolio thinking are less focus on articulating and managing capacity (i.e., bandwidth, resources, and money) and little awareness about the importance of proper prioritization—both for the objectives and constraints within the project, as well as for cross-project prioritization and urgency assessment.

## Resource Planning

Related to portfolio management is the area of resource planning and management. Resource allocation is the *wildcard* of the constraints and can be a significant source of conflict in projects and organizations, as well as a cause for project failures. Resource planning is a key step toward building a realistic schedule and it needs to be managed closely by the PM with support from—and collaboration with—the sponsor.

## Lessons Learned

Despite the awareness around it, relatively few organizations follow through with meaningful action to not only capture lessons, but also apply them properly and in context. Most sponsors would argue that they do not have time to go through a proper lessons learned process, nor to successfully document and subsequently retrieve the lessons in context. With that said, what is the solution? Agile methods call for an application of lessons at the end of every iteration (i.e., sprint)—so it is often enough, covers a short period of time, and is limited in both volume and scope. It is essentially bringing the concept of continuous improvement (i.e., Kaizen) to life. However, a focus on the tactical aspects of the project is too limited to make an impactful difference on the performance of the organization. A more meaningful lessons learned process that should be facilitated by the sponsor is performing a proper post-project study that circles back to the business case and reviews what really happened throughout the project, including trends with scope and change control, risks, impact on the organization, benefits realization, and a review of whether and to what extent the original intent was delivered—and why. This type of analysis will also provide insight into the project selection criteria, definition of success, selection of the PM, and alignment to strategic needs.

## Product Support and Integration

Under project (*siloed*) thinking, PMs tend to focus on the current project, even if some of their decisions may be counter to long-term organizational needs. This is not to imply fault with the PMs. In fact, the fault is on the organization because the mandates, messages, and reward systems all veer the PMs toward maintaining short-term thinking that heavily favor their projects—almost no matter what. This problem also manifests itself when it comes to implementation, integration, and product support since short-term performance and meeting specific objectives may prevail over doing the right thing for the organization. These short-term considerations may often favor items that are associated with the PM's career, growth, or even rewards. A more product-related approach can help ensure maximization of the product benefits, which are in greater support of long-term organizational needs.

## Long-Term Planning

Integration of products, ensuring support, and maximizing the longevity of the product should all be common objectives across the organization. This does not imply that PMs intentionally build products that do not last, but it is imperative to incorporate a common view across the organization that works toward product integration and support, as well as long-term planning in product strategy, continuity, alignment, and a systematic definition of the view of organizational needs.

# SPONSORSHIP IN AGILE ENVIRONMENTS

Agile is not new, but its growth and increasing rate of adoption introduce new challenges (and opportunities) on an ongoing basis. Agile is also not the solution for all problems, but it is an approach, an umbrella, and a state of mind that if done properly, can yield significant benefits for the performing organization. With that said, if agile is introduced in the wrong way, in an unsuitable environment, and under the wrong circumstances, it will cause more harm than good and there will always be someone who puts the blame on agile.

## What Is Agile?

Agile is a pragmatic approach that recognizes that both the project team and the client do not know everything that has to be done up front in a project and that things will change along the way. Agile is an empirical approach—or observation-based. It is open to changing needs and is evolutionary by nature as multiple iterations (or sprints) each produce a *shippable* product increment that is grouped into releases, where the customer actually receives, accepts, and, if needed, uses the released product increment. Agile addresses many of the challenges that were introduced by practices related to the waterfall approach, also known as a deterministic approach, where the team finalizes the requirements early on and then goes about building the agreed-upon product. Agile combines two approaches: incremental (where product increments are released along the way) and iterative (where adapting to change is continuous). Agile is not simply about breaking a large project into many small waterfall phases.

It is not that agile is simply better than waterfall. Although it addresses many bad practices that have been enabled by waterfall, there is still a place and time for a more deterministic approach. If a project has a set scope that will not change and if the client does not need to benefit from early releases of the product by using it along the way, a waterfall approach may be suitable. Also, because agile tries to fix some of the problems associated with waterfall does not mean that waterfall is at fault for project failures. Waterfall simply enables some bad behaviors by allowing them to *hide* for too long before they are realized. For example, because there are no interim releases and iterations along the way, the customer only sees the product at the very end after testing has been completed—and only then can they provide feedback. It could be that customer updates did not portray the actual picture of how the project was progressing, so the client had no chance to realize the issues at hand. This does not imply that the project team deliberately misled the client, but it is possible that information was communicated in a way that was misunderstood by the client. Good business analysis work and effective communication between the project team and the client can minimize the risk of such problems, but there is no guarantee communication gaps won't exist.

## Agile Roles

All agile methodologies have specific views about the roles within an agile team. More specifically, a Scrum team (type of agile) requires three roles: the product owner, the Scrum Master, and team members.

*The product owner* is essentially the equivalent of the project sponsor. Many organizations will engage the use of both a product owner and a sponsor and this section covers the interactions and challenges between the two roles. According to Scrum.org,[5] the product owner is the sole person responsible for managing the product backlog, which is the prioritized and estimated scope of the project. As the person who calls the shots, defines the mandate, and accepts (or rejects) deliverables, the product owner is the *single wringable neck*. He/she is where the buck stops and is accountable for the project.

The product owner is one person, not a committee; he/she may represent the desires of a committee in the product backlog, but those wanting to change an item's priority on the backlog must address the product owner. For the product owner to succeed, the entire organization must respect his/her decisions. The product owner essentially acts as a sponsor, but must play a much more involved and engaged role than what most sponsors demonstrate. It is therefore important to ensure that when someone is appointed as a product owner, he/she has the capacity, the ability, and the intent to perform this role as needed. Agile environments are unforgiving in these two senses:

1. *Whatever organizational problems exist, they will surface and hinder the project*—any issues around processes, roles and responsibilities, resource availability, decision making and sign off, mandate, change control,

acceptance, accountability, estimates, or cost management will quickly become hurdles in the way of delivering success on agile projects.

2. *When things start heading sideways, failure comes quickly*—agile is *unforgiving* in the same way that waterfall is *forgiving*—because waterfall enables us to kick the can down the road and procrastinate about problems until later. In agile projects, there is no *later* since the iterations are short and by the end of the iteration, it is necessary to be able to show something of value to the customer.

It is therefore important that the product owner is available frequently throughout every iteration; on the first and the last day of the iteration for planning and backlog maintenance; as well as on an ad hoc, as-needed basis for anything that may come up that requires the product owner's involvement, decision-making capacity, or feedback. If the sponsor cannot act as a product owner, the role should then be split into both a product owner and a sponsor. In this case, a clear role definition must be affirmed, along with an understanding of the touchpoints and the interactions between the two roles. A common split in the roles occurs where the product owner provides a more hands-on approach with the agile team and works within the mandate provided by the sponsor. The sponsor, in turn, acts more as an executive sponsor with only limited involvement and interaction—which will be mostly with the product owner. The sponsor gets involved in some matters related to the acceptance of major deliverables, decisions about releases, or when there are significant issues with the product backlog.

The *Scrum Master* (sometimes known as an Agile Coach) can be viewed similarly to the role of the PM. The *fathers* who introduced agile in 2001 were adamant about not calling the Scrum Master a PM since they did not want the reputation of PMs as firefighters or police officers to stick to that of the Scrum Master. In other words, in many instances PMs are known to be mostly consumed with reacting to situations and "herding cats," and the agile creators wanted a role that is focused primarily on the agile process. Since many Scrum Masters are mandated to focus almost solely on agile processes, artifacts, and ceremonies, many organizations also include the role of the PM, creating a need to ensure that the two roles are clearly defined, boundaries are set, authority levels are in place, and that each of the roles knows where one ends and the other begins. It is common to see the Scrum Master facilitating the agile process while the PM acts more outward toward the organization, the change, governance, and reporting. Either way, and especially when dealing with both a PM and a Scrum Master, the sponsor needs to define the roles and ensure that they work effectively together.

*Team member* is the third type of role and it refers to anyone on the team who produces value. The primary intent here is to reference the developers and testers (in a technology project) who make up most of the *team*. It is important to ensure the team is cohesive and no "us versus them" sentiments exist.

In recent years, the notion of the BA has finally started to trickle into agile projects and agile practitioners are beginning to realize the need for either having a BA role or at least making sure that team members possess business analysis skills. An extensive review of the role of the BA in an agile environment can be found in my book, *Agile Business Analysis*.[6] The book also explores the interactions between the BA and other roles in and around the project. When it comes to the interaction with the product owner, there can be significant benefits—including the ability to consolidate information, articulate messages and impacts, provide relevant context, and serve as the eyes and ears of the product owner. It is important, however, to ensure that the BA is not confused with the product owner and to not get tempted to *replace* the product owner with a BA. Although BAs are an important component that enables agile project success, the BA lacks the formal authority, seniority, strategic thinking, clout, visibility to other initiatives, and the context to actually act as a product owner.

## The Product Owner as Sponsor of an Agile Project

The product owner is the leader who is responsible for maximizing the value of the products being created by an agile team, and he/she also needs to take on the responsibilities of a business strategist, a product designer, an analyst, a customer liaison, and sometimes even a PM. Whether acting as just the product owner or also as the sponsor, he/she defines and owns the vision for the project, prioritizes the needs, serves as the final decision maker on anything related to the product backlog, oversees the delivery of value to the customer, proactively works with the customer to address their needs, and accepts/rejects deliverables.

In most organizations the roles of the sponsor and the product owner are not combined unless it is a small agile project. While both roles represent the voice of the business and of the organization, a sponsor typically brings a more formal and hierarchical power mix. In most cases, it also benefits the team when the roles are separate, as the seniority of the sponsor may compromise the team's ability to communicate and act openly in the presence of the sponsor, especially considering the team's need to work closely and regularly with the product owner.

## The *Proxy*

Project sponsors are not PMs or Scrum Masters and when they are not product owners, there has to be a clear distinction between the roles. It is likely that the sponsor/product owner is not going to have the capacity or availability to attend to the project as required. In these cases, the sponsor needs to delegate some of the mandate, roles, and responsibilities to a proxy who can have a more hands-on approach. When the sponsor cannot provide the support that the agile project needs, he/she should delegate part of their role to someone who acts within their authority and mandate and on their behalf. In a way, it is like appointing a junior sponsor, where he/she will act on behalf of the sponsor, report back to the sponsor, and escalate decisions to the sponsor that he/she is unable or not authorized to make.

The proxy must not only act on behalf of the sponsor, but also report back and demonstrate a consistent approach that does not challenge, question, or undermine the mandate or leadership of the sponsor. In such a case, clear and ongoing touchpoints need to be established and escalation procedures must be put in place so there is a clear path for the information, decisions, and sign-offs to flow.

Introducing a proxy to the mix does not need to be limited to agile projects. It is clearly more urgent to have a hands-on representative for the sponsor in agile projects, but even projects with more deterministic life-cycle approaches can benefit from a sponsor proxy who can guide the team on smaller matters and/or when the sponsor is not available.

# MORE ON EFFECTIVE PROJECT SPONSORSHIP

## Career Path and the Professional *Sponsor*

There are career paths for PMs, BAs, change practitioners, and multiple other roles and professions; however, there is no career path for project sponsors. Exacerbating this problem is the fact that the role of the sponsor is a *secondary* role. In other words, the individual appointed to become the sponsor is first and foremost a member of management and has a primary managerial role. These roles produce a high work volume and lead to over-allocation and conflict over capacity. Since people tend to default to their primary roles, the secondary (sponsor) role ends up suffering.

The career path for sponsors is something that needs to be promoted by those who act as sponsors, but there is also a need for senior levels of the organization to support it. Such a career path should involve a set of concepts, along with a job description and growth path:

- Introduce specific jobs and a list of competencies that can help people progress toward their goals
- Establish best practices and introduce consistent tools
- Identify a set of competencies for sponsors so it is easier to identify and hone in on skills and experience for candidates
- Design and deliver training programs that are tailored to sponsors' needs
- Create a sponsorship certificate

The creation of a career path can help *advertise* the role of the sponsor in order to attract suitable candidates, and it may encourage people to focus on this path and pursue career and development choices that will help them progress to a sponsor role. It is important to note that in most cases sponsors are members of senior management and by this virtue they become the sponsor. They typically have the seniority, clout, access to information, and oversight to act as a sponsor. With that said, although most members of senior management are qualified and suitable for the job, they often lack the capacity and awareness to become a sponsor. A career path can help them focus on the sponsor role. Alternately, it would be beneficial to look into introducing the *professional sponsor*, who will be an individual who is brought into the organization based on their relevant skills to perform the role of sponsor. This may introduce some challenges around seniority and clout, but these sponsors can also be a proxy—acting as the sponsor on the ground and working within the mandate of the senior member of management who is too busy to attend to the project's needs.

Naturally, the sponsor, who is an existing member of management, not only better understands the fabric of the organization, but he/she also brings passion to the role. This passion comes with the personal involvement the sponsor has with the initiative and with the stakes involved. Of course, the sponsor's involvement and passion might be split due to their primary managerial role. When it comes to professional sponsors, they will most likely not be all-in on every change since it is not their baby and there is no personal involvement with the initiative. With that said, professional sponsors bring focus and relevant capabilities to perform their role, along with less residue as a result of organizational politics, or due to relationships and involvement in other initiatives. These sponsors can channel their dedication to the initiative and focus on their role as a way to replace a lower level of passion. As the initiative moves forward, professional sponsors are likely to develop the passion as if it was their own to begin with.

## Growth Mindset

The project sponsor needs to have a *growth* mindset: individual and organizational growth, process improvement, collaboration, and focusing on capturing opportunities. The sponsor needs to drive this type of growth through coaching, developing suitable attitudes and aptitudes for growth, and enabling people to leverage their strengths. All this needs to be done while focusing on the project objectives and in support of business needs.

As a leader, the sponsor needs to create a working environment that fosters that growth, along with increasing buy-in, motivating, and enhancing people's conformity to the processes, the team, the goals, and the organization. How does someone achieve these ambitious goals? The sponsor needs to focus more on the following:

a. Select the right PM who will project positive, can-do attitudes and drive toward the team
b. Encourage team members to support and help each other
c. Streamline and oversee communications and ensure that there are no gaps or confusion
d. Establish an environment that is based on trust and openness, where people feel safe to challenge each other, disagree, and innovate while remaining positive, constructive, and professional (as opposed to personal)
e. Work with the team on introducing team norms to enable creativity and interaction

f.  Introduce routines and symbols to help people feel safe and familiar with the ongoing structure
g.  Establish clear and transparent decision-making and escalation procedures for issues and problems
h.  Demonstrate accountability while maintaining transparency
i.  Show respect and ensure that people act nicely toward each other
j.  Build extracurricular activities into the team's routine to maintain interest and to have something to look forward to; incorporate rewards and recognition
k.  Keep your style, handling, and responses consistent and hold back before responding to tight or emotional situations
l.  Lead by example

## Systematic Approach

Sponsors should develop a systematic approach to ensure that when it comes to the work of the project, all aspects are covered. While some may say that this should be done by the PM, it needs to start with the sponsor's due diligence. The way to ensure a systematic approach is through the creation of a context map or a mind map. Early on in the project, the sponsor needs to make sure that the PM and the team end up looking at everything that there is to do—without missing anything. All of the deliverables, their associated requirements, and the individuals who own these pieces must be identified or accounted for. This process is also not about duplicating the business analysis effort; although, the contribution of a BA here may be beneficial.

## Topic or Deliverable

The mind map starts with listing the main deliverables. Using an example of building a house, the mind map allows us to lay out the needs in the following manner:

1.  List the primary deliverable that needs to be produced (e.g., framing for a house); this is generally produced by the sponsor
2.  Work with a BA and SMEs to identify sub-elements of this deliverable (e.g., walls, roof, and foundation); this is generally done by interviewing the business
3.  Get from the BA a list of high-level requirements to produce the items listed previously (e.g., wood, wood framing, shingles, and concrete); this is done through engaging the technical team or SMEs to figure out what they need in order to deliver the business needs
4.  Link these requirements to an owner (e.g., roofer or contractor); there is no need here to identify an individual or a particular resource who will do the work, but rather the ownership of each area

This mind map provides an initial context for what needs to be reviewed and who will be working together; and since the team works with the business and with the technical experts, the map will grow by deliverables, by requirements, and accordingly, by ownership.

Here is a series of items (can be viewed as a checklist) for the sponsor to consider when working on ensuring that a high-level understanding of the scope of work is maintained, as well as knowing who should own or oversee each piece (once again, there is a business analysis component here, so the sponsor should seek the help of a BA):

1. Articulate the business needs through a business requirements document, along with a sign-off.
2. Engage SMEs to map out the tools and technology that are required to fulfill the business needs. This may not be a complete list and it may include options, but it should capture what is known at this point.
3. Identify the type of resources that will be needed to lead, oversee, and perform the work. This is not about specific individuals, but rather resource types and skill levels.
4. Build a RACI chart (or RASCI, where the S is for Support).
5. Look into building another RACI for project management activities (involving those who will subsequently act as PMs, BAs, and decision makers).
6. Engage the areas' managers of those roles identified in the RACI chart and start working on identifying suitable individual names.
7. Have the PM book a kickoff session where the sponsor will introduce the decision-making and escalation procedures. These include thresholds and criteria (e.g., specified impact on budget, security, or end use).
8. Empower the PM to work with the RACI chart on a rolling wave planning basis—one period at a time.
9. Pick the right life-cycle approach: if agile, work with the team to prioritize, sequence, and identify logical groupings and minimal feature set; if waterfall, identify major milestones.
10. With this guidance, the PM can pick up from here.
11. Establish which meetings and events the sponsor must attend and what level of involvement is required.
12. The sponsor identifies goals, metrics, and reports to track independently of the PM.

## Risk Management

The area of risk management in projects is lacking. Although there are strong methodologies to identify and manage risks, a lack of time, lack of awareness, and a failure to follow the processes often lead to surprises and the introduction of risks at a level that is beyond what the organization can handle. Although project risk management is under the responsibility of the PM, the mandate, focus, and rigor of the risk management processes should be established by the sponsor. Moreover, the sponsor needs to ensure that risks that are beyond the project are looked at—including business or operational risks, as well as cross-project risks. The latter type of risks includes those that are introduced by one project but their impact is on other projects (e.g., resource-related risks). Risk management should also consider any problems that may arise due to communication challenges and gaps, or to interactions with and among stakeholders.

Keeping in mind that risk management is much more difficult to manage in reality than in theory—due to emotions and to personal agendas—sponsors also need to establish a new and more proactive look at risk management to incorporate the following considerations, or at least to establish a framework for these items:

- *Readiness*—a review of the team's and the organization's readiness for the project. Readiness includes areas related to organizational support (decisions, mandates, governance, resources, and budgets); leadership; capacity to handle the project's workload; team readiness; definition of success; strategic alignment; and organizational change considerations.
- *Complexity assessment*—gauge the level of complexity that the current initiative is facing, generally in relation to previous, similar initiatives. Any area of concern from the readiness assessment may introduce complexity. Otherwise, complexity could be introduced from the following areas: technical or product-related, organizational, environmental (external), or stakeholder-related. Project duration and size, constraints, internal dependencies, overall level of uncertainty, and dependencies with other initiatives should also be considered.
- *Stakeholders*—a stakeholder environmental scan must be performed in order to learn who the stakeholders are, their expectations, expected influence, conduct, contribution, and overall involvement in the project. Although stakeholders were mentioned as a potential area in the complexity assessment, special attention needs to be given to this area since stakeholders' attitudes, conduct, and involvement are likely to play critical roles in the project's success or failure.
- *Reporting*—ensure that there are specific measurements for both schedule and cost performance. It is important to ingrain the concept of earned value and ensure that PMs track actual cost versus planned cost, and all in the context of the amount of value created in relation to the money spent.
- *Quality and the cost of quality*—the sponsor needs to ensure that the PM will maintain a sufficient level of awareness toward planning for, ensuring, and measuring quality. The problems that exist around quality management are primarily cultural because quality is sought after, but PMs have limited awareness as to how to achieve or measure it. It is also important to know how much quality costs (through prevention and appraisal) as part of delivering value and doing the right thing. It is also vital to understand how much nonconformance and quality problems/failures cost. Despite the

strong collective knowledge of quality concepts, there is still a lag in ensuring that the right action is taken to achieve quality, especially when it comes to competing demands—such as time and money.

Sponsors need to send a clear message to their PMs that a contingency is in place to cover for weak planning (e.g., when not enough money was budgeted to perform an activity so the contingency fund must be tapped into in order to complete it). Contingency is where money (or time) is set aside to account for unexpected events that may derail the project.

The more prepared the team is for things that might hit them throughout the project, the better all of the objectives and success criteria that may be impacted are understood, and the better the chance for delivering project success. Therefore, risk management should be second nature for a PM—ensuring that they have the awareness and the capacity to look after it.

## RECAP

This chapter reviewed multiple considerations that can help project sponsors perform their role more effectively. Although this chapter refers to project sponsorship, the change sponsor can also benefit from applying the concepts discussed here since they are applicable to all types of projects, including change projects. Also examined here were the characteristics that are necessary in order to be a good sponsor, along with some activities that sponsors need to perform prior to the project (specifically, business case analysis and ensuring there is a strategic alignment). Additional considerations included portfolio management (capacity management and prioritization), the selection of the PM, and establishing a cross-project collaboration mechanism.

As part of the discussion of the sponsor's role in agile environments, the idea of the proxy sponsor was reviewed. It is important to note that a proxy sponsor is not something that is only suitable for agile projects because projects of all lifecycle approaches can benefit from a proxy when the *real* sponsor is not sufficiently available.

The chapter ended with the call to establish a career path for sponsors, the need to get the sponsor to be growth oriented, and to ensure that there is enough focus on the product—not only on the project. This was followed by a list of things to consider as part of establishing a positive work environment and concluded with a short discussion on the role of the sponsor in ensuring risk management is performed properly.

Chapter 7 will pick up exactly where this chapter left off. Since Chapter 6 provided more of a high-level review of concepts, Chapter 7 will detail a few checklists and more specific things that the sponsor should engage in, look for, inquire about, and measure.

## NOTES

1. From the *Project Management Body of Knowledge, (PMBOK® Guide)—Sixth Edition*, Glossary, Project Management Institute, 2017.
2. Source: https://www.smithsonianmag.com/smart-news/what-50-lane-traffic-jam-looks-180956912/.
3. Source: http://thepeakperformancecenter.com/development-series/tool-box/seven-management-planning-tools/prioritization-matrix/.
4. https://www.toc-goldratt.com/en/product/Critical-Chain.
5. https://www.scrum.org/resources/what-is-a-product-owner.
6. Aguanno, Kevin and Ori Schibi. *Agile Business Analysis: Enabling Continuous Improvement of Requirements, Project Scope, and Agile Project Results.* J. Ross Publishing, 2017.

# 7

# KEY TIPS AND CONCEPTS FOR EFFECTIVE SPONSORSHIP

## THE EFFECTIVE SPONSOR

Chapter 6 introduced and elaborated on a series of considerations that help foster effective project sponsorship. With the increasing realization among many project practitioners and organizations that there is a sponsorship problem, it is necessary to take meaningful steps to improve performance around this important role in the organization. The problems with sponsorship, as discussed earlier, originate mainly from a lack of focus on the importance of the role and the lack of training, guidance, or clear expectations that goes with it. The performance of the project sponsor is critical to project success. The word *performance* here not only refers to tangible activities, but also to the availability of the sponsor, the level of support he/she provides to the project manager (PM) and the team, and the leg work that the sponsor does in relation to working with stakeholders and promoting the cause of the project against competing organizational demands.

Due to the seniority of the sponsor and the important contribution the sponsor makes to project success, the shock waves of weak and unengaged sponsorship have a significant impact on the organization by way of project failures. This reinforces the need to provide solid and consistent sponsorship for virtually all projects, including and especially change sponsorship. This chapter takes us further into our journey to improve sponsorship with a series of specific tips, actions, and thoughts that provide sponsors with a solid toolbox to use and exploit.

## Sponsorship and Project Failure

There is no argument that overall organizational capabilities, capacities, and performance have significantly improved throughout the years, but the rate of project failures and of challenged projects is still too high. This is despite the knowledge of the high cost associated with project and sponsorship failure *and* that solutions exist to fix project issues. A large number of projects fail because of reasons that are commonly known and uncomplicated, including:

a.  *Requirements*—a lack of proper understanding of the product's needs
b.  *Stakeholders*—a lack of understanding of stakeholders' needs, how to engage them, and how to set and manage realistic expectations
c.  *Resources*—a failure to realistically plan for resource allocation and utilization based on proper capacity management and prioritization
d.  *Success*—an unclear mandate and definition of objectives and success criteria; setting unrealistic expectations and focusing on time and cost over delivering value
e.  *Planning and coordination*—a lack of appreciation for planning, looking for shortcuts, and thinking in silos, rather than properly coordinating across projects
f.  *Short term*—pursuing short-term wins that provide visibility over investing in doing the right things
g.  *Communication*—a systemic lack of focus on communication and failing to engage in transparent and candid communication

Organizations keep stumbling over and over again on the same things; every time projects fail to deliver on their intended benefits, the reaction is surprise, as if the outcome was not already known. Then, we proceed to the next project and follow pretty much the same path that failed before—hoping that this time better results will be achieved. There are two things to be said about this approach:

1.  Doing the same thing again and again and expecting different results is one of the ways to define insanity
2.  Hope is not a strategy and hope alone will not replace skills, experience, competencies, and planning

An unscientific survey that I conducted over an extended period of time, and among hundreds of sponsors, PMs, and project practitioners, validated my own findings from over two decades of experience. In well over half of the projects that ended up falling short of their expectations, it was obvious that the project was not going to deliver success—and that outcome could be determined at its very early stages, sometimes as early as initiation. It does not take an expert to see when things do not add up, when the expectations are unrealistic, and when the organization does not provide the necessary support. Further, too often it was possible to see projects drifting toward failure. It was somewhat like watching a slow-motion train wreck, where there is little that anyone (PMs or sponsors) could do to change the course of events despite knowing what to do to fix it. On the one hand, the failure to act was due to cultural, political, and communication barriers, but it was also a result of a lack of clear understanding of the true extent of the situation, as well as a lack of understanding of (and ability to articulate) the available options. Due to the constant rush and pressure that PMs and sponsors are under—along with the reality of consistent and severe over-allocation and overwork of resources— little attention is paid to anything that is beyond what is mandatory to focus on or report. As a result, the response is to turn reactive, causing problems to be noticed too late, when the project is already engulfed in flames.

## Resource Management

One of the most difficult things for a PM or sponsor to get is more resources. Whoever makes the request faces a brick wall from the level above them because the decision maker only sees the short-term cost consideration. Almost always it comes down to looking only at the direct cost of adding a resource with no consideration toward the value that the additional resource will create (e.g., increased revenue or cost savings). There are multiple other ways that an additional resource can add value toward:

- Improving customer relations or satisfaction
- Helping to complete a task or a deliverable on time
- Helping to complete a task or deliverable to quality standards
- Providing support for existing efforts and reducing the workload of other resources
- Helping to distribute work to free up someone else's time so that they can perform their work properly, or to reduce their overtime, stress, and distractions

Adding resources does not just mean hiring. Hiring people introduces additional challenges that are associated with cost, effort, the time it takes to onboard them, the additional time it takes to bring them up to speed, and the chance that after all of that—they could fail. Effective resource management (see Table 7.1) also includes the proper sharing and allocation of resources toward high-priority initiatives and items.

**Table 7.1**  What is resource management?

| Resource Consideration | What and How (Driven by the Sponsor) |
|---|---|
| Capacity | Learn to measure and understand capacity (individual, team, project, and organization). Set realistic expectations about the ability to deliver on the needs and commitments. Capacity is about measuring the time available per person per day and what each individual can do with their time to add value. The availability is then factored by allocation, utilization, productivity, and the number of people available. |

*continued*

**Table 7.1**  *continued*

| Resource Consideration | What and How (Driven by the Sponsor) |
|---|---|
| Prioritize | It is virtually impossible to identify resource needs if the work is not prioritized. Prioritization needs to be systematic and both across initiatives (which project is more important) and within the project (elements of success, requirements). It is necessary to also consider urgency (timelines, impact, stakeholders). Additional considerations for prioritization include cost, complexity, risks, area of impact, and visibility. |
| Realize needs | Once there is an understanding of the capacity and priorities, it is necessary to articulate our resource needs. Start with a RACI chart and proceed to building a schedule, then communicate the need and set expectations around the impact if the needs are not met. |
| Gain commitment | The organization needs to provide commitment and, subsequently, the resources that were requested. |
| Collaborate and stagger projects | Collaboration happens at more than one level:<br>1. Sharing resources as needed based on changes and circumstances.<br>2. Cross-project collaboration, as was discussed in Chapter 6, ensures coordination and resource sharing by maximizing and optimizing resource utilization.<br>3. Stagger projects and activities to accommodate and work around the availability of the shared and most scarce resources. |

The items here serve almost as a roadmap for performing effective resource management. This is something that needs to be led, facilitated, and driven by the sponsor who, in turn, also serves as an escalation and decision-making point.

## Resource Management and Another Look at Prioritization

In Table 7.1, there is an item that may raise a question about whether or to what extent it belongs there: prioritization. This item made it to the table since it serves as a key consideration in effective resource management and as a part of reducing waste by focusing on what matters and what needs to take place next. In many environments, this has become a *sensitive* issue since it is hard to tell stakeholders that their item is of a low priority. Keep in mind that when a stakeholder says that something is important, the validity of their claim should not be questioned, but it is still necessary to discuss the sequence of their high-priority item based on technical considerations, other constraints, and logic.

It is also essential to remember that stakeholders tend to confuse whatever they view as important with the need to get it early. It is true that the later an item is slated to be delivered, the greater the chance that it will be scoped out; it is also true that the high-priority and high-complexity items need to be performed earlier if possible. However, with that said, many stakeholders' high-priority needs do not necessarily make the product viable; further, many of these items are more about the finish or the trim and it may not be feasible to deliver them early, or in *priority order*. For example, when a homeowner tells a custom home builder that the aquarium is a high-priority item, no one expects the aquarium to be built first in the empty field that is the site of the future home. It is also important to recognize that when it comes to certain key scope components, many stakeholders do not label these items as high priority. It is therefore important to ensure that stakeholders keep the prioritization process free of agendas and emotions, and that they focus on properly prioritizing items against each other.

Most exercises that attempt to prioritize items (e.g., requirements) yield a list where roughly 90% are considered high priority. When all items are considered high priority, nothing is high priority and the process of prioritization is essentially meaningless. It is therefore important to do two things when prioritizing:

1. Clarify that prioritization is about relativity, which means that even if an item is considered to be a low-priority item, it does not mean that it is unimportant, but rather that its relative importance is lower than the other items it is considered against.
2. Instead of using the term "prioritization," engage stakeholders by using "sequencing." It appears less emotional and less loaded. After all, the process of prioritization does not intend to question whether an item is important, but rather determines the order (or the sequence) of value delivery.

## A DAY IN THE LIFE OF THE PROJECT SPONSOR

It is very hard to identify an off-the-shelf set of activities that the sponsor should follow; even more so when it comes to their activities within each day. However, this chapter introduces a series of checklists that help sponsors identify and focus on what they need to do in order to improve their performance as sponsors. The sponsor needs to review these lists and then identify which items apply to their specific needs when it comes to addressing their projects. It is expected that each project demands different things from the sponsors, but beyond identifying the needs, the checklists also help sponsors in determining the amount of rigor and effort that these activities require, along with the frequency of their need to attend to each project. Since many sponsors end up sponsoring or overseeing multiple projects, identifying the needs and frequency of involvement will help sponsors plan and manage their time and priorities, as well as figure out how much of their time each project needs—on the way to performing effective capacity management.

When sponsors look at what their projects need from them and translate it to total effort, too often the amount of time they need to spend attending to a specific project ends up being higher than they assumed. Further, when adding up all the attention they need to pay to their projects, the combined effort ends up being beyond their available capacity, or even beyond their total capacity:

- *Available capacity*—most senior managers have a *day job* in addition to being a sponsor. When tallying up the total amount of effort needed for all tasks, it ends up being more than what they can allot. If, for example, a senior manager has 60% of their capacity dedicated to their day job and 40% to projects, but the projects require more than 40% of the sponsor's time, it can lead to the inability to provide timely decisions or make informed decisions. This problem is exacerbated when more than one project demands the sponsor's attention at the same time.
- *Total capacity*—in some cases, projects take up more time than the sponsor's capacity altogether, even if the sponsor does not have a day job.

Since many project problems originate with sponsorship, and a large percentage of sponsorship problems relate to sponsor availability, it is important for sponsors to focus on managing their own capacity. Since it is almost inevitable that multiple projects will max out the sponsor's attention, it is important for the sponsor to establish the mechanisms in Table 7.2 to minimize the impact of not being able to attend to all of the projects' needs.

**Table 7.2**  Minimizing the negative impact of sponsor availability issues

| Minimizing Fallout Due to Sponsor's Availability | Details |
|---|---|
| Timely decision making | Set protocols and expectations with the PM about milestones, timing of expected involvement, and ensuring that the sponsor is available at the specific times and intervals needed. |
| Clear and informed decision making | Ensure clear and concise reporting of project status and other related information to be received by the PM. In addition, the sponsor needs to establish lines of communication that are independent of the PM to get a proper picture of what is taking place in the project. The sponsor also needs to establish a checklist of questions to ask and things to focus on so he/she can stay informed and ensure that information flows in, as opposed to needing to pursue information. He/She must ask open-ended questions to understand the true state of the project. |
| Governance | Establish clear project governance: decision making, authority level, areas of responsibility for the PM versus the sponsor, and escalation criteria; thresholds and procedures. |
| Expectations | Ensure the PM knows what to expect regarding involvement, engagement, questions, escalations, and availability. Also, establish a course of action on what to do when the sponsor is not available. |

*continued*

| Minimizing Fallout Due to Sponsor's Availability | Details |
|---|---|
| Capacity, prioritization, and urgency | The sponsor needs to measure his/her own capacity and prioritize what needs to be done and in what order. Also, work with the PM to agree on prioritization and urgency criteria. The sponsor also needs to educate the PM, the team, and other stakeholders on how to sequence their work and their needs from the sponsor. |
| Proxy | The need to minimize the impact from the sponsor's lack of availability is a reminder of the benefits of naming a proxy sponsor who can help alleviate some of the sponsor's workload and free up some of the sponsor's availability. |

Since most sponsorship-related problems are related to sponsor availability, he/she needs to establish mechanisms that work on their own volition to make information available without the need to pursue it. Ensuring that information flows on a regular and ongoing basis can also help the sponsor maintain perspective, put things in context, and identify exceptions. Note that sponsorship-related problems often inflict significant damage on projects due to lack of direction, untimely and uninformed decisions, and confusion.

## High-Level Focus Areas for the Sponsor

Another step toward helping sponsors manage their days properly is determining what exactly are their responsibilities based on the project stage (see Table 7.3):

1. Initiating and kickstarting
2. Planning
3. Executing and control
4. Closing

There is no getting around these things since they serve as the foundation of project's needs. During the early stages of the project, the sponsor needs to set goals and priorities. The prioritization process cannot be skipped, and it needs to be performed in collaboration with other stakeholders, subject matter experts (SMEs), and any team members who are assigned to the project.

During planning, the sponsor needs to oversee the planning process and ensure that the PM and the team do not skip important steps or take too many shortcuts. This does not imply that the sponsor should micromanage or get too involved in the process, but rather the sponsor must make sure that enough time and focus are allowed for it. The sponsor also needs to work with stakeholders and the team to set *realistic* goals that will ensure that *realistic* expectations are put in place.

During the executing and control phases, the sponsor almost takes a step back as the more consistent type of involvement from the earlier stages of the project is replaced by a more as-needed type of involvement. This does not mean that the

**Table 7.3**   Sponsor's activity by project stage

| Project Stage | Key Sponsor Behavior |
|---|---|
| Initiating stage | • Set performance goals<br>• Select and mentor project manager<br>• Establish priorities |
| Planning stage | • Ensure planning<br>• Develop relationships with stakeholders |
| Executing stage | • Ensure adequate and effective communication<br>• Maintain relationships with stakeholders<br>• Ensure quality |
| Closing stage | • Identify and capture lessons learned<br>• Ensure capabilities and benefits are realized |

This a high-level breakdown of what the sponsor needs to focus on per project stage. Note that it does not imply that the sponsor needs to perform these activities; most of these things need to be delegated (mostly for the PM or lead to perform).

sponsor disengages, but that he/she supports the PM to ensure proper communication is taking place with stakeholders and that information is flowing. The sponsor needs to keep an eye on how the project is performing and to what extent the objectives are being met. When information is missing, late, or not in line with expectations, the sponsor needs to become aware of it in a timely manner and act accordingly.

When the project is coming to an end, the sponsor has to ensure handoff and benefits realization take place so value from the project's product can be achieved. Lessons learned is another area for the sponsor to oversee (performed by the PM, reviewed and accepted by the sponsor) with focus that goes beyond the project lessons to include lessons that pertain to the organization, business case, project selection, and approach taken. These lessons are of a more strategic nature than the *traditional* project lessons or post-implementation review.

## Things to Focus on and Measure— by Project Stage

### Initiation

Table 7.4 provides a detailed look into the activities that the sponsor needs to obverse, address, and measure during the initiation stage. Chapter 6 provided a review of the project charter and whether the sponsor or the PM should write it—concluding that the charter is the sponsor's document and is owned by the sponsor. Therefore, even if the sponsor does not write the charter, he/she needs to provide guidance and support. It is common for the PM to write the charter, but

**Table 7.4**    hings to observe, address, and measure during project initiation and kickstart

| Things to Observe | Things to Address | Things to Measure |
|---|---|---|
| • Charter (guide and oversee) <br> • *Sell* the project and relate it to business objectives <br> • Set realistic expectations <br> • Define and articulate success criteria <br> • Is the project purpose clear and understood? <br> • Check for acceptable levels of readiness and complexity <br> • Project initiation documents | • Select the right PM (and provide context and support) <br> • Verify that the charter covers the business case <br> • Ensure appropriate project organization is in place <br> • Allow sufficient time for the project <br> • Provide input to charter as needed <br> • Establish guidelines and expectation for planning <br> • Define criteria to get the most suitable resources <br> • Consider other options to address the project purpose <br> • Participate in kick-off and make go/no-go decisions | • Understanding of the project purpose by key stakeholders and the PM <br> • The purpose is properly addressed by the project <br> • Number and type of concerns about the charter <br> • Interlocking: check for other projects and initiatives in the organization that may impact/be impacted by the project <br> • Benchmarking: which past initiatives have been referred to for comparison? |

During initiation, the sponsor's focus is not on tangible things for the most part, but rather on setting the tone and ensuring there is proper setup and support for the project.

the sponsor cannot and should not pass it off to the PM and expect the charter to be written without his/her approval. In addition to the charter, the sponsor has to articulate the success criteria and work with the PM and stakeholders to ensure that they are clear and realistic. Also, check for any organizational considerations that may interfere with the project—through dependencies, resource allocation, and objectives.

## *Planning*

Key activities in the planning stage (see Table 7.5) include ensuring that the PM produces a realistic plan with clear milestones that are spread properly across the project. The sponsor should also make sure that the PM pays sufficient attention to project risks, and that the risk management activities consider the project activities' impact on business and operational matters. While the PM focuses primarily on project needs, the sponsor must guarantee that project considerations do not negatively impact the organization.

The sponsor needs to also work with both the PM and the business analyst (BA) to ensure that the requirements elicitation and management process gets enough focus and resources so that quality requirements are in place. In addition,

**Table 7.5**  Things to observe, address, and measure during project planning

| Things to Observe | Things to Address | Things to Measure |
|---|---|---|
| • Plan is realistic with clear milestones<br>• Consider both project and business risks<br>• Quality requirements built into each activity<br>• Realistic estimates aligned with objective<br>• Clearly stated project completion, success criteria, and sign-off requirements | • Check if plans are realistic<br>• Ensure that the team is not forced to commit to unrealistic expectations<br>• Allow sufficient time/capacity for planning<br>• Serve as an escalation point and be accessible as needed<br>• Ensure prioritization<br>• Optimize team's dynamics and effectiveness<br>• Document and manage assumptions, risks, constraints, and issues | • Who are key stakeholders?<br>• What do they think of the plan?<br>• What are the most critical project success factors?<br>• What trade-offs are required?<br>• How were project resources/time/cost estimates derived?<br>• Have functional managers agreed to the staffing plan?<br>• Is there a plan B?<br>• What the PM requires of the sponsor<br>• Do you think the project will be successful? Areas of concern? Challenging stakeholders? |

The sponsor needs to provide support and enable the PM to build a proper plan that will address project needs. At the same time, the sponsor can utilize the items in this table to gain an understanding of the quality of the plan. The sponsor also provides the mandate for planning activities and must ensure it is realistic and that any adjustments reflect the plan's findings.

the sponsor needs to enable the PM (along with the BA and the team) to produce realistic plans that are designed to deliver the product based on the requirements. An additional item to observe includes acceptance criteria and sign-off of the requirements and, subsequently, the deliverables.

There are many areas for the sponsor to check and address, including that the plans are realistic. This requires the sponsor to seek and explore additional information from other sources that can serve as a point of reference, a benchmark, or a reliable source of input to the planning elements that are under consideration. The extent of how realistic the plans are also depends on circumstances that are related to resource allocation and the level of organizational support. The sponsor should have influence over some of these items, while others are within the sponsor's areas of oversight or visibility. Based on findings from the planning process, the sponsor needs to determine whether the plans and the expectations are realistic and then make the necessary adjustments to ensure that they are.

During the planning process, the sponsor needs to be available to serve as an escalation point and a decision maker, and despite the pressure that the sponsor applies to move forward, he/she needs to allow sufficient time for planning. The word *sufficient*, when it comes to planning, is difficult to measure because there is a fine line between too little and too much—and the PM will typically ask for more time to plan. The sponsor needs to be able to determine not only whether there is sufficient effort and focus put into the planning process, but also whether the effort invested in the planning is efficient and pays off. It is important to minimize waste around planning and ensure a focused process. The activities listed in this section and in Table 7.5 can help the sponsor maintain a level of involvement and oversight over the planning process that will give him/her an idea of the quality of the planning process.

As planning is taking place, it is the sponsor's responsibility to oversee the prioritization process and ensure there is clarity around it. It is critical for the sponsor to facilitate it and provide clear guidance for the PM and the team to understand the order by which to perform the work—based on the sponsor's guidance. Proper prioritization is also key in supporting good team dynamics since it helps streamline the planning process and determine when value is going to be produced. Additional effective team engagement activities include:

- Establishing a direct line of communication with team members
- Ensuring transparency in decision making and being available for escalations
- Providing thresholds and guidelines for performance and exception management
- Making sure there is support for the PM in managing communication
- Supporting the PM in the establishment and following of ground rules
- Complementing the PM in engagement and communication activities

Another item to address during planning is to provide the PM with support (and if needed—legitimacy) in identifying and managing assumptions.

The sponsor needs to either ask about or measure several items during the planning process, including that the PM has a clear understanding of who the stakeholders are and what their view is of the project and the approach. The entire stakeholder engagement process needs to be a joint effort between the PM and the sponsor, and the two must ensure that their activities complement each other and that they produce a sufficient understanding of stakeholders' needs. These needs will help articulate the critical success factors for the project that, in turn, will provide a foundation for planning and the approach for making trade-offs throughout the project.

While most planning activities are led by the PM (based on the mandate provided by the sponsor), when it comes to resource planning—the sponsor needs to be more proactively and directly involved. Resource planning is often not done properly by the PMs because time estimates and commitments are produced based on hope and on the assumptions (not assurances) that resources will report to the project. The sponsor needs to work with the PM to ensure that he/she remains realistic in the resource planning process and that specific measures occur (i.e., RACI charts and assumption management). Beyond the challenges in planning for resources, the sponsor needs to support the PM in ensuring that the project's resource needs are met and that requests for resources are answered with the appropriate resources. While the sponsor is not involved in every transaction associated with resources, the sponsor serves as a decision maker and an escalation point when there are resource-related conflicts—especially between the PM and the resource owners. Generally, the sponsor needs to serve as an escalation point in support of the PM for anything that is beyond the PM's authority. Another item for the sponsor to observe is whether the resource owners or functional managers agree to the staffing plan and how resource needs are going to be met.

A sponsor also needs to inquire about a plan B. This does not refer to a plan B regarding the project itself or the approach to the project (these questions should be asked pre-project—or at the latest, during initiation); but rather about exploring options based on needs that emerge during the planning process. For example, what are the possible alternatives if there are resource constraints, technical dependencies, or organizational considerations (e.g., cross-project dependencies)? When items are introduced or imposed on the project, the sponsor has to help formulate a plan B and provide approvals for the proposed courses of action that are formulated by the PM.

In an effort to ensure alignment with the PM, the sponsor needs to check with the PM on any additional areas to address, including needs and expectations between the two during the next stages of the project. The sponsor needs to review the project plans and assess whether the project is on track or whether there are any areas of concerns that require the attention of the PM or other stakeholders.

### Executing and Control

During project execution and control, the sponsor should be evaluating reports and performance, handling changes, and making decisions in support of the project, among other things (see Table 7.6). Obviously, not all reports should get to the sponsor; only high-level ones, as well as specific reports that include information that the sponsor needs to know. This formal information must allow the sponsor to learn about the state of the project and make informed decisions accordingly. In addition, the sponsor also needs to obtain reliable information from informal sources, such as conversations, observations, and other ways to connect the dots. Looking for informal signs and signals involves asking to see some of the lower level detailed reports (randomly), participating in some team meetings, and having conversations with stakeholders. The sponsor also needs to track the outcome of completed change requests, as well as review assumptions, risks, and issue logs. The intent here is not to interfere, replace, or overlap with the PM's work, but rather to see things as they are impartially—not through the *lenses* of the PM.

The sponsor also has to check team performance and cohesiveness to ensure that the PM is leading them effectively. Any issues with team performance will soon (if they haven't already) impact the project work; and these things need to be addressed effectively and quickly if possible. In the process, the sponsor can also evaluate the PM's style and execution effectiveness and address any associated

**Table 7.6**  Things to observe, address, and measure during the project execution and control phases

| Things to Observe | Things to Address | Things to Measure |
|---|---|---|
| • Evaluate reports and performance<br>• Look for informal signals<br>• Check team performance and cohesiveness<br>• Track crisis situations, issues, changes, risks, and their handling<br>• PM style and control level<br>• Opportunities<br>• Is working relationship with PM effective (e.g., sufficient involvement; no micromanagement)?<br>• Are conflict resolution processes for the project team and stakeholders in place?<br>• Team follows processes and does not bypass scope change mechanisms or other project processes | • Ensure clear boundaries are in place and that processes are followed<br>• Evaluate progress and guide appropriately<br>• Empower, motivate, acknowledge/celebrate<br>• Identify underlying factors and root causes to address issues<br>• Celebrate milestones<br>• Document and realistically manage assumptions, risks, constraints, and issues based on actual conditions<br>• Motivate PM(s) and team members to identify and address their own project-related problems and facilitate effective escalations | • Tools/Training to improve team effectiveness<br>• Number of change requests made versus approved; compared to previous projects<br>• Biggest outstanding risks?<br>• Can performance be improved? The plan?<br>• Activities that add little/no value<br>• Have conditions/assumptions changed?<br>• Issues: what are they and what is the approach?<br>• Do any stakeholders pose challenges?<br>• Is the project getting the resources it needs? |

Sponsors' activities during project execution focuses on reviewing reports, approving changes and actions, providing sign-off on deliverables, supporting the team, and working behind the scenes to address issues, identify trends, solve problems, and connect the dots.

concerns. Working with the team and with the PM, along with ongoing stakeholder engagement activities, gives the sponsor perspective as to whether or not the PM or the team face unnecessary distractions and, if so, protect them from those distractions.

The sponsor needs to provide oversight; making sure that clear boundaries are in place when it comes to the PM and stakeholders, as well as ensuring that processes are being followed. Although process adherence responsibilities fall under the responsibility of BAs, SMEs, PMs, and other process owners, the sponsor can identify, even through sporadic reviews, whether there are process adherence issues since these things may negatively impact team performance, project work, and the organization as a whole. On a more positive note, while tracking performance and guiding accordingly (with directions, decisions, and sign-offs), the sponsor has to look for opportunities (efficiencies, project improvement, processes, and organizational) to exploit, milestones to celebrate, and that progress and performance are recognized. Depending on the roles and responsibilities and the division of work, many of these *positive* activities do not fall under the direct responsibility of the sponsor, but the sponsor needs to enable them and provide support and permission to allow them to take place.

The sponsor, as a leader, needs to ensure that actions related to empowerment and motivation take place in support of team members; mostly by delegating and directing others to perform them (e.g., the PM), but also through informal conversations and coaching if possible. In addition to team growth and improvements that these actions may lead to, it is an opportunity for the sponsor to use informal conversations to identify trends and root causes of problems. Additional support activities for the team include ensuring that the necessary tools are available to support the team's work and that appropriate training is also in place to develop and grow the team as required.

While project work is taking place and results are coming in, there are more specific measurements for the sponsor to track. These include issues, changes, and risks *and* any associated trends or comparisons to previous projects. These could be related to the number of occurrences, their magnitude, their reach, or their rate of resolution. There is no need to measure everything, but it might be useful to compare, for example, the number of change requests against the number of accepted changes or the number of change requests made in the current project against a similar one (per the number of requirements). The goal here is not to overburden the sponsor with unnecessary measurements, but to provide opportunities to gain insight on anything that can be meaningful for project success.

The sponsor also keeps track of how major risks and significant assumptions are managed or impact the project, and whether there are any *smoldering* areas in relation to project conditions, work, or stakeholders. When it comes to stakeholders, it is important to not only check to what extent their needs are met, but also how they feel and conduct themselves, as well as whether there is any known friction among stakeholders. Timely acceptance of deliverables, sign-offs, and decisions will help the project progress toward completion.

## Project Closure

Upon the completion of milestones and acceptance of project work and deliverables, the sponsor decides whether and when to bring the project to an end and start the closing activities. Project closure involves a series of administrative activities that are mostly performed by the PM, along with activities that have a more strategic impact, such as lessons learned. Table 7.7 provides a review of the items the sponsor needs to focus on as part of project closing.

Closing a project happens for one of three primary reasons:

**Table 7.7**   Things to observe, address, and measure during project closing

| Things to Observe | Things to Address | Things to Measure |
|---|---|---|
| • Check for project completion and the extent of meeting project success<br>• Check if the client is satisfied with the results<br>• Evaluate adherence to processes; whether processes enhance/detract<br>• Look for *surprises* at project close<br>• Ensure capture and implementation of lessons | • Check what extent we delivered on the business case; was this the right project/approach?<br>• Participate in post-project evaluation<br>• Ensure handoff is done properly and sign-off completed<br>• Foster a constructive discussion | • What should we do differently next time?<br>• Root causes for project's troubles and successes?<br>• What would have made your job easier?<br>• What could I have done differently to increase success?<br>• How can we make our next project even better?<br>• What went right? What went right as a result of luck, rather than good planning? |

The sponsor's role during closing is more about ensuring a smooth handoff, benefits realization, and the capturing of meaningful lessons learned.

1. The project is meeting its goals and milestones and it is ready for completion
2. The client decides to stop the project before completion (for convenience)
3. The project is failing to meet its goals and there is a decision to end it prematurely

In any case, the formal decision within the organization to end a project lies with the sponsor. Once the project is ready for a decision on whether to close, the sponsor checks for project completion and the extent of project success. This includes determining the level of client satisfaction with the state of the project and the results. From a process perspective, the sponsor needs to ensure to what extent the processes were followed and whether there has to be any change with processes to improve them. He/She also needs to allow for one of the most important aspect of closure—lessons learned—and that administrative aspects of the closure are performed (mainly by the PM), including final reports, handoffs, integration of the project's product with operations, and benefits realization. An extension of the lessons learned process is for the sponsor to perform: a review of whether or to what extent the project met its original intent as stated by the business case. When it comes to asking and measuring, the sponsor needs to encourage a constructive conversation on what could be done differently if this had to be done again, explore the root cause of problems, and check what would have made things easier.

### Filling up the Sponsor's Day

The role of the sponsor needs to be taken seriously by the organization and by those who perform it. Therefore, it is important to gain an understanding of what the sponsor needs to do, ask, look for, and measure. The information in this chapter can also serve as a checklist for sponsors to consider, picking whatever is applicable and to what extent based on project needs, rigor, and level of complexity. When compiling all of these actions, it is possible to get an idea of what a day in the life of a sponsor should look like. Next, sponsors need to check the nature and the amount of work that is required of them—and determine to what extent they can perform it based on their capacity. When the individual who acts as a sponsor has a day job, it reinforces the need to check their volume of sponsorship work to make sure he/she has enough capacity to handle everything. Either way, a failure to articulate what the sponsor needs to do will almost inevitably lead to sponsor capacity problems and trigger many of the issues associated with project sponsorship.

## THE SPONSOR AND THE PM

Having a good project sponsor and a good PM are both critical to project success; however, there is also a need for the sponsor and the PM to work well together, otherwise their talents and experience are going to be wasted on misunderstandings and confusion, and will ultimately lead to project performance issues. Working effectively together is achieved by setting clear expectations and breaking down roles and responsibilities. The need to have a clear role definition is reinforced when it comes to anything that both the sponsor and the PM are engaged in—but at different levels and extents. The split between the sponsor and the PM on who leads what has to be determined between the two of them based on project needs and circumstances. The following sections will break it down by project phase.

## Initiation

- *The sponsor initiates the project*—at this point there may not be a PM in place yet, and once there is, the sponsor needs to establish who does which part of the initiation. The work breakdown should be based on project needs and organizational considerations. The sponsor needs to lead the chartering effort and determine the role of the PM in it; and the same goes for stakeholder identification and analysis.
- *Goals and objectives*—the sponsor provides the fundamental purpose and justification and the PM supports this effort.
- *Establishing touchpoints and escalations with stakeholders and steering committees*—should be done by the sponsor and the PM should support as needed.

- *Definition of success criteria*—this item starts during initiation and should be led by the sponsor. The PM supports this effort and may provide input. Articulating success is an activity that repeats during planning, where it takes a more detailed and specific form (per requirement). The planning portion of defining success criteria is led by the PM with a support and approval role by the sponsor.

## Planning

- *Building the project plan is the primary role of the PM*—the sponsor oversees and approves as needed.
- *Putting together the project team is a split role*—the sponsor provides guidance and approvals, along with assistance as needed. The PM leads parts of it.
- *Building reporting mechanisms*—the sponsor provides guidance and establishes specific needs and the PM leads the way accordingly, asking for help as needed.
- *Detailed resource allocation and task-based planning*—the PM leads this and the sponsor gets involved on an exception or problem basis.

## Execution and Control

- *Managing the project and team performance*—this is the job of the PM under the guidance of the sponsor with escalations as required.
- *Accountability*—based on areas of ownership, the PM is accountable for performance and has product and operational accountability. The sponsor has corporate accountability.
- *Reporting and controls*—the PM is in charge of the detailed reporting, while the sponsor relays report highlights to senior corporate management and other stakeholders.
- *Risks, issues, problems*—corrective action. The PM is in charge of all of these at the project level and the sponsor handles anything that *spills* beyond the project to the organizational or corporate level.

## Closing

Pretty much all of the closing activities are led by the PM. Guidance, capacity, and approval are provided by the sponsor. While many PMs are aware of the need to perform proper lessons learned and complete the handoff as required, they often lack the capacity or the mandate to do it properly. It is important that the sponsor enables the closing processes and ensures that they are performed properly and in a meaningful way.

A good practice for the sponsor and the PM would be to go over each item that has to be done and determine to what extent each of them is involved. They can quantify their respective levels of involvement—for example, from zero to five, where zero is completely uninvolved and five is leading that area or task. There can be any type of mix of involvement to maximize benefits for the project.

Part of working well together includes the sponsor and the PM needing to connect and maintain alignment. Several pieces of research have shown that it is common to find significant differences and misalignments between how sponsors and PMs perceive the role and involvement of the sponsor. A Project Management Institute report from 2014 pointed at a significant disparity between how often and to what extent sponsors demonstrate their skills and perform effectively. The report pointed at four areas where the sponsors thought their own performance was much better than the grade the PM would give them. Those areas were:

1. Sponsor frequently motivates the team
2. Sponsor frequently listens actively
3. Sponsor frequently communicates effectively
4. Sponsor manages change

Now, let's circle back and check the key focus areas for sponsors mentioned earlier in the book. Are these problems areas covered? Does the sponsor:

a. Help manage resource allocation as required
b. Serve as an escalation point for issues and problems
c. Proactively explore and support the team and the project
d. Ensure organizational and executive support for the project
e. Show interest in regular reports and make timely decisions
f. Manage stakeholder engagement and expectations beyond what the PM can do
g. Promote and champion the project
h. Grow and develop the team
i. Seek and provide feedback

## Do Not Be a Difficult Sponsor

The sponsor needs to be aware of his/her role, contribution, and style. No one deliberately tries to sabotage their own project, but sometimes circumstances, actions, and personal styles may stand in the way of delivering success. In those cases, PMs and other stakeholders may have the perception that the sponsor is being difficult—not realizing that it is most likely the result of the circumstances and the fact that the sponsor is either unaware of how his/her actions appear, unaware of the need for action, or simply out of capacity. There are also situations where the sponsor's style is too overbearing or imposing. Some sponsors want to show their involvement, exert their authority, or just demonstrate that they are there. Unfortunately, it may come across as too strong and become counterproductive to the team's efforts. Informally checking with the PM (or with other team members or stakeholders) can be done to gain a better understanding of such a lack of balance with the sponsor's involvement.

There are also the cases where the sponsor is not sufficiently involved, engaged, or even present. This may have similar, or an even more damaging effect than when the sponsor is too involved or overbearing; here too, the sponsor needs to explore appropriately and check what level of involvement is sufficient.

When *exploring* with others on appearances, styles, or levels of involvement, sponsors must ensure that the act of checking is not perceived the wrong way—as a lack of confidence or weakness. Confiding with the wrong people may send the wrong message and completely backfire in the sponsor's attempt to gain traction or show leadership. Here, the word *wrong* refers to the nature of their relationship with the sponsor and how trustworthy these people are in both understanding the context and nature of the question, as well as keeping it from *leaking* to others. Done correctly, informal check-ins between the sponsor and the PM or other team members may lead to success in aligning the sponsor with project needs and demonstrating the right type of leadership and style.

Most important, the sponsor needs to separate his/her emotions and accept feedback in a constructive manner, rather than as push back or criticism. Maintaining emotional faculties can also help the sponsor make informed decisions without allowing emotions to get in the way.

## HOW TO PROPERLY CONNECT THE CHANGE AND THE PROJECT

One of the main challenges that organizations face is to properly connect the change initiative and the project(s) associated with it. This need circles back to Kotter's findings that over 80% of organizational change initiatives fail to deliver to a satisfactory level. The reasons behind this high and disturbing number are not necessarily poor project management skills or choosing the wrong initiatives. The main reason for the failure is the lack of alignment (connection) between the change and the project. It is therefore not enough to have a great idea to pursue, a great project team to perform it, or strong organizational support. Those are all needed, but there are several factors that contribute to the lack of alignment between the change and the project:

- Unrealistic change objectives
- A lack of organizational capacity to support the change initiative
- A lack of project context in support of the change
- Misalignment due to the breakdown of the roles between the change manager and the PM
- A lack of the sponsor's presence and support
- A failure to follow basic best practices when it comes to change and projects (e.g., charter, realization of the stages of the change curve, etc.)
- Confusing need and desire with capacity and ability
- A failure to enable sufficient capacity and resources

- A lack of proper prioritization
- Optimistic and aggressive planning with little regard to risks
- Assuming everyone is supportive and failing to communicate and address stakeholders' needs
- Being locked in paradigms and failing to manage assumptions

That said, here are some remedies to improve alignment:

- Do things properly (charter, planning, risks, communications)
- Define the change and its goals and ensure alignment to project objectives
- Use proper project management practices with the right sense of urgency
- Connect the roles of PM and change manager
- Set realistic expectations and manage them throughout
- Ensure sufficient sponsor guidance support throughout
- Set clear objectives and success criteria and ensure they are aligned with organizational needs and team capacity and capability
- Communicate
- Reduce politics, ego, and siloed thinking
- Collaborate within and across projects and initiatives
- Use proactive and realistic resource planning
- Do not be afraid of making, documenting, and managing assumptions

## RECAP

This chapter provided a series of guidelines regarding what sponsors should look for, ask about, and measure. These can serve as checklists for sponsors to introduce and maintain their projects based on the surrounding circumstances and the needs that their organization (as a whole) and the initiatives introduce. There were also discussions about the ways to strengthen the connection between project and change initiatives in order to reduce the losses due to handoffs, gaps, and misunderstandings. The chapter then circled back to the role of the sponsor and what it takes to improve the working relationship between the sponsor and the PM.

## NOTE

1. Partially adapted from http://www.ownerteamconsult.com/what-are-the-sponsor-key-roles/.

# 8

---

# SPONSORSHIP IS COMMITMENT

---

When it comes to project and change sponsorship, the emphasis is on organizational commitment—commitment for success, value creation, accountability, and commitment towards the customer. Throughout this book, it has been shown that the role of the sponsor is critical to project and organizational success. *Proper* sponsorship is not difficult to achieve; nor is it about knowing what it takes, but rather about a lack of awareness and commitment. Ensuring that the right sponsor is in place demonstrates that the organization is *walking the talk*. It makes certain that the project or change initiative gets the amount of focus and attention it needs—based on its priority, sense of urgency, and organizational goals.

The types of project sponsors can be equated to the types of leaders in organizations. There are those leaders who start the organization, the organization belongs to them, and since it is their success or failure, they show a strong commitment to organizational success. There are also the *agent leaders*, who are installed at the top of organizations, and these are *leaders for hire*. They bring expertise and relevant experience to the organization, but the organization is not *theirs* and, therefore, their level of commitment may be different and will essentially be a by-product of their compensation. Project and change sponsorship are similar in this sense: there are sponsors who *own* the initiatives; they have a personal and emotional involvement in the initiative and their level of commitment is high. It is not all good, however, because the *initiating sponsor* may lack specific skills, experience, or drive to lead (or sponsor) the initiative effectively to the next level. In addition, despite having the skills and experience, the sponsor for hire (*agent sponsor*) often lacks the personal and emotional stakes, and with that the required level of commitment.

The discussion surrounding an initiating versus agent sponsor is important when looking for a project/initiative leader. Related to this matter is the reality that sponsors often change, and it introduces the question of what might happen to the project or the change initiative as a result. In theory, since the initiative is *owned* by the sponsor, if he/she moves on, it could spell the end of the initiative. However, as sponsor

292 Effective Project and Change Sponsorship

movement and departures are common, if a sponsor leaves his/her role, the initiative will proceed forward since it is part of a set of organizational considerations that are bigger than the individual who sponsors it. Clearly, when an initiating sponsor leaves, the extent of changes to the direction of the initiative will be greater.

It is important to have a proper handoff of responsibilities from the departing sponsor to the new one (if possible) and it is critical for the organization to ensure as much continuity as possible when it comes to communication and expectations, as well as with leadership and direction. One of the first actions of the new sponsor is to communicate the direction and leadership style that is expected under their tenure. New sponsors, like any new managers, often have a need to leave their mark and make changes quickly. These changes are often done in a rush and without the sponsor getting a chance to learn the lay of the land or to realize the impact of their actions—or at least the message they are sending. It is therefore important for the sponsor to first learn more about the initiative and the organization before introducing too much change. Sponsors can have tremendous impact by acting responsibly and reiterating their commitment to the initiative's success. Performing due diligence on the project will instill more confidence and trust in team members and stakeholders than trying to rush change.

It is also important to note that the organization, the stakeholders, and the team are likely already struggling with the change components of the initiative, and a variation in direction midway may further erode trust and support. Another important step for the sponsor to make is to reach out to the project (or the change) manager and quickly reset some norms, expectations, and ground rules. In some cases, personality differences, styles, and views may deem the relationship between the sponsor and the project manager (PM) incompatible. In these cases, the problem that the new sponsor faces is compounded since there is now an additional need—to replace the PM.

## SO, WHAT'S NEXT?

The conversation about project and change sponsorship is still fairly young. Although there is an increasing awareness around the importance of the sponsor's role, there is no consistent or productive discussion about where sponsorship goes from here. It is likely the result of the entire discipline still being so unorganized. Before talking about how to build a great sponsorship future, it is necessary to establish the current state of sponsorship, overcome the challenges that are already known, stabilize the situation a little, and then work on improving it.

### Current State and Challenges

The current state of sponsorship is weak, overall. On a scale from one to ten, it is probably at a four. It is not that there are no sponsors in place, but most organizations still lack the basic awareness of the importance of the sponsor's role, and sponsors often lack the awareness regarding how important their involvement in the projects is. As was established in Chapter 1, one of the primary reasons for sponsorship challenges is related to capacity issues; sponsors are, in most cases, senior managers who have a day job and, in addition, are being expected to fulfill a second role as a sponsor. Since sponsorship is their secondary role, in most cases they default to their day jobs with little awareness of the negative impact it may have on their projects. Further, with little guidance as to what is expected of the sponsor, and, therefore, virtually no key performance indicators or performance measures, it is easy to drop the ball when it comes to filling that position.

## Improving Sponsorship

It is important to have a strong sponsor who works both at the front of the stage and behind the scenes to promote the initiative, support it, and be there for decisions, sign-offs, and escalations. Improving sponsorship therefore almost guarantees improving project and organizational performance. But doing that requires a few actions:

- Increase the awareness around the role of the sponsor
- Ensure enough capacity is in place for sponsors to perform their work effectively
- Develop a set of guidelines on what it takes to be an effective sponsor
- Set clear boundaries between the sponsor and the PM

In addition, it is necessary to break the silos that still drive people's decision making in organizations. This ensures cross-project collaboration and the true application of big-picture considerations at virtually every decision point. In fact, breaking silos is also something that needs to be done on a strategic level—across the organization. It involves changing the compensation and incentive structure for sponsors and PMs and ensuring alignment between project/change objectives and the rest of the organization. Another mechanism for breaking silos involves proper prioritization processes for the sponsor, along with a greater sponsor involvement in managing stakeholder expectations.

Improved collaboration between the sponsor and the PM, along with a more systemic look at the initiative, are essential for bettering project timelines. This systemic look means properly managing and communicating the CRAIDs—constraints, risks, assumptions, issues, and dependencies. With these things managed properly, the number of misunderstandings will be reduced and it will allow the focus to be on value creation and minimizing silos.

Improving sponsorship can also be achieved by focusing on business analysis activities in order to ensure proper diagnosis and problem definition with less *solutioning* (a term used when the focus is more on the solution, rather than on figuring out and fixing the problem). The business analysis actions will help improve value creation, the customer's ability to define their needs, and maximize product and solution alignment to the actual objectives.

A lack of capacity and time for planning, along with overly optimistic planning, will lessen the impact of the change/initiative and set unrealistic expectations. The sponsor needs to ensure that there is sufficient focus on properly understanding and addressing stakeholder needs and on handling issues and problems. With more capacity and realistic expectations, the sponsor can focus more on building commitment and aligning the sense of urgency around the initiative.

Another item that will improve sponsorship is establishing a proper reporting mechanism that has a feedback loop built into it. Candid reporting and ongoing feedback help to ensure that the sponsor and other stakeholders have a proper understanding of any issues and their severity, as well as maintain a more proactive position to identify exceptions and respond to them effectively.

## THE SPONSOR AND THE PROJECT MANAGEMENT OFFICE (PMO)

Part of a sponsor's success lies in collaborating with other stakeholders and governing bodies, including the PMO. The PMO provides various levels of support and guidance to PMs; and to ensure there are no gaps, inconsistencies, or duplications of efforts that lead to waste, the sponsor needs to establish rules of engagement with the PMO. Similar to the relationship between the sponsor and the PM or with any other stakeholder, there is a need to define boundaries, authority levels, and areas of responsibility. In the absence of a strong sponsor or when there is no sponsor at all, the PMO can act as a sponsor—especially for smaller projects where the stakes are lower. The PMO acting as sponsor applies even more where the projects are about process improvement or enhancing capabilities that are related to project performance. Clearly, the PMO is unlikely to be able to provide what a sponsor offers the project, but with no sponsor in place, the PMO can at least partially fill that void.

When there is a sponsor in place, it is important to utilize the PMO's capabilities for guidance, governance, and support—including coaching, advice, and facilitating the process of collecting, sharing, and even implementing lessons learned. The PMO can also provide support in stakeholder engagement, ensuring alignment to organizational strategy, risk governance, and at least part of the benefits realization activities. These come in addition to PMO support for the PM and for the project—such as clarifying issues, dealing with resource challenges, and assisting with decisions. However, whatever level of support the PMO provides has to be coordinated and in line with project needs and, specifically, with the sponsor's view of the PMO's appropriate level of involvement. Many organizations struggle when it comes to PMOs since their level of support, engagement, and involvement in projects may not be properly aligned with specific project needs. That coordination should start with the sponsor providing the initial guidance for the project-PMO relationship, along with tweaking and adjusting those relationships as required.

Coordinating the sponsor's needs with the PMO also increases the organization's ability to articulate the capacity that it has to work on the project. Understanding the organizational and team capacity will allow for a proper prioritization process across initiatives and resource planning. With the majority of sponsors struggling to understand the project's true needs and with an unclear prioritization process, most organizations engage in initiatives that require more resources and needs than what the organization can provide.

## The PMO and the Change Management Office (CMO)

Many firms are developing CMOs to facilitate organizational change initiatives. Since change and project sponsorship are similar when it comes to the skills and experience levels the sponsor needs to demonstrate, organizations may want to consider merging the PMO and CMO to create an entity that looks at projects and change initiatives together. This will generate a series of benefits:

a. A better understanding of the impact of projects on the organization
b. A way to properly prioritize projects and initiatives against each other
c. The opportunity to manage organizational resources and capacity more effectively
d. A chance to provide consistent support across initiatives

In addition, change initiatives may be bigger than projects—or they may appear as projects. Regardless, it is important that although they may be different, one body will look at them, provide them with guidance and support, and even name names and address their symbolic aspects. When there are two governing bodies that oversee these very closely related areas, it is likely that definition, priorities, a sense of urgency, and issues will be managed in an inconsistent manner. More layers of governance and sign-off should not be added to our already convoluted complex organizations, but rather things should be simplified to promote consistency and stability in our projects and initiatives. Staffing and other considerations will not only be more consistent, but it will also help reduce unnecessary friction by removing the partial duplication of effort of having both a PM and a change manager (CM) in place.

When it comes to duplication of effort, the concern is not only with the PM and the CM, but with a series of roles. Once again, these roles all interfere with each other—partially due to the lack of consistent governance because of silos and multiple bodies overseeing different aspects of the organization. Examples of roles that are likely to have duplication of effort among them include the following:

1. PM
2. BA (business analyst)
3. CM
4. Sponsor
5. Product owner (in agile environments)

6. Scrum Master or coach (in agile environments)
7. Delivery manager

When there are roles that overlap (or at least partially overlap) with each other, there is an increased chance for confusion, gaps, duplication of efforts, slow downs, and other inconsistencies; all of which may increase the chance for performance problems. Whether the sponsor directly facilitates the boundaries and role definition process or delegates it to someone else, it is important that all of these roles (or those who are part of the project/initiative) understand each other and work well effectively. Depending on the situation, the sponsor may want to reduce the number of duplicate roles to ensure that communication is streamlined and that the team's performance is optimized.

## WHERE DO WE GO FROM HERE?

It is not enough to install a strong PM or a high-performing team because the focus, commitment, and tone starts from the top. This tone, along with the mandate, communication, clarity, and direction, cascade through the organization and resonate with various stakeholders, middle managers, and team members. The effective sponsor is both a leader and a manager, and his/her level of commitment is critical in delivering project and organizational success.

The message that comes from the sponsor involves a few components—from small to large:

- Communication
- Leadership
- Conduct and reinforcement

Communication must be consistent and suitable for the situation, the nature of the message, and the audience. Strong leadership skills must be demonstrated and the sponsor's conduct needs to be consistent and reinforce the sense of urgency and direction of the project or change initiative. This speaks again of the need for having just one sponsor, as opposed to multiple ones. With large initiatives, it is customary to have an executive sponsor, along with a lower level sponsor for the various areas within the initiative. However, when there are multiple sponsors, specifically when a committee sponsors a project, problems ensue. With committees, the old adage comes to mind that "committees take minutes and waste hours." In my experience, in the majority of cases where a committee sponsored a project, it ended with results that fell significantly short, mostly because the decision-making process was almost always much slower than that of a single sponsor. In addition, the quality of the decisions was, for the most part, noticeably lower because there was no one *single wringable neck* where the buck stopped, but rather a group of individuals who each pulled in their own direction.

Since it is sometimes inevitable to have multiple sponsors, a series of considerations must be in place to reduce the noise and increase the chance for success:

- All sponsors or committee members must be aligned on the intent, success criteria, and objectives
- Decision-making criteria has to be in place for when there are cross-functional changes or impacts
- Clear understanding on the overall project/initiative priority and the sense of urgency around it

## Education and Training

To ensure that senior managers who become sponsors know how to perform their role, they need to be provided with some direction and guidance. This could be through conversations, training, or coaching. Few question a senior manager's skills, experience, or clout, but all of these factors need to be in place in the right dosage for effective sponsorship, along with specific knowledge on the sponsor's role, responsibilities, and actions.

Providing guidance for the sponsor is the first step in showing that sponsorship is taken seriously. Proper role definition and areas of focus are an important start in ensuring that the sponsor performs both effectively and efficiently, especially considering that the sponsor's primary role as a senior manager will consume most of their time. Part of the role definition of the sponsor is to help him/her define and realize what they need to look for, measure, and ask about—in a similar fashion to the areas that were covered in Chapter 7.

In the event that the *natural* sponsor—the senior manager who is the initiator and the champion of the initiative—does not have the skills or the capacity to sponsor the project/initiative, the organization can keep them as an executive sponsor and appoint someone else as a proxy, or there may be a need to bring in an agent sponsor from the outside. That agent sponsor will have the skills and experience to drive the initiative on behalf of the executive or the original sponsor.

We should also ensure that sponsors do not have any type of conflict of interest concerning the initiative. This is not referring to an ethical conflict of interest, but rather to situations where the sponsor oversees other initiatives that may conflict. While having sponsors who oversee multiple initiatives is a common situation, it is important that there is both alignment with the initiatives' objectives (portfolio considerations), as well as clear decision-making criteria when it comes to dealing with conflicting needs across initiatives. The sponsor needs to be politically savvy because overseeing projects and change is a constant exercise in power and politics. The sponsor needs to be able to influence customers, stakeholders, decision makers, and resource owners and be able to do so while navigating the delicate landscape of their conflicting needs. This is especially true when the needs and priorities are not clearly defined or articulated.

# In Short: Define Success

Although multiple areas have been listed in this book for the sponsor to focus on, if nothing else, sponsors need to ensure that they focus on at least this handful of items:

1. *Define project success*—since it is the sponsors' initiative, no one else can properly articulate what success should look like. This does not refer to the details of each acceptance criterion, but the sponsor is the most suitable individual to set the tone about the objectives and success criteria.

2. *Articulate timelines and other major objectives*—the sponsor needs to provide guidance on the major milestones for the project/initiative. Regardless of whether these milestones are realistic or not at this point, or whether they are customer-facing or self-imposed, the sponsor cannot leave it to the team and he/she needs to set these expectations. There may be subsequent adjustments or changes, but it is critical for the sponsor to set that mandate in the first place.

3. *Foster a conversation of what could go wrong*—in relation to defining success, sponsors should think about what could go wrong and what to do if and when things go sideways. Risks, assumptions, and issues are important to manage and they are an extension of the success criteria. If an event does not have an impact on success, it should not be considered as a risk and scarce resources should not be spent on addressing it. The sponsor is likely to express a few significant areas of concern, and the rest of the risk-related conversations will happen on the project level.

4. *Provide the project/initiative the resources it needs*—most PMs plan their projects assuming that they will get the resources they need, with the right skill set, at the right time, and for the right duration. However, this is not the case. Resource allocation and management is one of the most volatile constraints on a project and needs attention from the beginning.

5. *Define what is needed of the sponsor and be there accordingly*—the sponsor must set expectations with the PM and the team; and it starts by asking them what they need from their sponsor. Based on the need, the parties should agree on the level of involvement and support that the sponsor needs to provide. Next, the sponsor needs to actually be there and provide the support that is necessary and has been agreed upon. It is common to see sponsors who appear to be involved, but are not truly engaged. The result is that although they are there and provide timely action, their decisions are uninformed.

Take projects and initiatives seriously and make sure that actions speak louder than words. It is not enough to talk about how important an initiative is or take symbolic steps. It is necessary to act meaningfully, including taking some tough and painful actions to show it. This means putting a strong and involved sponsor at the top, understanding and articulating needs, providing the necessary capacity, and prioritizing—which means both prioritizing the project/initiative against other organizational considerations, as well as prioritizing the needs and objectives within the initiative (including the requirements).

## The Future of Sponsorship

The future of sponsorship means three things: a clearer role definition for the sponsor, increased awareness around the role of the sponsor, and increased focus on sponsorship overall. There is also a good chance that within the next couple of years a new professional certificate will emerge that deals with project and change sponsorship. Perhaps the most likely reason why a sponsorship certificate is not available yet is because it is harder to get a senior manager to pursue certificates with their time constraints than it is for BAs, PMs, and CMs. With that said, it is necessary to realize the importance of the role of the sponsor, as well as the reality that project sponsors often underperform—and with that revelation, the likelihood for a certification process grows.

Without an improvement in sponsorship, project and change initiatives should be expected to continue to perform as they have been—poorly. Agile and other methodologies and approaches have managed to introduce improvements to project performance, but most of these improvements have been tactical. Improving sponsorship will make a strategic difference regarding the way projects and change initiatives are performed. When it comes to change initiatives, it is necessary to go back to Kotter's number from the 1990s—that about 80% of all change initiatives fail. It is a mystery as to why, in a quarter of a century since that claim, it has not been possible to significantly improve the performance percentage on change initiatives. Methodologies, concepts, theories, certificates, and concepts galore have been introduced, but change initiatives still struggle mightily—maybe even at a worse rate than 25 years ago.

It is, therefore, time to reframe the discussion and look at developing the area of sponsorship as a way to jump start overall organizational continuous improvement. The cost of doing so will not be significant; and definitely not higher than any of the costs that organizations have expended to improve performance thus far. It is also noteworthy that sponsorship is one of the roles that is least expected to be directly impacted by automation. While many processes and work products can be automated, the roles that require a higher level of human interaction and the ability to potentially process many subjective situations with hard-to-predict combinations will still need an individual with strong communication and leadership skills. Sponsorship requires the ability to form relationships, understand human interaction, and make informed and timely decisions.

The sponsor can handle situations much more effectively than any machine, but it requires the sponsor to be engaged and have a clear understanding of his/her role and level of involvement that is expected and necessary. Sponsors will need to evolve their focus and shift into a model that combines more engagement into the traditional reporting and escalation role of the sponsor as we know it.

As part of this focus, sponsors will need to not only engage the stakeholders who are already more involved, but also to bring stakeholders into the conversation earlier on. Many sponsors and PMs procrastinate when it comes to engaging certain stakeholders with the hope that waiting will help, even though it has been proven time after time that delaying stakeholder engagement is almost always detrimental to project success. It is therefore important for the sponsor to perform an environmental scan and work with the PM and other stakeholders in starting a conversation as early as possible that includes all of the possible stakeholders. Early engagement does not mean that everyone needs to be involved from the start, but it helps set expectations, express and hear needs, and helps everyone plan more effectively for when they need to get more actively involved. The effort required in organizing such a conversation is relatively low, especially compared to the clear benefits that are achieved.

## The Future of Change Management

In recent years, there has been a significant increase in the awareness around change management, as well as with change-related designations and certificates. Change management is not a new discipline, but the increase in awareness appears to have picked up when organizations got disillusioned with the relatively tame impact that agile methodologies had introduced. From 2010 to 2019, the use of agile concepts significantly increased. With that increase came the hope that agile will fix most of the ailments of our projects and organizations. However, the extent of the fix was far below expectations and the improvements have been more tactical by nature. There are a few reasons to consider as to why agile has fallen short of delivering on its promise:

- *Unrealistic expectations*—people thought that agile was going to save the day, but it was not meant to fix all of our organizational problems.
- *Agile is unforgiving*—Whenever there are any organizational issues that cross the path of an agile project (e.g., resource allocation, processes, accountability, planning and estimating, governance, etc.), agile tends to amplify them and even help these problems surface. The nature of agile's short cycles brings problems to the forefront sooner than later and prevents them from being covered up.
- *Agile done the wrong way*—many organizations introduce agile the wrong way and despite that, they expect agile to help achieve results. It is hard to find the right approach to take when it comes to agile so when the wrong approach is chosen, people tend to blame agile. Agile is not right for all environments, so when it fails it is necessary to find the root causes.

The growth in change management has introduced a significant challenge regarding duplication of effort and other conflicts between the change initiative and the project staff. While Chapter 5 provided an overview of how to handle change initiatives, there are a lot of commonalities between change and projects since projects are the likely vehicle to deliver the benefits of the change initiative. The areas of change management and project management have been in significant need of coordination and collaboration; but instead, change and project staff are now competing for resources and are engaged mostly in friction, conflicts, and misunderstandings. While it is important to give the right amount of focus to the change initiative, it is also important to enable the projects around it to deliver on their objectives. Further, the separation of these two disciplines is artificial, forced, and ineffective overall.

Proper communication, training, and managing attitudes are critical to success in change management. With that said, a PM who performs his/her work properly should cover training and communication. These two areas make up the core set of activities of any change initiative, as well as part of ensuring projects are successful. Training and communication are also keys to managing attitudes. When it comes to introducing change to organizations, stakeholders' attitudes are critical for buy-in and success. It has been learned over and over again (sometimes the hard way) that the success of an initiative is not just about the quality of the product, but also about the attitudes of the stakeholders for acceptance and adaptation.

Unfortunately, it is likely that in the coming years the chasm between the people who lead projects and change will widen because both sides will play the *us versus them* game, while focusing on territories, egos, and silos. However, as organizations look to improve all-around efficiencies, they will start trying to bridge the gap between project and change management—similar to the way they will look for improvements in sponsorship. Bridging the gap will occur by consolidating the roles of the PM and the CM. Within perhaps 10 years, there will once again be one individual leading these initiatives, instead of PMs and CMs butting heads on a regular basis. Consolidating these roles will reduce waste and ensure more consistency in performing these two important—but highly related—areas. This does not imply that change and project management will blend into each other, but with a more holistic view by the PM, it will allow the organization to cover the basic aspects of the change management portion of the project; allowing those who directly engage in organizational change to focus their efforts more effectively.

One of the problems with the change side of things is that training and communication often happen at a later stage of the engagement. This makes it hard for many stakeholders to anticipate them or to bring themselves to perform any meaningful planning or consideration about these items during the early parts of the engagement. In reality, it is necessary to plan and design those areas early on, even though they occur later in the game.

The new reality that is being forced upon us as we recover from the corona shock will further push us toward a search for efficiencies and savings, along with a need to streamline project and change management. Whatever process improvement organizations will go through, these will have an elevated sense of urgency and will be expected to show results rather quickly. In addition, the improvements will need buy-in from the very top of the organization, along with a push and meaningful support and facilitation by the sponsor. This book discussed the need to strengthen the role of the sponsor in projects and change initiatives, and the emerging needs of the new post-corona world further call for this leadership role to deliver on its promised and overdue value.

## Center of Trust

The sponsor does not only need to build *trust*, he/she must be a trust center of excellence. At the foundation of every high-performing team there is trust—and on it, the team has the ability to:

- Effectively communicate and create constructive conflict
- Build commitment
- Be accountable and accept ownership
- Be results orientated

Trust can be viewed as the expectation that a person can rely on another individual. More formally, trust is "the willingness of a party (truster) to be vulnerable to the actions of another party (trustee) based on the expectation that the trustee will perform an action important to the truster, regardless of the truster's ability to monitor or control the trustee."[1]

Trust allows people to act in a series of ways that foster collaboration and performance, including the following:

a. Getting closer and developing productive relationships
b. Opening up and feeling safe
c. Allowing people to put themselves in vulnerable situations knowing they will not get hurt
d. Innovating and daring to propose new things or new ways of doing things
e. Working better together
f. Acting in a consistent manner
g. Being transparent
h. Recognizing and rewarding, while also criticizing and providing feedback constructively
i. Inspiring and getting inspired
j. Communicating openly
k. Pointing out problems
l. Exploring solutions

With all of these great things in mind—trust is hard to establish, difficult to maintain, and next to impossible to regain, once it is lost. When people trust and feel trusted, they can also do something that is a critical ingredient in relationship building—including interpersonal relationships—the ability to admit when he/she is wrong. Most people have a major problem doing this. It is about ego, saving face, self-confidence, self-awareness, and pride. It took me years and countless arguments—along with possibly some missed opportunities—to learn to admit when I am wrong. Although no one likes to be wrong, developing the ability to admit when it happens is crucial, not only in building trust and relationships, but also in everyday conduct.

## Why Relationships Do Not Work

Another important ingredient in building trust is the ability to explore why some relationships do not work and how people should look at themselves and their part in it. When a person does not get along with someone, they default into blaming the other person—their style, personality, or values—in the failure to develop good relations. However, it is not always the other side's fault and people need to look at themselves, as well as the situation, in order to learn more from it. Not getting along with someone can be the result of a combination of things, including the circumstances or the personalities involved. But learning about themselves can help to minimize some of the differences and address them effectively. The sponsor, as a leader, needs to minimize the number of occasions where he/she does not get along with people; and he/she needs to maximize the ability to leverage relationships, work together with people, and influence others. Sponsors (and, in fact, all of us) also need to constantly look at themselves and determine what it is that they can do better or differently to improve. We all have a hard time looking candidly at our own actions and then changing the way we do things, but developing the ability to do so is critical for self improvement. Further, we should do it not only when we fail to achieve our goals, but also when we accomplish them.

## Back to Trust: the Trust Formula

Building trust means being accountable for your actions, being reliable, maintaining credibility, doing what you say you are going to do, being candid, and being there for others. There also has to be something more tangible to it and, like everything else in life, there is a formula that helps identify the ingredients of trust, as well as the interactions among them (see Figure 8.1).

With one variable in the denominator and three in the numerator, it establishes self-orientation, which sits alone in the denominator, as the most important variable in the formula. People who have low self-orientation are virtually free to honestly focus on those around them and become more effective and better at building trust. People become more effective when they do not directly focus on their own needs, but rather when their focus is on helping others.

The trust formula covers the most common meanings of trust that are encountered daily, but its meaning is personal, rather than institutional—and it is therefore about people. Although companies are often described as credible and reliable (which are the first two components of the trust formula), it is the people within the companies who make those companies what they are. Let's break down the

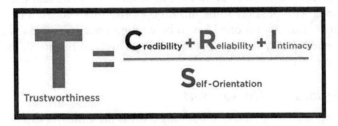

The trust formula, or equation, has one variable in the denominator and three in the numerator. Increasing the value of the factors in the numerator increases the value of trust, while increasing the value of the denominator (self-orientation) decreases the value of trust.

**Figure 8.1**    Trust formula[2]

variables in the trust formula to better understanding what can be done to increase trust in our relationships:[3]

- *Credibility* (*words*)—content expertise and presence (how people look, act, react, etc.). This is the most common trust factor. Most people get this one right. Credibility is about what people say and how believable they are to others. In order to be a good leader, a person must be credible.
- *Reliability* (*actions*)—whether people are thought of as dependable and can be trusted to behave in certain ways. Increasing reliability takes time. People tend to trust those whom they have interacted with regularly. People need to know that their leaders will be there and come through for them.
- *Intimacy* (*emotions*)—the extent to which a trustee can discuss difficult topics/agendas with someone else. This is a high-risk/high-reward variable with a huge gray area. Intimacy considers how safe people feel sharing issues with you.
- *Self-orientation* (*motives*)—anything that keeps the focus on oneself rather than the person he/she is trying to get to trust him/her. Having a high self-orientation can manifest itself in several ways with selfishness being the most common. When people focus too much on themselves, it lowers their level of trustworthiness.

Once again, since self-orientation is the only item in the denominator, it has the highest weight of all the items in the formula. For every marginal increase in self-orientation that occurs in a relationship, it is necessary to work that much harder to rebuild trust. Conversely, focusing on others first is the single most effective way to increase trust. It is hard to assess our own trustworthiness since it is a subjective measure. However, it can and should be done as part of our process to self-improve, and it can be very useful for those people who feel that they are trustworthy, but at the same time they struggle to develop relationships or to get other people to follow and trust. Trust is essential to developing relationships with other people, and people who cannot inspire trust cannot lead because they will have no followers.

## FINAL WORDS

This book has taken the area of project and change sponsorship and shed light on what it takes to become a good sponsor. What is a good sponsor? One who leads, manages, directs, mandates, decides, and acts—as required. This book started by defining what sponsorship is; discussed problems and challenges in relation to sponsorship; identified actions to consider in an effort to prevent, address, or alleviate sponsorship challenges; and elaborated on what it takes to be an effective sponsor. It looked into what the sponsor needs to do to set realistic expectations and to work effectively with others, and discussed the all-important task of engaging and understanding stakeholders. The focus was then shifted to change management concepts and to specific things for the sponsor to consider as part of sponsoring projects. Although these are not identical, project and change sponsorship are closely related in a similar fashion to the close relationship between the *disciplines* of project and change management. We then reviewed a set of key tips and advice for the sponsor on things to consider, look at, measure, and inquire.

The last chapter of this book took a slightly different path, where the discussion included ways to improve sponsorship, considered where sponsorship goes from here, and looked into additional areas within the organization that will need to improve, alongside sponsorship, in order for organizations to remain competitive. The topic then circled back to one of the most rudimentary and foundational elements of leadership—trust. There was a discussion as to what it takes to improve trust, along with information about the innovative, yet simplistic concept of measuring trust through a formula.

Sponsorship has been a growing area of focus in many organizations as people come to the realization that it is not only about the product quality, the processes, or the ways to deliver things (i.e., project management, agile, change management, and business analysis); it is also about leadership—and this starts at the very top. It is becoming more and more clear that many organizational problems originate from up high—and specifically from the sponsorship layer. Ironically, the problems are not due to a lack of knowledge or qualifications, but rather due to insufficient awareness and attention by the sponsors because of a lack of capacity.

Without awareness and tangible changes in the way project and change sponsorship are referred to and treated, meaningful improvements cannot be expected in this area. Doing the same things over and over again and expecting different results is the definition of insanity.

Improving sponsorship is not easy: sponsors are senior managers and it is hard to tell them when they do not perform their roles effectively; there is little literature and structure around sponsorship; the awareness of this role is limited; and most organizations look for problems elsewhere. Therefore, it is safe to say that improving sponsorship is quite the tall order; however, doing so will yield substantial benefits to organizations. Several firms I have worked with have shown significant improvement in their performance due directly to improvements within their project and change sponsorship areas. So, although it is not easy to articulate what and how to improve sponsorship, putting our minds to it is the first step; bringing up the level of awareness around sponsorship is next; introducing structure follows; and then comes coaching, training, and guidance.

It is perhaps time to take the information laid out in this book and turn a new and better page in the story of our organizations by putting structure and awareness around improving project and change sponsorship. And if the only way to do it is by establishing a new certificate or designation in sponsorship, something along the line of a Sponsorship Management Institute—then so be it.

## NOTES

1. Davis, James H., et al. "The Trusted General Manager and Business Unit Performance: Empirical Evidence of a Competitive Advantage." *Strategic Management Journal*, vol. 21, no. 5, 2000, pp. 563–576. doi:10.1002/(sici)1097-0266(200005)21:53.0.co;2-0.
2. https://trustedadvisor.com/articles/the-trust-equation-a-primer.
3. https://robertgreiner.com/the-trust-equation/.

# INDEX

Page numbers followed by "*f*" refer to figures and those followed by "*t*" refer to tables.